BACKROAD
ADVENTURING
in your
sport utility
vehicle

Jonathan Hanson and Roseann Beggy Hanson

McGraw Hill

Camden, Maine • New York • San Francisco • Washington, D.C. • Auckland • Bogotá •
Caracas • Lisbon • London • Madrid • Mexico City • Milan • Montreal • New Delhi •
San Juan • Singapore • Sydney • Tokyo • Toronto

This book is dedicated to responsible four-wheel-drive use and
to wilderness preservation. While we encourage backroad explorations,
we also support the protection of our many roadless areas.

Ragged Mountain Press

A Division of The McGraw·Hill Companies

10 9 8 7 6 5 4 3 2 1

Library of Congress Cataloging-in-Publication Data available
Hanson, Jonathan.
Backroad adventuring in your sport utility vehicle/Jonathan Hanson and Roseann Beggy Hanson.
         p.   cm.
    Includes bibiliographical references (p.) and index.
    ISBN 0-07-158186-3 (paper)
    1. All terrain vehicle driving. 2. Automobile travel—United States. 3. Automobile travel—Canada.
4. Automobile travel—Mexico. I. Hanson, Roseann Beggy. II. Title.
TL235.7.H36 1998   98-35797
796.7—dc21   CIP

Questions regarding the content of this book should be addressed to:
Ragged Mountain Press
P.O. Box 220
Camden, ME 04843
(207) 236-4837
www.raggedmountainpress.com

Questions regarding the ordering of this book should be addressed to:
The McGraw-Hill Companies
Customer Service Department
P.O. Box 547
Blacklick, OH 43004
Retail customers: (800) 262-4729
Bookstores: (800) 722-4726

Printed by Quebecor Printing Company, Fairfield, PA
Design by Faith Hague
Project Management by Janet Robbins
Production by Faith Hague and Shannon Thomas
Edited by Tom McCarthy; Jack Sanders

Contents

Acknowledgments

We'd like to thank the staff of Ragged Mountain Press for supporting this project. Foremost we'd like to thank Katie McGarry (again!) for letting us convince her not all drivers of four wheel drives are land-destroying, beer-chugging fanatics. Jeff Serena provided helpful support, and Tom McCarthy's cheerful demeanor (even while under fire) was greatly appreciated.

A number of companies and land agencies provided products for photography, as well as photographs and art. Thanks to the folks at: Bilstein USA; Bloomfield Manufacturing; Bureau of Land Management Arizona office; Discount Tire Company (Tucson, Speedway location); Hella; High Gear; Packasport; Performance Products; Sierra Designs; Tread Lightly Inc.; USA VenturCraft; Warn Industries; Yakima Products.

Introduction

Naturalist and scientist Edward O. Wilson coined the term *biophilia* to describe the deep attraction most humans feel for the natural world. Sure, there are exceptions to this biophilia—a very cosmopolitan American writer once described the Great Outdoors as "the region between the doorman and the taxi." Pity those poor souls like her whose world consists only of concrete and glass.

But most of us are regularly drawn to soak up nature, even if it's just for quick trips to our city parks at lunchtime so we can smell the grass, watch the birds, and listen to the breeze blow through the trees. On our weekends and vacations we head out of the city confines to visit seashores, forests, deserts, and grasslands, in the hundreds of national forests, parks, and wildlife refuges with which our continent is blessed.

If you're the lucky owner of a sport utility vehicle—the four-wheel-drive station wagon of the '90s—then you own a passport to endless backroad adventuring. You can explore miles beyond the standard, crowded vacation spots, in places motor homes and minivans can't reach, where campsites aren't numbered or reserved (and are never filled), where the glow of your campfire is the only light between you and a horizon filled with stars. In the United States there are millions of acres of public land with roads suitable for exploration, areas where the distance between you and the next visitor might be measured in miles instead of feet. And then there's Canada and Mexico . . .

But if you are short on time, even day trips with a sport utility allow you to get away from the bulk of holiday traffic and find a corner of peace and quiet. All those interesting but rugged side roads that folks in sedans have to pass up are now your jumping-off point for backroad adventure. It is this potential for adventure that has attracted many people to sport utility vehicles—but, in many cases, the potential goes unrealized. This book is designed to help you get out and explore.

We've organized *Backroad Adventuring in Your Sport Utility Vehicle* so each chapter offers information independent of the others. If you just want to learn four-wheel-drive techniques, you can go straight to Chapter 2; if you want to learn about camping, you can read Chapter 3; and so on. Whenever possible, we cross-reference information so you're just a thumb-flip from finding what you need to know.

To whet your appetite for backroad adventure, throughout the chapters we tossed in stories of backroad adventures in Baja, the Canadian Arctic, Canyonlands, Death Valley, the Rocky Mountains, the North Woods, and Michigan in winter. Many outdoor pursuits are perfectly suited to partner with sport utility exploration, so we've also included primers on getting started in sea kayaking, mountain biking, and bird watching.

The chapter subjects are arranged as follows:

Chapter 1, "Four Wheel Drive Fundamentals," is an introduction to the sport utility phenomenon and to the mechanics of four-wheel-drive vehicles in general, to help you understand how they work and what they can and can't do.

Chapter 2, "Backroad Driving Techniques," is all about using four wheel drive effectively, both on normal roads when snow and ice create hazardous conditions and on backcountry trails where ordinary vehicles can't travel at all. You'll learn both basic and advanced techniques, a few interesting tricks, and recovery strategies in case you or someone else actually gets stuck.

Chapter 3, "Planning and Preparing for a Backroad Adventure," talks about finding places to go, essential vehicle equipment, maps and books, plus pre-trip maintenance and vehicle checks.

Chapter 4, "Backroad Tripping," gets down to the nuts and bolts of touring: camping equipment and techniques for setting up a really comfortable home away from home, food and cooking for great meals on the road, plus many tips for making trips go smoothly.

Chapter 5, "Modifications and Accessories," discusses ways to improve the backroad performance and reliability of your vehicle, plus modifications to turn your vehicle into a real expedition workhorse—not to mention making it look really great (we're honest: When your city life has you half-crazy, you can at least *feel* adventuresome every time you hop in your SUV).

Chapter 6, "Maintenance and Repairs," deals with easy ways to increase your self-sufficiency regarding simple repairs and preventive maintenance. You'll learn the best technique for changing flat tires and how to do your own checks of oil, belts, and other vital parts of your vehicle.

In addition, there's information on driving in Mexico and Canada, ideas for traveling with dogs, many safety tips, plus sources for equipment suppliers, and contact information for land agencies, four-wheel-drive clubs, and driving schools.

Throughout the book we encourage environmentally sound driving—with instructions for minimizing your impact on the land (often, engaging four wheel drive significantly reduces impact on dirt roads), as well as a suggestion to park your sport utility during the week (they're gas-guzzlers).

Our hopes for the reader remain the same: Have fun, stay safe, enjoy the beautiful lands with which our country is blessed, and, finally, use your vote to help protect them.

CHAPTER 1

Four Wheel Drive Fundamentals

BY JONATHAN HANSON

- Why Four Wheel Drive?
- What Does "Four Wheel Drive" Really Mean? (And When is Four Wheel Drive Not Four Wheel Drive?)
- What Four Wheel Drive Can—and Can't—Do (and What it Shouldn't Do)
- *Road Trip: Baja Backcountry*

A New Kind of Station Wagon

The skyrocketing popularity of sport utility vehicles caught a lot of manufacturers by surprise and sent many scrambling to introduce their own models. Most in the industry thought the booming sales would be a short-lived fad, but the opposite has proved true. Sport utilities have become the station wagons of the '90s—an adventuresome version—and show every sign of remaining popular well into the next century.

Why the boom? First is the extra security of all wheel drive in inclement weather. Second is the versatility: Even the smallest four-wheel-drive station wagons and compact sport-utes such as the Toyota RAV4 have a lot of usable space. Third, in the case of larger models, is the commanding view of traffic, along with the collision-safety factor of driving a vehicle with a heavy frame and a lot of sheet metal.

However, it's the fourth characteristic we will concentrate on for much of this book: the vast potential for adventure intrinsic to the sport utility. Surveys conducted by several magazines have confirmed that well over half of the people who buy a sport utility vehicle express a desire to use it to explore beyond their normal highway vacation routes. Since the U.S. Forest Service alone maintains dirt roads eight times the length of the interstate highway system, obviously there's room for a lot of people to get out and use these vehicles as they were intended. We're not talking about plowing through mud bogs or ripping up sand dunes: We're talking backroad exploration, with a serious lean toward low-impact use.

Why Four Wheel Drive?

Simply put, four wheel drive gives a vehicle twice as much traction as two wheel drive. It's really not *that* simple, as I'll explain later. But it's sufficient at the moment.

There are two major benefits to the extra traction provided by four wheel drive. First, it is safer in many situations, especially those involving snow, ice, or other slippery surfaces. Second, it allows you to reach places ordinary vehicles can't, on very rough or steep roads. Some four-wheel-drive vehicles are not designed for use on rough trails, however—they are intended for adverse conditions on ordinary roads. In Chapter 2 we discuss the capabilities of different styles of sport utilities.

But how does someone whose previous vehicle was a minivan or sedan go about tackling a whole new facet of driving? It's actually quite easy to get started—you just have to learn a bit about the vehicle: How it works, what it is, and isn't, capable of, and how to get the most out of it.

Perhaps the most important thing to begin with is a basic understanding of how four wheel drive works. I know what some of you are thinking, but don't skip this section. Even if you are not mechanically inclined, you can grasp the basics of what follows.

What Does "Four Wheel Drive" Really Mean?
(And When is Four Wheel Drive Not Four Wheel Drive?)

Even to someone unfamiliar with mechanical terms, this sounds like a trick question, and in a way it is. Just stick with me for the next few hundred words, and I guarantee you'll have the essentials well in hand.

Almost all of the sedans in which we commute around town are two wheel drive—the engine delivers its power to either the rear or the front wheels, hence the designation "rear wheel drive" or "front wheel drive." In a front-engined, rear-wheel-drive car, for example, the power from the engine is delivered through the transmission and then a driveshaft to the rear axle.

To make a four-wheel-drive vehicle, the engineers add a second driveshaft from the transmission to the front axle so it, too, receives power from the engine. In addition, they often add a second transmission, called a transfer case, which drops the ratios in the main transmission to allow the vehicle to travel very slowly in difficult conditions. An analogy is the gearing on a mountain bike: The gears on the rear wheel are like the transmission; the chainrings at the pedals are like the transfer case. You do most of your shifting on the rear gears, but if you hit a very steep hill, you shift down to a smaller chainring in front—just like shifting the transfer case into low range.

So far so good. Now, there is a very important component of every vehicle, whether it's two or four wheel drive, called the differential. Here's what it does.

Imagine turning in a circle in your car. You can easily see that the outside wheels make a larger diameter circle than the inside wheels. This means that the outside wheels must turn faster than the inside wheels to keep up. If the two driven wheels were

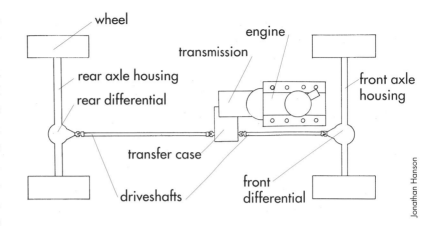

Schematic Drawing of a Four-Wheel-Drive System

connected to each other by a solid axle, obviously something would have to give—in this case, the tread on the tires would quickly be worn away, as the outside tire tried to force the inside tire to turn faster, and the inside tire did the opposite to the outside tire.

The solution is a differential, so called because it allows each wheel to turn at a different speed. The differential takes the power from the driveshaft and splits it in two, half to each wheel.

Here's the big catch. Under normal conditions, the differential sends power to both wheels. However, if one wheel loses traction and begins to spin, the characteristics of the differential cause it to send all the engine's power to *that* wheel—the wheel with no grip. Even if the opposite tire has plenty of traction, the vehicle will go nowhere.

A similar situation can occur even with four wheel drive if, for instance, the left front and right rear tires are caught in soft sand or mud. Both those tires will spin and, again, the vehicle goes nowhere. Another situation can happen when someone pulls the right side of the vehicle off the pavement onto a patch of ice or slick mud—both right tires will spin helplessly, while the tires still on the pavement do nothing.

This answers our question *When is four wheel drive not four wheel drive?* In certain circumstances, your four wheel drive might be only two wheel drive. If that's a bit disillusioning, remember that, in the same spot, a two-wheel-drive car would only have *one* wheel drive. So, no matter what, you still have twice as much traction available in a sport utility vehicle as you would in a regular car.

Why bother with this? Because if you're ever in a situation where one or more of your tires has lost traction, you'll know exactly what is happening and why. And when you know what is happening, you'll have a better chance of knowing what to do about it.

Incidentally, it's possible to prevent or minimize the traction loss inherent to a standard (also called "open") differential by installing a limited-slip or locking differential, which allows the wheels to rotate at different speeds in turns but can fully or partially lock the axles together if one wheel starts to spin. See Chapter 5, pages 134–135 for more information.

ROAD TRIP: BAJA BACKCOUNTRY

Shortly after we left San Felipe, with the Sea of Cortez shining deep sapphire on our left, the road started getting rough. The farther south we drove, past the expatriate gringo camps on the beach, farther away from the spring-break haunts of California college students, the worse the track deteriorated—which was just fine with us; that's why we came this way. Soon the only people we saw were Mexicans driving ancient Ford and Chevy pickups, missing fenders, bumpers, and exhaust parts from the constant pounding of the rutted and rocky path. Even they began to thin out until hours would go by without sight of another human.

In the meantime the stunning, unearthly flora of the Baja desert had taken our breath away. Even native Arizonans, used to saguaros and cholla, react with wonder to the sight of boojums, like gigantic upturned parsnips stuck in the earth. Our photo album shows a comic progression: We jumped out and took our picture next to a huge boojum, at least 30 feet high, only to find a 40-footer a few miles later. Another photo. Then, a 45-footer a mile farther on. Eventually we discovered boojums more than 50 feet tall—still well short of the 70-foot record.

The roads we followed—purposely as far off the main track as possible—continued to deteriorate, which left us seemingly alone in the world. The stretches through mountain passes were essentially paved with jagged rocks, while the level valley sections had degraded into truly awesome washboard. The only two ways to drive washboard are: (1) Very slowly, with the vehicle bouncing up and down as if it were on pogo sticks rather than wheels; or (2) Very quickly, which allows the tires to skip over the crests of the ridges. The latter is supposedly much harder on the vehicle, although I swear if you get the speed and frequency just right the suspension hardly seems to flex at all. The trouble is getting up to that speed or slowing down—then everything goes berserk. And sudden braking initiates such a violent oscillation that ice chests and duffel bags

Jonathan Hanson

North America has some of the best backroad driving in the world. Nearly all access to the best beaches of Baja, Mexico, is on rough backroads: perfect for sport utilities such as the authors' classic Toyota Land Cruiser.

(continued on page 6)

Full-time Versus Part-time Four Wheel Drive

Most early four-wheel-drive vehicles, and many newer ones, employ a part-time four-wheel-drive system. The engine normally drives only two wheels; when four wheel drive is desired, the driver must engage it manually. The advantages to a part-time system include saving gas, since the engine isn't always working to drive an extra set of wheels and in the process having to overcome the internal friction of the differential and axles, as well as reducing wear on those same parts. Additional savings are possible if locking hubs are used at the front wheels. Locking hubs completely separate the front wheels from their driveshafts and the differential, reducing friction and adding a little gas mileage. Without locking hubs, even though the front driveshaft is not being turned by the engine, the front wheels are still connected to the axles and the driveshaft so that, as the wheels turn, they have to drag the rest of the parts with them.

Keep in mind that most part-time four-wheel-drive systems are not meant to be driven on pavement with the front drive engaged. Doing so will cause the transfer case gears to bind, since the front wheels rotate at different speeds from the rear wheels through turns, just as they do from side to side. This can seriously damage the transfer case. Part-time four wheel drive should be engaged only on dirt, snow, or other surfaces that allow some slippage in the tires.

Full-time four wheel drive has the benefit of—well, being full-time. *(continued on page 7)*

THE FIRST SPORT UTILITY

What was the first sport utility vehicle? That is, the first enclosed four-wheel-drive vehicle designed for recreational, rather than military or industrial use? Many people consider the Ford Bronco and Chevy Blazers of the mid-1960s to be the pioneers of the class; others point to the older Chevy Suburban and Willys station wagon. And let's not forget the Land Rover, introduced (in hardtop form) in 1951—although the early Land Rovers were marketed

The 1938 Ford Woody four-wheel-drive station wagon may have been the first "sport utility vehicle."

Courtesy of Open Road

strictly as working vehicles, in sharp contrast to their posh descendants. But one vehicle, older than any of these, arguably holds the ultimate title: the 1937 Ford "Woody" station wagon, converted to four wheel drive by the Marmon-Herrington Company of Indianapolis. The M-H conversion was offered as a factory option on several Ford vehicles in the late 1930s, but the 85-horsepower V8 station wagon became a favorite of hunters and fishermen, not to mention country doctors and mailmen.

Amazingly, the M-H Ford boasted a fully automatic four-wheel-drive system. A gear-driven actuator engaged drive to the front wheels whenever the rear tires began spinning.

appear in the rearview mirror, alternating only infrequently with glimpses of the road behind.

That night a family of coyotes serenaded our camp, reminding us of home, while the hiss of small waves on the beach and the occasional poofs of passing dolphins provided an exotic counterpoint.

The first part of the next day involved a long stretch of sandy trail, so I reduced the tire pressure to about 20 psi (pounds per square inch) from the normal 40, thus increasing the amount of tread in contact with the road and adding flotation over the soft surface. When the trail climbed back into rocky desert, we stopped and used the portable compressor to pump the tires back up, necessary to avoid damaging the sidewalls on sharp-edged stones. Then things got steep quickly, and we drove the next 15 miles in low range, rarely exceeding 10 miles per hour. Our reward was a pristine, isolated inland camp, with a new family of coyotes, and a pair of great horned owls that called softly to each other across a small canyon.

The Land Cruiser was running perfectly; morning oil, water, and suspension checks seemed a mere formality. The tires, however, were showing scuffs and scars from the pounding. They were off-brand tires that the previous owner had installed. Our intention had been to wear them out before putting on a set of good ones. It appeared we would rapidly facilitate that plan on this trip. Indeed, a couple of days later as we pulled onto Mexico 1 for some of the only paved-road mileage of the journey, in the rear-view mirror I thought I saw something fly out from beneath the car. Going back to check, I found a chunk of tire—a whole block of tread—had torn loose and been flung off. The hole in the tire showed bare steel casing, although it still held air.

We changed to the spare and continued on to Bahia de los Angeles, where we stayed for a few days before heading south once more to Bahia las Animas. There we set up an idyllic beach camp under a mesquite tree just yards from the storm tide line. At low tide, reddish egrets danced in the shallow puddles, fanning their wings to scare up fish and crustaceans. When the tide returned, dolphins followed the water to hunt where the egrets had stood hours before. We took out our sea kayaks and paddled along the cliffs that line the south shore of the bay, looking down through the clear, cold water at rock bass and opaleye cruising among huge submerged boulders.

This part of the Sea of Cortez is subject to massive upwelling of cold, nutrient-rich waters from deep offshore trenches. As a result, sea lions, dolphins, and whales find a rich feeding ground. We paddled out to watch several fin whales, the second-largest whales in the world, feeding in their characteristic clockwise circles.

At night we sat in our camp chairs watching the stars wheel overhead—thousands more than are visible from our cities; it was a truly deep black, vastly black sky punctuated by

(continued on page 8)

Whenever you need the extra traction, it's already there. You do, however, lose a little fuel economy with the engine continually turning the extra parts. The differential problem we talked about in the last section also crops up—in a turn, the front wheels describe a different arc than the rear ones do, and thus move at a different speed. So a full-time four-wheel-drive vehicle must have some sort of differential in the transfer case as well as in the axles. Some vehicles accomplish this with gears; others use a fluid coupling that allows the right amount of slip. Most center differentials can be locked at very low speed or on dirt roads, to divide the engine's power equally between front and rear axles. Otherwise you run into a situation similar to that with the axle differentials: The center differential will send power to the *end* of the vehicle that is slipping.

More sophisticated center differential systems can sense whether a front or rear wheel is losing traction and shift power to the axle with the most grip.

What Four Wheel Drive Can—and Can't—Do (and What It Shouldn't Do)

Lest you suffer any delusions of invincibility in your rugged four-wheel-drive vehicle, keep in mind what I refer to as the 4x4 Prime Directive:

**Four wheel drive doesn't keep you from getting stuck—
it just gets you stuck in worse places.**

That's not meant to put you off, but it's a good phrase to remember. Although four wheel drive gives you an extra margin of traction and safety, it is *not* invincible.

Ironically, more people in sport utilities probably get into trouble in fairly normal situations of ice and snow on urban roads than do so on rough trails. Inclement weather is the one situation where people seem to *over*estimate the capabilities of all wheel drive. While four wheel drive does provide superior traction, steering, and engine braking on slippery surfaces, it cannot overcome the laws of physics. A surface that is difficult to *stand* on comfortably is bound to be difficult to drive on, too.

However, the same driver who is disappointed when his or her supposedly invincible vehicle gets stuck on a perfectly flat road covered with a skin of ice will be astonished—and even terrified—at what that vehicle will do on a steep, rocky trail. When sufficient traction is available, many four-wheel-drive

This is one of our favorite signs when exploring on backroads: "No Services" usually means no crowds and lots of scenery.

(continued on page 9)

ROAD TRIP: BAJA BACKCOUNTRY, CONTINUED FROM PAGE 6

glittering pinpoints of light. The silence was immense, broken only by the gentle sounds of the sea and the calls of coyotes and owls. Kangaroo rats and deer mice, the cute but impudent scavengers of desert camps, hopped between our feet, looking for dinner crumbs. We toasted the camp with Mexican beer and ate chicken fajitas with green and red peppers, onions, and salsa.

We left the bay reluctantly, heading out the sandy beach road to the coastal route with its sharp-edged rocks. Halfway back to Bahia de los Angeles, we felt the unmistakable floppiness of a flat tire. It was punctured too badly for our plug kit to fix; the only recourse was to re-install the tire with the damaged tread and continue slowly.

We had come to Baja during the pre-run schedule for the famous Baja 1,000 race. As I worked on the tire, a heavily modified Ford Bronco scout vehicle for one of the teams blasted by just feet from us, shooting gravel everywhere. Since this was not the actual race, the justification for such rudeness was slim indeed; later we gained some satisfaction to learn that the Ford team had been trounced by the Toyota entry. Ha!

We made it back to Bahia de los Angeles on the bad tire and got the other tire repaired at a *llantera.* The pre-run scouting was in full swing, with motorcycles and tube-framed, unlimited-class buggies screaming through town, apparently intent on duplicating race speeds as closely as possible. We left and continued our loop up to the U.S. border and San Diego.

As much as both of us enjoy backcountry camping, it's always a treat to come back to civilization. After a two-hour wait to get across the border, we booked a hotel, then went out for Italian food and ice cream. Delightful.

The best time to venture to Baja is in late fall (November) through April. Summer can be blessedly free of other travelers, but not insects and high temperatures.

Always carry lots of spare water, food, tools, and parts when traveling the Mexico backcountry. Tire repair shops are very common, even in remote towns, but an extra spare would be a wise addition. As in any country where you are a newcomer, filter your drinking water and wash market produce well in filtered water if you want to avoid the dreaded *turista.* It is advisable not to eat uncooked seafood. (Ceviche, a popular—and delicious—Mexican dish, includes lime juice, chiles, onions, and uncooked shrimp or other white-fleshed fish. We make our own by precooking the meat, then marinating in lime and chile.)

U.S. dollars are usually accepted throughout Baja, but carry pesos as well for tips, supplies, and small grocery items in backroad towns. Occasionally gasoline can become short in supply; always carry jerry cans and keep them topped up in case of a shortage. Gas is no longer a bargain in Mexico, by the way. Expect to pay prices similar to those in the States.

For Information: See Chapter 3, page 46, for contact information for Baja travel, and page 47 for travel guide and atlas suggestions.

vehicles can negotiate grades you would have trouble walking up.

That said, the essence of this book will not be about "conquering" formidable terrain, but simply exploring rough roads and trails that would be difficult or impossible in a normal sedan. One of the biggest problems with the image of four-wheel-drive vehicles in general is the perception that they are destructive. However, like many other inanimate objects, it is the operator who determines what the vehicle does. We'd like to think that the interest in sport utility vehicles might spark a resurgence in the appreciation of nature, as more and more owners explore and learn to value the wild lands now accessible to them. Looked at in this way, the sport utility vehicle might pave the way, so to speak, toward a wider conservation ethic.

One other criticism leveled at sport utilities deserves attention: fuel economy. Particularly in reference to full-size models, four-wheel-drive vehicles are castigated for wasting gas, a claim that is, frankly, quite true. Even considering their great passenger and cargo space, the big sport utilities suffer when compared to, say, a minivan (yuck!) of essentially the same capacity. However, the disparity can be mitigated in several ways. First, stick with the base engine when buying; it's usually powerful enough for any normal use. Second, exploit all that interior space by carpooling with friends and co-workers for commutes and other errands. And third, leave the thing at home once in a while and walk or bike to your destination.

Finally, while taking advantage of all that four wheel drive can do, keep in mind what it *shouldn't* do.

Nowhere in this book will we refer to four-wheel-drive vehicles as "off-road" vehicles. "Off-pavement," yes, "backroad," sure, but no vehicle should ever be driven off existing trails or roads. The scars left by irresponsible drivers can last for decades; worse, wildcat trails can erode and damage far more land than is actually covered by the vehicle.

As with many other activities, it's the selfish acts of a few that give a bad name to the entire group. And it's not just the beer-swilling guys in jacked-up trucks who do the damage— recently we talked with a well-dressed, mid-fifties birdwatcher who bragged to us how close she drove her new Jeep to the nesting site of a rare gnatcatcher: "Everyone else walked up the last mile of the trail, but I just drove right in." Marvelous.

The best solution is policing from within our ranks. If you see people driving where they shouldn't, take down their license numbers and *report them*. If you come upon a trail that has obviously been recently bashed through by selfish slobs, don't take it. Look for four-wheel-drive clubs in your area, which will often organize projects to block off illegal trails.

If you're interested in doing some real backcountry exploring, consider taking a class in backroad driving skills. You'll learn under the direct observation of an expert, in a controlled environment, and will be taught how to minimize the impact of the vehicle on the environment. A couple of manufacturers, such as Land Rover, run their own classes; others are considering the possibility. There are many independent schools across the country as well.

Another possibility is to join a four-wheel-drive club in your area that offers classes or outings for beginners. See Appendix II, starting on page 166, for more information on contacting schools and clubs.

CHAPTER 2

Backroad Driving Techniques

BY JONATHAN HANSON

Engage

There are two broad categories of situations in which you might benefit from the four-wheel-drive capabilities of your vehicle. The first involves travel on graded dirt or even paved roads, when conditions such as snow, ice, or mud have reduced traction. Depending on where you live, you might find such conditions on your regular commute to work.

The other situations arise on rough, backcountry trails, where high ground clearance and extra traction are necessary at all times (and where the added complications of mud or ice can make any progress at all next to impossible).

Although each of these situations demands many similar driving techniques, there are enough differences that we are going to discuss them separately.

Basic Four-Wheel-Drive Techniques for the Road

Even a four-lane-wide stretch of paved superhighway can become treacherous when snow or ice renders the surface as slick as a skating rink. The best strategy in these conditions is to *stay home*. However, that's not always possible, and many times such situations can develop with frightening suddenness, turning a pleasurable road trip into a white-knuckle epic within hours. This is when the extra security of four wheel drive could quite literally prove to be a lifesaver.

If You Have Four Wheel Drive, Use It

If your vehicle has a part-time four-wheel-drive system, don't hesitate to use it when snow, ice, or mud cover significant parts of the road. Just because you see other drivers out on the road in two-wheel-drive sedans is no reason not to optimize your own situation. Men, in particular, are often susceptible to a strange macho reluctance to admit they might need four wheel drive. The same men wouldn't hesitate to pilot a vehicle with full-time four wheel drive, but apparently reaching down and consciously pulling that lever is seen as a sign of some sissy lack of skill. For more on this syndrome, see the Tread Lightly section later in this chapter.

While you shouldn't hesitate to use it when conditions dictate, remember that most part-time four-wheel-drive systems are not designed to be run on dry pavement. Snow-covered pavement or wet pavement with frequent icy patches allow enough slippage to prevent the transfer gears from binding (see Chapter 1, page 5). In vehicles with shift-on-the-fly four-wheel-drive systems, you can shift back and forth between two and four wheel drive (high range) while moving, and can thus select more traction as needed. With full-time four wheel drive, of course, the traction is always there, and the transfer case is designed to allow the necessary slippage.

Four-wheel-drive conditions can vary from snow and ice on pavement, to very difficult dirt roads, such as this steep section on a Bureau of Land Management four-wheel-drive-designated route in southern Arizona.

Jonathan Hanson

Easy Does It

When you walk across an icy sidewalk, you do so slowly and carefully, avoiding sudden movements and abrupt changes of direction. That's exactly the way you should drive on slick roads, too.

BASIC RULES FOR LOW-TRACTION CONDITIONS ON THE ROAD

- Don't be afraid to use four wheel drive.
- Avoid rapid acceleration or deceleration.
- Avoid using low range if possible.
- Use as high a gear as possible.
- Keep your speed down.

When driving on ice, snow, or slippery mud, the traction available to each wheel is drastically reduced. That means that any abrupt application of power or brakes is likely to break the fragile bond between tire and road. Once that bond is lost, the tire has no grip at all and acts more like a luge than a tire.

The way to prevent this from happening is to be very smooth in your use of both the accelerator and brake pedal. Gradual applications of power and braking will help prevent the tires from breaking loose. If you do accelerate and feel or hear a tire spinning, back off gently on the pedal; similarly, if a tire locks under braking, back off slightly on the brake pedal to regain control. In high-end vehicles equipped with a device called traction control, a computer senses wheel spin and automatically reduces power to the wheels when accelerating. Vehicles with antilock brakes have a similar sensor to prevent the brakes from locking a wheel.

Another way to avoid power-induced traction loss is to use as high a gear as possible for the situation. In vehicles with automatic transmissions, if you leave the gear selector in drive ("D"), the car will normally start from a standstill in first gear, which results in a lot of torque to the wheels. If your selector has "one" and "two" positions in addition to "D," try using the two position to start the vehicle in second gear, reducing the torque to the wheels and thus the chance of slipping. With a manual transmission, try starting in second gear as well. You'll need to slip the clutch a bit to avoid stalling the engine, but again the chance of losing traction is reduced.

A corollary to the above is to keep the transfer case in high range if possible. Low range doubles the torque at the wheels—a good thing when climbing steep hills, but not when driving on a flat but slippery surface.

Needless to say (isn't it?), keep your speed down on ice, snow, and slippery mud. Not only does this reduce the chances of losing traction, but it certainly reduces the consequences if you do so.

Stuck on a Flat Spot

Sometimes, no matter what you do, you'll find yourself in a situation in which the vehicle refuses to move. Maybe it's on a patch of ice or hard snow, perhaps it's a mud-slicked dirt road—whatever, any attempt at acceleration just spins the tires. There are a couple of things to try before calling a tow truck.

First, don't exacerbate your predicament by spinning the wheels wildly. The odds are strong you'll just make things worse. The instant you realize you're stuck, stop everything and evaluate the situation.

If you're on ice or snow, and the tires haven't dug themselves below the surrounding surface, try turning your wheels all the way to one side and applying gas gently. Sometimes this allows the front tires a bite at a fresh surface. Moving the wheel all the way back and forth sometimes helps. Also, don't forget to try *reversing* out of the spot. If you have a manually locking differential, engaging it now might help, but disengage it as soon as you are free—a locked differential can be a hazard on an icy road.

One exception to the no-spinning rule is if the vehicle is stuck on a small, very thin patch of ice or snow. In such cases, the heat generated by a spinning tire will sometimes melt the ice beneath it, resulting in firm contact with the pavement. If the tires are kept spinning *slowly*, they can melt their way off the ice patch. This technique requires caution, however, so the vehicle doesn't accelerate out of control when it hits clear pavement. Also, if tried on a side slope, the vehicle might slide sideways when the tires begin to spin.

The surest way to get the vehicle moving is to put something under the tires to add traction. For ice, sand works very well; a covered bucketful kept in the cargo area is a good idea. Auto stores sell various mats to roll out in front of the tires. In a pinch, many things will work—carpeted floor mats are excellent, so are old blankets or even items of clothing. Beware, however—it's doubtful you'll be wearing the clothes again after they've been cuisinarted under your tires.

Using Chains

Even the most aggressive tire tread designs are still just rubber, and rubber leaves much to be desired for traction on slick snow and ice. One excellent solution is a set of tire chains, sturdy metal links that wrap around each tire and really bite into the surface.

Don't go halfway—if you buy chains, buy them for all four wheels. If conditions are bad enough to use chains at all, you should have them at every corner, and it's very little extra trouble to install four chains instead of two. Generally, the metal link chains are stronger and

HIGHWAY ROBBERY

Several years ago, our friend Bruce and his girlfriend were touring the Pacific Northwest in a two-wheel-drive sedan. Outside Portland they got caught in a freak blizzard that covered six states with snow drifts and ice. The interstate was littered with both stuck vehicles and those that had careened into snowbanks after their drivers lost control. Since he had to be back in Arizona in several days, Bruce was determined to continue, but the car was virtually unmanageable.

Then, on the side of the road, he found two men in a freight truck selling snow chains—for $75 a set, at least triple what they would have cost at the time at an auto parts store. The chains looked pretty flimsy at that, but Bruce shelled out the cash and continued on in much greater safety—for about 30 miles, when the pot metal links simply disintegrated. Of course, there was no way to go back and confront the con artists, so Bruce limped into the next town and found one of the last pairs of good chains left at an auto parts store.

The moral is: Be prepared, and carry your own equipment. If you visit a different area of the country, be sure you have the right tools for the climate.

more effective than the cable type; the advantage to the latter is that they are quieter and don't thump as much on hard surfaces. Some cable chains can be driven over pavement without ill effect; trying to do the same with link chains sounds and feels like a moving car wreck.

The best link chains are constructed so that the chain sections cross the tire diagonally, rather than straight across like a ladder. The ladder pattern allows the bare tire to contact the surface intermittently, which could result in a skid if the brakes locked with the bare tire on ice or snow. With the diagonal chain pattern there is always steel in contact with the road.

Four-Wheel-Drive Techniques for Trails

There comes a time when you're ready to tackle your first stretch of rough trail—a stretch difficult enough to make your palms sweat a little, even though you might have seen other vehicles negotiating the same route without any problems. Knowledge of some basic skills will help you look like an expert the first time out.

Get a Grip

On rough trails, rocks, ruts, and other obstructions can cause the front tires to jerk suddenly sideways. When this happens, the steering wheel can spin out of your grip with surprising force, even with power steering. Always use two hands on the wheel, at nine and three o'clock, and keep your thumbs outside the rim, so the spokes can't whack them if you lose your grip. Don't laugh—people have had their thumbs broken this way. When you need to turn the wheel more than 90 degrees, don't maintain the same grip and get your arms crossed over each other; shift your hands to keep as close to a nine-and-three position as possible.

Needless to say—at least I hope it is—you should be belted in at all times, even on one-mile-per-hour sections of trail. Make sure you've got the seat adjusted to give you maximum control; you might want it a little closer to the steering wheel than when driving on the road. You should be able to brace your left foot on the floor next to the clutch pedal (or the brake in an automatic). Incidentally, I've heard a spurious rumor that the bouncing and banging of rough roads might set off the air bags on

---

BASIC RULES

- Keep your thumbs outside the steering wheel.
- Slower is usually better.
- Watch where your wheels are going.
- Drive over big rocks, don't straddle them.
- Use engine compression instead of braking to control speed.
- Use the clutch only for starting and shifting.
- Approach small ditches and drop-offs at an angle.
- Scout questionable stretches before driving through.

DEFINING THE BACKCOUNTRY SPORT UTILITY

As the market for sport utility vehicles continues to broaden, so does the very definition of what constitutes such a vehicle. More and more models are being developed that are oriented toward secure on-road traction than rough backcountry ability. Some of these have more clearance and features than others, so it becomes difficult to easily evaluate the backroad potential of any one. But here are a few ways to judge what to expect from yours.

■ **Does it have a transfer case with a low range?** Low gearing is one of the most important features of a vehicle designed for rough and steep trails. If your vehicle has only a regular transmission with standard ratios, it was not intended for serious backcountry use. Note, however, that some models with no transfer case do have an extra-low first gear. This is a compromise that does help in situations needing slow speeds.

■ **How much ground clearance is there?** Many four-wheel-drive sedans and station wagons stand no farther off the ground than their two-wheel-drive counterparts; obviously they are meant to be used on relatively smooth tracks.

■ **How vulnerable is the undercarriage?** Look underneath the vehicle. Are the exposed pieces of running gear thick and sturdy or protected by skid plates, or do suspension struts, exhaust pipes, and engine parts hang down where they could be damaged?

There is a lot of middle ground for the latter two criteria, so you'll have to use your own judgment in deciding where to go exploring. If you go cautiously at first, and scout questionable stretches, it's unlikely you'll get into too much trouble.

new vehicles. Nonsense. The threshold of impact necessary to trigger an air bag is far, far beyond even the roughest jostling possible by a driver.

Slow is Best

In about 90 percent of all trail situations, it's better to go slow than fast—that's one reason the transfer case has a low range. Going slow allows you to place the wheels—and thus the whole vehicle—accurately, avoiding damage to the underside and helping to stay on the proper line through and over obstacles. You might think, approaching steep sections of trail, that you need to accelerate to make it up, but in low range the power of the vehicle is multiplied greatly. Generally just a bit of gas is sufficient to climb most slopes. Experience will soon improve your judgment.

Learn to be aware of where your tires are at all times. They are your contact with earth, and you want to offer them the best places to be at all times. The skill of proper tire placement is, more than any other single factor, what separates average drivers from experts in the backcountry.

Jonathan Hanson

Drive slowly but steadily when in low-range four wheel drive, and keep careful track of your tire placement; leaning out of the window helps you get a better perspective.

I've seen two drivers cover the same stretch of trail with technique so different they appeared to be driving two different routes. The novice essentially went straight up the path, so the tires dropped into every rut and hole, and the vehicle bounced around and threw dirt from the tires. The more experienced driver smoothly guided the wheels around the drop-offs, picking a more level route that made the stretch seem easy.

Know Your Clearance

Do yourself a favor before you go exploring—get down on the ground and familiarize yourself with the underside of your vehicle. It helps to know where the highest and lowest spots on the chassis are.

Often the lowest spots on the vehicle will be the differential housings, at least if you have one or more live axles (see Chapter 1, page 2). Sometimes the housings will be in the middle of the axle, sometimes offset to one side. If you know where they are, you'll be better able to keep them from dragging on heavily rutted or rocky trails.

Jonathan Hanson

When negotiating rocky roads, you must know the ground clearance of your differential housings. Shown in this photo is the front differential, between the wheels; if in doubt, get out and check before proceding.

Other points to watch out for are low-hanging shock absorber mounts and suspension and steering struts. Check the middle of the vehicle, halfway between the front and rear axles. If you drive over a sharp hill crest or over a ledge, the center of the vehicle can drag or hang up. Getting stuck in this position is called "high-centered." Some pretty vulnerable parts are exposed under the vehicle near the centerline. The transfer case outputs, where the driveshafts to the front and rear axles emerge, hang down in this area. Other items include the transmission and transfer case housings. Sport utilities designed for real backroad use will have skid plates or crossmembers protecting breakable pieces.

One vulnerable component of many vehicles is the exhaust system. Often the muffler, catalytic converter, and pipe itself are poorly protected, if at all, and are prone to damage. If the exhaust runs down one side of the vehicle, keep it in mind when choosing a line through a rough section so you can take extra precautions against rocks on that side.

If you're on a trail and you're not sure if a rock or ridge will clear the underside, get out and check with the vehicle right up close to the obstruction. You'll look like a golfer lining up a putt, but you'll be able to see if and where you can make it over. You'll also gain experience judging the next obstruction, until you rarely need to get out to verify your gut feeling.

Often it's better to drive the tires over an obstruction than to straddle it. When you drive over, the whole vehicle is lifted up and over, and the lower sides of the body under the doors, called the rocker panels, usually have more clearance than the underside. Do this slowly, so the vehicle doesn't bounce when the tire rolls off the rock, thus making it more likely that

AIRING DOWN

The contact patch of the tire—that is, the amount of rubber actually in contact with the surface over which you're driving—is the key to traction and flotation. On soft surfaces such as sand, a larger contact patch means the weight of the vehicle is spread out over a larger area, so the vehicle is less likely to sink.

An easy way to temporarily increase the size of your tires' contact patch is to reduce the air pressure in the tires. Reducing pressure from, say, the normal 35 or 40 pounds down to around 20 flattens the tire a bit, putting more tread on the ground. This technique is suitable *only* for low-speed driving, under ten miles per hour. At higher speeds an underinflated tire can overheat and destroy itself. Also, it's not advisable to air down in areas of sharp rocks, since the danger of sidewall damage is increased. But it's amazing how well it works—many times I have seen vehicles stuck in sand that were subsequently driven free after reducing tire pressure.

There is a lower limit to airing down. If you go too far, the tires can actually spin on the rims. For safety's sake, keep the pressure above fifteen pounds per square inch.

Of course, if you air down, you'll have to air back up when you hit the highway. That requires a portable air compressor of some type. See Chapter 5, page 142, for more information.

the rocker panel hits the object. Again, don't hesitate to get out and check or even measure the clearance before attempting the move.

Another facet of ground clearance is the approach and departure angle of the vehicle. Crouch down about 20 feet from the side of your vehicle, and draw an imaginary line between the bottom of the front tire and the lowest point of bodywork or the front bumper. This is the approach angle; a similar line drawn from the back tire to the rear bodywork defines the departure angle. The approach angle determines how steep a rise your vehicle can climb before the front valance, air dam, or bumper contacts the ground. Use caution: On most vehicles the departure angle is shallower than the approach angle, meaning you might successfully get the front of the vehicle up a steep rise, only to find the rear bumper digging in and halting progress.

Don't Use the Brakes

Did I get your attention? Good. Of course, I don't mean *never* use the brakes. However, in many trail situations, it's better to let the braking effect of the engine slow the vehicle instead of using the brake pedal.

Try an experiment. Shift your vehicle into low range, and accelerate in first gear. Let off on the gas pedal, and note how abruptly the vehicle slows. This is what the normal compression of the engine can do when its torque is multiplied by the low gearing in the transfer case. In most sport utilities, the engine braking in low-range first gear will safely control the speed of the vehicle down even the steepest descents.

Why use engine braking instead of the brake pedal? Because the engine applies equal decelerative force to all four wheels, and does so very steadily. On a bouncy descent of a rough trail, it is extremely difficult to modulate the brake pedal with your foot while paying attention to everything else. Even if you could do so, with the vehicle on a downhill angle, most of its weight is over the front wheels, unloading the back wheels and making it much more likely that the rear brakes will lock. If this happens the rear of the vehicle will try to slide *ahead* of the front—an unhappy situation.

Note that engine braking works better on vehicles with manual transmissions than on those equipped with automatics. The slippage inherent in an automatic reduces the amount of braking effect somewhat. To gain any engine braking at all with an automatic, the gear selector needs to be in the "one" or "low" position. Experiment while exploring easy trails to see how effective your vehicle is at slowing itself. For more on engine braking, see the section on steep descents, page 25.

Stay Off the Clutch

If you have a manual transmission, you should use the clutch pedal for three purposes: starting, stopping, and shifting gears. That's it. There's a tendency to transfer some things you do with a road car to backroad technique; these not only don't work very well, they can hurt the vehicle.

Driving a sedan on pavement, we habitually let the clutch pedal part way out ("slipping" the clutch) to hold the vehicle on a slight hill, and to move off from a stop on a hill we'll slip it even more. But hills on backroads tend to be much steeper than urban roads. If you're in a position on a back road where you find it necessary to slip the clutch to get the vehicle moving, you're probably in high range on the transfer case when you should be in low range. Shift down and let the gearing work for you. Likewise, when downshifting to descend a steep hill, do so quickly (but smoothly) so the gears and not the clutch do the work of slowing you. See the box on page 25 for more information.

Driving Obliquely

One of the most common obstacles to encounter on a trail is a small ditch or rut, or a short ledge you must climb or descend, oriented directly across your line of travel. The best way to tackle such an obstacle is by approaching it at about a 45-degree angle. In this way only one wheel at a time crosses the obstruction, which helps traction. If you enter a shallow but steep rut straight on, you increase the chances that, first, your air dam or bumper will catch on the opposite side and, second, you will become high-centered when both front wheels drop in and the chassis behind the front axle catches on the edge of the drop-off. The same thing can happen when climbing a small ledge. Think about driving off a curb as an example (or go try it)—it's easier to go off one wheel at a time than to drop straight off. The same thing is true climbing the curb, with an additional factor—it's easier for the engine to push one tire at a time up the obstruction.

Always approach ditches or drop-offs at an angle.

Jonathan Hanson

The only problem that can occur with this technique is if the obstruction is big or deep enough so that one front and one rear tire lose traction. If this happens, and your vehicle is not equipped with a locking differential, the proper solution is to approach the obstruction slowly. Then, just as the first wheel climbs it, tap the gas to give the vehicle a bit more momentum. This will usually carry you far enough over so that both front tires regain grip.

Scouting and Spotting

Never, ever be afraid to get out and inspect a questionable stretch of trail. This is particularly vital if the stretch in question leads out of your sight; you might make it just around

PARKING ON A SLOPE

A couple of tips will help ensure safety when parking on a severe slope. These work well both on back roads or steep city streets.

■ With an automatic transmission, stop the vehicle, leave your foot on the brake pedal, and apply the parking brake firmly, then shift the gear selector into "Park" and turn off the engine. This ensures that the parking brake is doing the primary job of holding the vehicle, with the transmission as backup. The park setting on the transmission has a single pin that locks the vehicle in place, so shifting into park first and letting go of the brake pedal puts a great deal of strain on the part, and can make it difficult to shift out of park.

■ With a manual transmission, stop the vehicle, shift into neutral, and apply the parking brake, then shift into reverse, turn off the motor, and release the clutch. Again, this puts the primary strain on the parking brake. Reverse is used because it is the lowest-ratio gear in the transmission and thus exerts the strongest restraining force against the vehicle.

■ To start from a parked position on a hill, step firmly on the brake pedal, start the engine, shift into the proper gear, then release the parking brake. See the box on page 25 for tips on getting underway on a slope.

the bend and find your way blocked, leaving you no choice but to reverse through the difficult part.

Scouting is also important if the trail appears to have been extended illicitly. When the passage has been easy and suddenly turns much narrower and rougher just past a wide turnaround, you can suspect that some slob has bashed his own road through where he was too lazy to walk. Once one vehicle shows the way, others inevitably follow, but you can refuse to contribute to this destructive behavior.

A useful adjunct to scouting is spotting. If you have a passenger, he or she can help guide you through difficult spots by standing outside the vehicle and watching your progress. Simple hand signals can help you place the tires more accurately than you could possibly do otherwise. Experienced spotters are used by clubs whose members challenge some of the most difficult—even dangerous—trails in the country, so there is no taint of the amateur in this practice.

Treading Lightly

Accompanied by two other vehicles, we had reached a lovely overlook off a trail in the mountains of southern Arizona. Below us a creek splashed through oaks and sycamores, and we began to deploy picnic supplies in the shade.

About 20 minutes later, we heard another vehicle coming up the trail. It was a weekend, and we hadn't expected to have the whole mountain range to ourselves, so no one thought much of it. But as the vehicle got closer, it was obviously having trouble negotiating the relatively moderate route. Out of curiosity, I walked back up to the main trail and waited.

In a few minutes, a four-wheel-drive pickup appeared around the corner and attacked the grade below me at full throttle, engine roaring, wheels bouncing into the air, gravel and dirt shooting from the rear tires. I could see the bed of the truck twisting out of alignment with the cab as the frame torqued under the stress. The truck pulled up next to me, the two young men in it grinning. I knew what they were going to say, but I waited for it anyway. Sure enough: "Made it all the way in two wheel drive!" the driver boasted.

This macho *made-it-all-the-way-in-two-wheel-drive* syndrome is sadly common, especially—at least in my experience—among the jacked-up-suspension, major-tires pickup crowd. What the participants think they're proving is unclear. The real results are threefold:

- They look foolish to experienced drivers, who are much more impressed with a graceful, smooth ascent of a difficult grade than an out-of-control charge up it.
- They stress the running gear and chassis of their vehicles, hastening wear and risking breakage—to say nothing of the chances of careening off the trail and really doing some damage.
- Most importantly for the rest of us, they significantly degrade the trail by tearing up the surface, digging ruts, and promoting erosion. Is it fair to assume that the yahoos who are willing to do all of the above are also more likely to drive off trails altogether, giving a bad name to four-wheel-drive owners in general?

It was partially to combat this poor image that the *Tread Lightly!*, Inc., nonprofit organization was established by the U.S. Forest Service in 1985. *Tread Lightly!* promotes responsible use of not just four-wheel-drive vehicles, but

Tread Lightly! represents environmentally sound practices: **T**ravel only on designated routes; **R**espect the rights of others; **E**ducate yourself; **A**void streambanks, meadows, wildlife, etc.; **D**rive and travel responsibly.

mountain bikes and snowmobiles as well, and even offers advice for low-impact hiking.

The *Tread Lightly!* pledge offers a good foundation for environmentally aware use of your vehicle:

> Travel only on designated routes.
> Respect the rights of others.
> Educate yourself.
> Avoid streambanks, meadows, wildlife, etc.
> Drive and travel responsibly.

Stay on the Road

It would have been much better if the term "off-road vehicle" had never been coined—it's just too suggestive. Throughout this book you'll notice we're careful to use terms such as backcountry or backroad or rough road. The fact is that, with more than 500,000 miles of backroads available to us just in the United States, there is no need for anyone to travel off an already established trail. And there's certainly no skill involved in bashing through bushes; in fact many people who do so are detouring around difficult spots along the proper route. Rather than ignore such behavior, other drivers should self-police it. If we can stop this selfishness with peer pressure, we'll face less outside pressure to shut down vehicular access to abused areas.

Certain circumstances encourage off-trail abuse:

■ When rain fills dips in the main trail with water and mud, it often results in a quagmire. These spots are difficult to evaluate and can easily mire most vehicles, so the natural reaction is to cut around the spot. The problem is that the new track develops mud holes of its own, encouraging people to detour yet again, until the area is a 50-foot-wide mass of tracks and muddy ruts. If you're not sure you can make it through on the main trail, *turn around* and come back when things have dried out.

Jonathan Hanson

Never drive "off-road" to explore, camp, or even park; the damage will take decades to diminish, or others will follow your tracks and create more damage.

LEAVE ROOM FOR WILDERNESS

At least one high-quality magazine devoted to serious four-wheel-drive vehicles and techniques spoils its image by ridiculing those who want to protect the remaining wilderness areas with which our country is blessed. The editorials continually brand wilderness advocates as "elitists" and accuse them of wanting to lock up millions of acres of public land. It's an ironic accusation: All anyone needs to enjoy a wilderness area is a good pair of walking shoes, yet this publication regularly features trails navigable only by vehicles modified with thousands of dollars worth of equipment. So who's being elitist? The magazine has even brought out the banner of "Handicapped Access"—a surefire political point-getter. If the editors are really interested in handicapped access, they should lobby to have all those challenging class 5 trails graded and paved so wheelchair vans can get through. We suspect that what they're really interested in is access for overweight middle-aged guys who don't like to walk. And to argue that four-wheel-drive owners don't have enough places to go is just stupid—the U.S. Forest Service road network alone is *eight times* the length of the entire interstate highway system.

We believe there is enough room for everybody. We also firmly believe there are many, many places where vehicles simply don't belong. Remember—it's easy to bash a trail through a wilderness, but once a wilderness is lost, it is lost forever. If sport utility owners spoke out for wilderness preservation, they would gain immense credibility when legitimate access problems for vehicles came up.

- On steep trail sections, ruts formed by spinning tires can erode into nasty trenches, which are tempting to avoid by going around. But the same expansion effect mentioned above then occurs. If you must get through, the solution is to fill in the ruts with enough rocks or dirt to ensure clearance.

- Now and then even flat stretches of trail will develop eroded fissures deep enough to swallow whole wheels. Again, short of turning around, the proper technique is to do some filling-in.

- Sometimes, a four-wheel-drive trail ends in a parking circle a few hundred yards from a scenic spot. Sooner or later, some bozo will decide that's too far to walk and will start forging an extension to the trail, until the parking lot winds up right next to the waterfall or stream or overlook. Lovely. Again, peer pressure might be the best prevention for this syndrome. Sometimes four-wheel-drive clubs work to block off spurious trails with large boulders. In the meantime, if you notice something like this happening, you can at least refuse to participate. Park in the original spot and give disgusted looks to anyone who drives past you.

Advanced Backroad Techniques

You might spend a lifetime exploring without ever getting into a situation where you need the following techniques. Most are appropriate for very difficult trails, well off the routes of the majority of vacationers. But occasionally you'll want to head into country where above-average skills are needed to successfully negotiate challenging terrain. Even if you don't plan on getting into such places, it never hurts to know more than you need to about the capabilities of your vehicle.

If you decide to challenge yourself in rough terrain, try to do so at first with someone more experienced than yourself, so you can watch how the veteran does it. Also, don't head off somewhere that would involve a 20-mile walk out if you get irretrievably stuck.

Lastly, keep in mind the design parameters of your vehicle, and don't try to make it do something for which it wasn't intended. To successfully negotiate advanced four-wheel-drive trails, you need plenty of ground clearance and tires designed for real backroad use. The vehicle should have a transfer case with a low range. Skid plates should be in place over vulnerable underparts, and you should be equipped with tools for self-recovery in the event you get stuck (see Chapter 5, page 131). If possible you should travel in the company of another vehicle, so one of you can help the other if a vehicle gets stuck, and so you'll have a way out if one breaks down.

Steep Ascents

I remember the first really steep hill I attempted with my old Land Cruiser. I looked at the slope and knew for an absolute certainty there was simply no *way* anyone could drive up it. Yet the evidence of numerous tire tracks leading to the top was irrefutable. So I selected low range first, gave it half-throttle—and motored up without a trace of drama. Since then I have completed ascents that made that first hill seem like a speed bump, yet I am always amazed just how steep a grade a 4x4 can climb with good tires and the correct technique.

That technique varies depending on the situation. For hills with a reasonably firm dirt surface, slow is best—first or second gear, low range. If the surface is very loose, such as a sand hill, you might need more momentum at the bottom, starting out at a higher speed and higher gear, dropping to a lower gear as you near the top.

Always keep your vehicle pointed straight up the hill. Getting sideways on a steep slope is an invitation to a roll. If the tires lose traction and the vehicle comes to a halt, *immediately* shift into reverse and let the engine compression back the vehicle straight down the hill; don't try to turn it around. If your vehicle has automatic transmission and little compression braking, use the brake pedal lightly to keep the speed down.

If the ascent is very rutted, pick the smoothest line possible for your tires. If you're applying a lot of power and one of the tires loses contact with the ground over a rut, it can spin wildly. When it hits the ground again and suddenly stops spinning, the impact can snap axles or strip differential gears. The chances of this happening are reduced if the vehicle is equipped with limited-slip or locking differentials.

STARTING ON A HILL

Getting started up a steep hill with a manual transmission can be a tense experience—even on pavement. Here are a couple of effective techniques.

■ Apply the parking brake firmly, so it alone will hold the vehicle stationary (the brake must be adjusted properly for this to work). Put the transmission in first gear, apply some gas, and let the clutch out slowly until you can feel the vehicle just trying to move forward against the brake. Release the parking brake and you will move forward.

■ If the parking brake will not hold the vehicle immobile, use the edge of your right shoe on the brake pedal to do so. Put the transmission in first, then roll the outside edge of your right foot onto the gas pedal to build up engine speed while you maintain pressure on the brake. As above, let out the clutch until the vehicle starts to move; then roll your foot off the brake pedal while applying more gas.

■ If the engine has stalled on a hill, it is sometimes possible to get underway without using the clutch at all. With the transfer case in low range, put the transmission in first gear. Let out the clutch pedal and release the parking brake, so the transmission alone is holding the vehicle stationary. With your foot lightly on the gas pedal, turn the key so the starter engages. The starter will jerk the vehicle forward and start the engine at the same time, and you will be under way. Note: Many vehicles have a "safety" switch that prevents the engine being started with the clutch pedal out. In that case you'll have to use one of the first two techniques above. A few vehicles have a "clutch start cancel" button that lets you temporarily disengage the safety switch to use the clutchless starting technique. Obviously this technique works only with manual transmission.

■ You can use the above tricks to get started on a steep downhill section as well, to prevent the vehicle accelerating out of gear.

Descending Steep Slopes

If going up vertiginous hills is scary, going down them can be downright terrifying. Sometimes it looks as though the vehicle might trip over some tiny obstacle and go tumbling end over end to the bottom. You feel as if you could fall through the windshield. Again, however, the capabilities of the vehicle are astounding.

As when ascending, keep the speed down as low as possible. With manual transmission, compression braking will do this for you in most circumstances; with automatic transmission you might have to augment the engine's restraining pull with a light touch on the brakes.

If you use the brakes going downhill, the rear tires often lock up, since the rear of the vehicle is very lightly loaded when it's pointed down at a steep angle. If the rear tires do lock, the back of the vehicle might try to slide around. It seems illogical, but locked tires can actually skate over the surface *faster* than slowly turning tires (the same thing occurs on pavement). When this happens, you have to ignore what your instincts are telling you and get *off* the brakes. Sometimes you might even have to tap the gas pedal to get the vehicle lined back up straight downhill. It's better to be heading down too fast than to be heading down sideways.

JUDGMENT

When you encounter a very steep or washed-out section of a backcountry road, it is always worth considering: Do I really need to go down this section? Sometimes a nearly impassable road is a sign that it should stay that way.

Water Crossings

My rule for fording unknown bodies of water is: *Let someone else go first.* I'll be blunt—I think anyone who crosses a stretch of water without being absolutely sure of the depth, bottom conditions, and current, if any, is being foolish. Look in any four-wheel-drive magazine that prints photos of "really, truly, badly stuck" vehicles, and see how many of them are up to their windshields in water.

Water can do serious damage to your vehicle in several ways. The worst is if you go in deep enough so water is sucked into the air intake and actually ingested into the running engine. The pistons will try to compress the water, which cannot *be* compressed. The result is usually bent connecting rods—time for an engine rebuild. This condition is known as hydraulic lock. Fortunately, it rarely happens, since the air intake is high on the engine—you'd have to be traversing really deep water. As a rule the ignition system will short out and stop the engine before the water gets inside. When this happens the engine will often start again once the distributor and ignition wires have dried out.

On newer vehicles, another expensive component to watch out for is the main engine computer. If water gets inside this, it will fry. On some vehicles the computer is mounted in the engine compartment; on others it is more protected. In our Toyota truck the computer is in the cab, behind the passenger footwell panel—well-isolated from normal splashing. If we're crossing a stream and water starts pooling on the carpet, we know it's time to head for land.

Water that gets into the transmission or differentials will cause problems, but only if they are not drained and refilled with oil shortly after the incident. Transmissions and differentials have to have breathers, since the air inside them expands and contracts as they get hot while running and then cool off while parked. Most manufacturers use a breather valve, which helps prevent water from getting in, but a better option is an extended breather tube that runs up to a point high enough to avoid submersion. Most Land Rover vehicles have extended axle and transmission breathers, admirable standard features. They can be retrofitted to most other vehicles.

Just how deep a puddle you can safely cross depends in large part on the vehicle. All else being equal, a taller vehicle has an advantage, since the ignition and air intake are higher. But some tall vehicles have distributors mounted low on the engine, and some short 4x4s have components higher up. So it's an individual question. Very few manufacturers publish official fording depths for their vehicles; if you're interested, call your company and see if you can pry it out of someone. You can also get some idea of your vehicle's capabilities by looking under the hood. Note where the air intake, distributor, and spark plug leads are located. The higher, the better. Don't, however, think you can cross any water as long as it's an inch or two below the vitals, because water gets thrown all over the place as it's scooped up by the bodywork and churned around inside the engine compartment.

For a rough-and-ready idea of your situation during a crossing, lean out the window and look at your tires. Water up to the hubs (the center of the wheels) is usually safe to cross. If it reaches the tops of the wheels, you're pushing it. If the tops of the tires are going under, you're really on the edge.

Most sport utilities can ford water 12 to 15 inches in depth with no problems. A few can handle 20 inches, and some large diesel-engined trucks (with no ignition systems to worry about) can exceed that—assuming there is little or no current.

Moving water is a whole different animal from a still pool. The force of water pressing against the side of the vehicle can be tremendous, even in a moderate current. If the bottom of the channel is mud, sand, or gravel, the current will constantly try to scour pits around the tires. Vehicles that have gotten stuck in stream beds (or below high tide line on a beach) have been nearly buried by this scouring action.

The proper way to cross a stream flowing over a soft surface is to keep moving yourself, at about a walking pace. If you stop, the water will immediately begin scooping the substrate from around your tires, and when you try to start again, you might find you can't.

As long as the water depth is below the level of your frame and bodywork, the current shouldn't exert too much pressure on the vehicle, but beware if it rises higher—the force will immediately multiply tenfold. In our state of Arizona, numerous cars are washed off roads, sometimes with tragic results, when their drivers try to cross dips filled by sudden floods. The depth of the water might be no more than a foot and a half, but it is moving at 10 or 15 miles per hour and exerts tons of force against a sedan foolishly piloted into it. Rugged four-wheel-drive vehicles are no guarantee of safety—one young man was swept to his death after he drove his Toyota Land Cruiser into a swift-moving wash nearly four feet in depth. The heavy vehicle was recovered *two miles* downstream. So pay close attention to both the depth and the speed of the water.

You're crossing a swift-moving stream and suddenly feel the tires losing traction (you can feel the vehicle start to dig its way straight down). What do you do? Try turning the wheel sharply downstream and giving it a little gas. Sometimes the push of the current will help just enough to get the vehicle moving again. If it's possible to exit the water downstream of your original goal, you can continue driving at a downstream angle; otherwise you'll have to use the momentum to turn back across the flow.

Sometimes, in spite of the most careful scouting and piloting, you might find yourself in water that is really frighteningly deep, like halfway-up-the-doors deep, with no option but to continue. Surprisingly, the best technique is to keep up a pretty good head of steam. The strategy is to build a good-sized bow wave in front of the vehicle, which creates a trough just behind it, actually lowering the water level in the engine compartment *below* that of the mean water depth. I've seen vehicles using this trick successfully driven through water that was washing over the hood.

Incidentally, it is possible to modify a vehicle so it will run with the engine submerged. The procedure involves extending the air intake to at least cab level and completely water-proofing the ignition system. Most vehicles intended to routinely cross deep water are equipped with diesel engines, which have no conventional ignition system to short out. A few owners of late-model Land Rover Defenders in the United States have equipped them with raised intake snorkels, imitating the look of the real expedition versions in Africa. But the U.S. Defender has a gasoline engine with a sensitive computer control and is not designed for submersion—so these accessories are strictly for style unless backed up by extensive further protection.

The driver of this Blazer failed to heed one of the most important tenets of backroad travel: Cross any water with extreme caution, and if you can't see the bottom, don't enter the water.

Sand

The only way to successfully drive in soft sand is to ensure the vehicle floats on top of it. Unlike some other substrates, sand retains essentially the same consistency well below the surface. So if your tires begin sinking or spinning and digging in deep sand, they will keep right on heading for the center of the earth until the vehicle is sitting on its doors.

Deep, aggressive tire tread is a disadvantage in sand, since the way an aggressive tire works is by biting into the surface. A shallow-lugged design—even a street-tire tread—is better, as is a wide tire, but of course you must balance different needs unless you plan to drive only in sand. In any case, airing down the tires (see box, page 17) is the single most effective way to assure adequate flotation with whatever tires you have.

SAND ETIQUETTE

When we talk about driving in sand, we don't mean driving across beach dunes or inland dunes—we are talking about sandy roads or dry river crossings. Sand dunes, while they appear "lifeless," are actually intricate ecosystems full of life: Specialized plants, insects, mammals, reptiles, and birds depend on them. Driving over dunes destroys their stability and causes erosion, and in beach areas you may destroy vital nesting sites of shorebirds and animals such as sea turtles.

When you drive into sand, you will immediately be able to gauge its consistency by the behavior of the vehicle. Some sand is so firmly packed that it is almost like driving on a dirt road; other times it will be so soft that the effect will be as though you'd hit the brakes, and the steering will feel mushy. The best technique is to keep up speed, as this seems to help the vehicle float. Keep the transmission in just a low enough gear that the engine doesn't strain—too low and the tires might spin if you apply gas. Avoid abrupt changes of direction, which cause the front tires to plow into the surface. And, as when driving on ice, do everything smoothly and gently, especially starting and stopping.

Mud

Mud is tricky, largely because it is so variable. It can take any form from firm clay to near-liquid soup. It can be inches or feet deep. Thick, gluey mud can stop a vehicle in its tracks and hold it as if it were nailed down.

If you drive in places where mud is common, consider installing mud tires on your vehicle (see Chapter 5, page 119). Most all-terrain tires quickly become clogged with mud, rendering them nearly tractionless. Mud tires are designed to minimize this problem with tread blocks that fling the mud out instead of trapping it.

No matter what kind of tires you have, driving through mud is one situation when spinning the tires is not necessarily bad. If the tread becomes clogged, you can feel the loss of control through the wheel and gas pedal. Sometimes a quick burst of power will restore control by freeing the tires of some of the mud load. This should be accomplished very quickly, so the tires don't dig into the surface.

Another useful technique is especially helpful in rutted mud. If you start to lose traction, move the steering wheel back and forth so the front tires bite at the edges of the ruts. Sometimes this extra grip will keep the vehicle moving. Use caution, however, as the tires can bite too deeply and fling the whole vehicle out of the path.

Recovery Techniques

It's easy to view getting stuck as some sort of failure, but that's simply not the case. In fact, if you push the limits of your vehicle at all, you *will* get stuck sooner or later. Experienced drivers accept the occasional loss of forward momentum as part of the fun. If you carry the proper equipment to rectify the situation, and learn the proper techniques, the whole process from "uh-oh" to back underway can take less time than changing a flat tire. Usually.

A vehicle gets stuck because the tires lose traction. That can happen in numerous ways: on a frictionless surface such as ice or snow; on a soft surface such as sand or mud where the tires spin and dig themselves in until the chassis grounds out (which unloads the tires, exacerbating the situation); or when part of the vehicle hangs up on a rock or something similar, and the tires cannot get enough grip to drag the vehicle off the obstruction. The task then is to give the tires the traction they need to get the vehicle moving again (for techniques on ice and snow, see page 12 earlier in this chapter).

RECOVERY EQUIPMENT

BASIC GEAR

- Shovel
- Hi-Lift jack
- Base plate for jack
- Tow strap or snatch strap

ADVANCED GEAR

- Winch
- Winch accessories: snatch block, tree strap, shackles, gloves
- Wheel chocks
- Sand ladders

Mud and Sand

The first thing to do in most situations when the tires have completely lost grip in a soft surface is *stop*. In the majority of cases, giving the engine more gas will only make the situation worse. I've seen dozens of drivers turn what would have been a mildly stuck vehicle into a well-and-truly stuck vehicle by gunning the engine and spinning the tires until they have dug graves for themselves.

Get out of the vehicle and evaluate the situation. If the problem is sand or mud, look closely at the surface around the tires. Occasionally a layer of mud or sand will lie over a firmer or drier surface, in which case spinning the tires down to the firmer material just might get you moving again. More often, however, the only fix will be getting the vehicle back up on top of the stuff in which it's sunk.

The first thing to do, if you haven't already, is air down the tires (see box, page 17). If you've not dug deep holes with the tires in a vain attempt to power out of the situation, very often airing down the tires will be all that's necessary to get you free. Even if it doesn't work immediately, the bigger contact patch will augment further techniques for getting unstuck. Take the tire pressure down to 20 psi or even a little lower, then gently apply power. You can feel the vehicle lift and grab if the tires get enough flotation. If the vehicle still won't move, stop immediately and try another option.

If you're traveling with another vehicle that can get close enough to you without getting bogged itself, a pull-out is the quickest way free. You can use a heavy-duty tow strap, rope, or chain, or an elastic nylon strap, commonly known as a snatch strap.

A snatch strap looks like a stout nylon tow strap, but it is actually elastic. This characteristic considerably reduces the strain on both vehicles—especially when compared to a chain—but the real trick is, it allows you to use a slingshot effect to free a vehicle that might not be freed with just a pull. However, snatch straps can be dangerous if not used carefully.

To use a snatch strap safely, both vehicles *must* have proper tow hooks to which to attach the strap. The little tie-down loops found under some vehicles, used to lash them down during transport, won't do. An inadequate attachment can become a lethal projectile if the strap rips it loose from its mount. If you have a receiver hitch, you can buy a slide-in fitting with an attached shackle that works perfectly. Don't, under any circumstances, attach the strap to a part of the vehicle not designed for heavy pulling.

Once you've attached the strap to both vehicles, attempt to free the stuck one with a simple pull, using low range first gear. If that doesn't work, pull the tow vehicle closer to the stuck one, so some slack in

Jonathan Hanson

Always attach "snatch straps" to strong frame-mounted tow hooks (or to frame-mounted bumpers with tow hooks). Never attach them to anything that wasn't designed to pull heavy loads.

the strap can be coiled loosely on the ground. Give the tow vehicle some gas so that it hits the end of the strap abruptly. There will be an elastic *BOING*, and, often as not, the stuck vehicle will pop free. If not, try again with more slack and a bit more speed. Don't, however, exceed a fast walking pace—you'll put too much strain on the system. While doing this, keep everyone except the drivers of the two vehicles well out of the way.

Never extend a snatch strap by attaching it to a length of chain. If the chain came loose from the vehicle, it would turn into a weapon. It's possible to extend the strap using another snatch strap, but I recommend against it.

If no other vehicle is available for a pull, and you don't have a winch, it's time to get out the shovel. You need to excavate a ramp to help each tire climb out of its hole. First, pick the direction you want to go; if you've just hit a small patch, you might continue forward, but if the path ahead looks like more of the same, it's time to back out. Then excavate a sloping hole down to each tire. Don't be tempted to scrimp on the holes to save time—if you don't get it right the first time, the vehicle will destroy your work while remaining stuck, and you'll have to start all over.

It will help immensely if you've got something solid to stick under the tires for extra traction. Genuine sand ladders are the best, of course. These are perforated sheets of metal that you see bolted to the roof racks of expedition vehicles. Unfortunately, they are decidedly awkward to carry around on an everyday vehicle (unless you're hopelessly into the *poseur* scene, with snorkels, tail-lamp brush guards, and similar accouterments bolted all over—or are actually on a serious expedition). Substitutes include floor mats (get someone else to loan you some if possible), boards, or sticks. Rocks can help, but often spinning tires will fling them into the undercarriage or bodywork, or at observers. Don't—as used to be accepted practice—cut limbs off shrubs or trees.

Incidentally, if you're stuck in mud that proves to be too soupy to dig effective ramps in, skip the shovel work and go right to the traction aids.

Hi-Lift Jack

A Hi-Lift jack has an astonishing range of capability. It can be used even as a winch if you carry two lengths of cable or chain and some shackles. This technique, however, is excruciatingly tedious. There are other ways.

First of all, to use a Hi-Lift jack, the vehicle must be equipped with heavy-duty bumpers that can easily support the weight of the whole car. The spiffy, vinyl-clad, body-color bumpers common on many vehicles these days are worthless for jacking. Several aftermarket bumpers, such as the superb ARB from Australia, are designed specifically for use with a Hi-Lift—the ARB even has a fitting to connect the jack tongue firmly to the bumper if needed.

An accessory you won't want to do without is a base plate for the jack. This is simply a large-diameter base to prevent the jack from sinking in soft surfaces and to offer a more stable platform. It can be a manufactured aluminum model, designed specifically for the jack, or something as simple as two pieces of ¾-inch plywood glued together to form a 1½-inch-thick base. It's also good to nail strips of wood on the plate to form a socket for the jack's own base plate to fit in; this helps stabilize the jack.

If one end of your vehicle is stuck in a hole or rut, with firm ground only a couple feet away, you can use the jack to raise the stuck end clear of the hole, then stuff big rocks underneath. There is, however, a faster and definitely more dramatic way, called "casting."

If the vehicle is stuck and there is firm ground to the side,

DEATH BY MUD

As this book was being completed, a woman died just outside Tucson after her truck partially sank in mud (it was night, during a torrential rain, and she had pulled off the pavement to wait out the downpour). After becoming hopelessly mired, she decided to wait it out in the cab because of the cold and wet weather, and she left the engine and heater running. She did not know that her tailpipe was buried in the mud, and her cab slowly filled with carbon monoxide, killing her during the night. The truck was still running when she was found.

you can jack up one end of the vehicle a foot or so to clear the rut. Then, you simply *push* the vehicle sideways off the jack, so the tires drop onto the firm ground. If necessary, you can copy the procedure at the other end of the vehicle. You can "walk" the vehicle several feet sideways if you repeat the process a few times.

The risks involved in casting should be obvious. Make sure everyone not involved is well clear of the action, and make sure the jack will not catch on anything as it tips across the bumper.

High-Centered

Once, on a rocky trail, I came upon a couple in a truck who had dropped one of the frame rails on a boulder, high-centering the vehicle. Although both were still in contact with the ground, the right front and left rear tires spun helplessly—the rock had lifted the vehicle just far enough to unload the tires. The couple had tried revving the engine and spinning tires until they smoked. The man had tried pushing, to no avail. I asked them to wait just a minute, and quickly located a flat rock about the size of a frying pan, which I wedged tightly under the left rear tire. I told the woman to try first gear and a little gas—and the truck rolled effortlessly off the boulder.

High-centering is a simple condition that results when part of the vehicle gets stuck on and partially supported by a boulder or ridge of dirt. The obstruction takes enough weight off the tires so they get little traction. The solution is to raise the ground under the tire with a rock or other object, the size being dependent on how far off the ground the tires are. If nothing else is available, the spare tire will often suffice.

Another way to regain traction is to add weight to one of the slipping corners of the vehicle. Had I and the gentleman in the above story stood in the bed of the truck over the spinning tire, our combined weight might well have accomplished the same end the rock did. Obviously there is a bit more risk involved in having someone hanging on the vehicle; caution is necessary.

Winching

The forces involved when using a winch to free a stuck vehicle are tremendous. Pay attention while using a winch!

If your vehicle is equipped with a winch, buy the accessory kit offered by manufacturers such as Warn and Ramsey. The kit includes a tree trunk protector strap, one or two large D-shaped shackles, a snatch block, a length of chain, and a pair of gloves. The gloves have loose wrists, so if by some chance they get caught, you can pull your hand out. This kit will enable you to use your winch safely and effectively in a variety of situations.

If a winch-equipped vehicle gets stuck, the simplest way to free it is to attach the winch cable to something solid, such as a large tree or another vehicle. The winch has a freewheeling position that allows the cable to be pulled out quickly. The anchor should be as nearly as possible directly in front of the winch, so it doesn't have to pull at an angle—the exception being if the vehicle *needs* to be pulled out at an angle, such as away from an obstruction or drop-off.

If you're using a tree as an anchor, always employ a protector strap around the trunk. Wrapping the cable around the trunk and hooking it to itself is bad for both tree and cable (you should always avoid hooking the cable to itself if possible). Position the strap right at the base of the tree and monitor it while pulling, in case the tree shows signs of being uprooted.

If another vehicle can be positioned in front as an anchor, make sure the cable is attached to a proper tow hook or receiver shackle, and block the wheels of the anchor vehicle. Someone should be inside as well to stand on the brakes.

The snatch block (essentially a stout pulley) included in the accessory kit effectively doubles the pulling power of your winch, while halving its speed (as well as halving the reach of the cable). The snatch block is attached to the anchor, and the winch cable is run through it and back to a tow hook on the stuck vehicle.

If the winch-equipped vehicle is assisting a stuck vehicle, the above procedures are modified to suit. The wheels should still be blocked to prevent sliding. If a snatch block is used, it is attached to the tow hook of the stuck vehicle, and the cable

WINCHING RULES

- Use gloves.
- Never straddle the cable.
- Use proper attachment points for cable hook.
- Use the remote control.
- Keep observers away from the vehicle.
- Never use nylon straps or rope to extend the cable.
- Don't hook the cable to itself.

is doubled back to the assisting vehicle.

If the winch vehicle cannot position itself directly in front of the stuck one, the snatch block can be attached to a tree, and the winch cable run through it to allow a straight pull. If the cable has to run over a dirt edge, position a log or something similar under it to prevent it from digging into the ground.

The remote control on the winch is not a labor-saving device; it is a safety feature, designed so you don't have to stand right at the winch to operate it. Ideally, it would be best to stay completely away from both vehicles involved; unfortunately, this is rarely possible. You'll need to run the engine of the winch-equipped vehicle to prevent the battery from being quickly drained. If you're using your winch to pull out someone else, you'll need to be in the cab to apply the brakes—relying on the parking brake and even wheel blocks is insufficient. Run the remote control unit into the cab so you can control the whole operation from the driver's seat.

Make sure everyone not directly involved with the procedure stays well away from the area. Under no circumstances

Warn Industries

Using a double line with a snatch block gives less stress on the winch and is better for the surrounding ground terrain.

WINCHING HAND SIGNALS

It's very helpful to have an observer standing outside the vehicle to keep an eye on the winch and the progress of the stuck vehicle. However, it's difficult to shout commands when the engine is running, so everyone should memorize a series of standard hand signals.

- A finger waving in circles above the head means "winch in"—that is, engage the winch to pull in cable.
- A finger waving in circles pointed down means "winch out"—that is, reverse the winch to pay out cable.
- A raised palm means "stop." (Two raised palms is generally considered to mean "STOP!!!!")
- Tapping the thumb and forefinger together signifies giving the winch control just a tap, to take in a couple inches of cable.

should anyone stand near the winch or—as I've witnessed more than once—stand *over* a winch cable that is taut with three or four tons of force. Yikes.

Don't use the winch to move the stuck vehicle farther than necessary to free it. Once back on firm ground, pay out the cable a bit if necessary to get some slack and rewind it under hand tension, using a glove to guide the cable into even layers on the spool. This helps prevent damage to the cable when the winch is working under load.

The physics of a winch results in greater pulling power with fewer layers of cable on the drum, so if you're pulling out someone else and the winch is laboring, back up enough so there is more cable out. However, *never* use the winch with less than four complete turns of cable on the drum, or it could pull free.

Each time you use the winch, inspect everything carefully, especially the cable, for signs of damage. Never use a winch with a frayed cable; likewise, never use a frayed or cut tree strap.

If, during the winching procedure, you detect a burning electrical smell, the motor is overheating. Stop and let the winch cool off for a few minutes.

You'll hear differing opinions, but generally it's best to let the winch do all the work and not to try adding power to the stuck vehicle's tires. They can spin and dig the vehicle in deeper rather than helping, or suddenly grab and cause the vehicle to run over the winch cable.

Getting Around on Forest Service & BLM Roads

With more than one-third of the land in the United States owned by the federal government (that's you and me), you won't have any trouble finding back roads to explore. Two of the biggest land management agencies are the Forest Service, with around 200 million acres, and the Bureau of Land Management, with 275 million acres or so.

Because BLM and USFS lands are multi-use, including logging, mining, and grazing, their roads are usually well-marked and easy to find. When driving on any public roads, some universal standards apply:

- Expect most roads to be low-standard, single-lane, usually unsurfaced except for occasional gravel.
- All vehicles should stay on existing roadways at all times.
- Keep speeds low to limit dust and impact on the road surface and surrounding wildlands (high speeds cause washboarding and other surface problems, not to mention increase the chance of killing animals). If traveling with other vehicles, keeping dust down is also an important safety feature, to keep visibility high.
- Never trim trees or alter other natural features if they are in the way. If you don't want to scratch your paint, it's best to turn around.
- Always close gates if you find them closed or leave them open if they are open. (And, if you come upon an open gate with a "Keep gate closed" sign on it, you

(continued on page 38)

PURSUITS: MOUNTAIN BIKING

The last 100 yards of the trail were steep and rocky. I had the bike in the lowest gear possible, cranking fast but moving almost too slowly to stay upright, dodging boulders constantly. I "dabbed" once, briefly touching a foot to the ground to avoid falling over, but made it the rest of the way in style. Meanwhile, my three companions had made it all the way without removing shoe from pedal and were waiting to rib me about the momentary loss of balance. Did I deserve this, just because I'd made one or two offhand comments about their own skirmishes with gravity?

The view that greeted us was worth the climb—a good portion of southern Arizona lay spread below. Even the astronomical telescopes on Kitt Peak, 50 miles away, were visible through the clear air. All around, oak trees gave tangible evidence of the elevation we'd gained since leaving the vehicles back down in the desert scrub.

The ride back down took about one-tenth the time, an exhilarating plunge with both hands gripping the brake levers until they cramped. We got the bikes back on the racks in time to enjoy sunset, then brought out the lawn chairs and watched the stars come out while the steaks grilled.

Four-wheel-drive vehicles are loads of fun, but it's also fun to kick the internal-combustion habit now and then. Mountain bikes are the sport utilities of the cycling world, and they'll take you places your two-ton vehicle wouldn't fit—and keep you in shape to boot.

WHAT YOU'LL NEED

The bicycle. You can buy bicycles called "mountain bikes" for under $200, but if you want one that will hold up to real trail use, you'll have to spend a little more. First, look for a frame made from aluminum or chrome-moly steel (rather than high-tensile steel, which is not as strong). Such models start at around $450, and go up—way up—from there. From about $500 to $1,000 or so, the quality of the components and wheels will improve rapidly, and the weight of the bike will go down as aluminum parts are substituted for heavier steel pieces. Beyond the $1,000 bracket you'll get better components (smoother shifting, more powerful brakes, etc.) and slightly lower weight, but the return for your investment begins to level off unless you're a real techno-weenie.

Suspension has become common on mountain bikes in the last five years, but not everybody needs it. If your riding will be confined to smooth dirt or even paved roads, your money would be better spent on an unsuspended model with higher-quality components. For rougher roads, however, a suspension fork will really smooth out the ride and increase control. You don't really need rear suspension unless you're a racer—for the money

(continued on page 39)

should close the gate). This is important in cattle country because managers rotate herds among grazing and watering areas, allowing regeneration of the resources.

- Camp only in designated or pre-used sites, and don't camp near water holes used by wildlife or cattle.

Forest Service Road Signs and Travel Tips

Nearly all Forest Service lands have corresponding maps produced and sold by the service. You can usually find them at local outdoor shops, or call or write your local Forest Service office (see Appendix II, beginning on page 165).

On the maps, all unimproved dirt roads are indicated with dashed lines, improved (stabilized) dirt roads are marked with solid unfilled lines and sometimes dots to indicate gravel, and paved roads are indicated by alternating color-blocked lines or solid dark lines (see Figures A and B). Roads, referred to as FSRs (Forest Service Road), are marked both on the maps and on the roads themselves with signs and numbers. The shapes of the signs indicate the types of vehicles suitable to travel on that road:

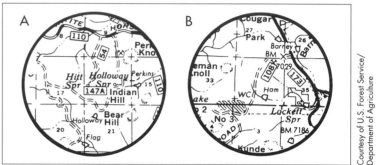

Courtesy of U.S. Forest Service/ Department of Agriculture

A) shows the barred (alternating color blocks) of a "Secondary Highway" (paved) and the dashed lines of unimproved roads.

B) shows a "Primary Highway" (paved) and solid lines indicating improved dirt. On some maps gravelled roads are indicated with dots over the solid lines (not illustrated).

- Horizontal markers (Figure C) indicate roads passable by passenger cars.

- Vertical markers (Figure D) indicate roads passable by high-clearance vehicles, including pickups and four-wheel-drives. Many of these roads are not indicated on the maps because logging or other industry activities change road placements fairly often. (For more on Forest Service roads, see page 40.)

Remember that sometimes the markers will not always jibe with the road conditions—weather happens, after all. But in general, the maps and markers are pretty accurate, quite a feat given *(continued on page 40)*

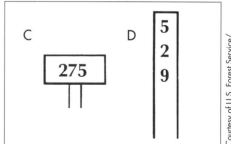

Courtesy of U.S. Forest Service/ Department of Agriculture

C) Horizontal markers indicate roads passable by passenger cars.

D) Vertical markers indicate roads passable by high-clearance vehicles, including pickups and four-wheel-drives.

(continued on page 40)

PURSUITS: MOUNTAIN BIKING, CONTINUED FROM PAGE 37

and weight that rear suspension adds, you could buy a much better, lighter model with just front suspension.

Helmet. Try an experiment. Run across the room and hit the opposite wall with your head. You've just approximated a fairly mild bicycling accident.

Modern bicycling helmets are lightweight, well-ventilated, and start at about 30 bucks. Any other excuses? Seriously, you should always wear a helmet when mountain biking; it could prevent a simple spill from becoming a life-threatening incident.

Gloves. A pair of padded bicycling gloves will significantly increase your comfort and grip and help prevent scrapes if you fall.

Tools and spares. Always carry a tube repair kit and a set of plastic tire levers for removing the tire from the rim. An extra tube is a good idea in case one gets really torn. Also consider a few wrenches for tightening and adjusting components; your bicycle shop can tell you what you'll need. Everything will fit in an underseat bag, a small zippered pouch that straps under the rear of the seat. You'll also need a pump; these are made to attach to the frame. Don't forget a tire gauge.

Racks and packs. On many mountain bikes you can add a rack that bolts over the rear wheel, to which you can attach panniers or a rack trunk. The latter is a very useful case that straps to the top of the rack and can carry lunch and cold sodas (some are insulated), plus books or binoculars. A handlebar pack can serve the same function, minus the insulating capabilities.

Carrying the bikes. There are two good ways to carry bicycles on your vehicle (stuffing them in back doesn't count): a roof rack or a receiver rack. A roof rack has the advantages of keeping the bikes out of your way and out of reach of casual damage or theft. On the other hand, getting the bikes on and off—especially on a tall sport utility—can be a real pain. And there's the ever-present danger of a low garage opening and an absentminded driver. A hitch-mount rack puts the bikes at an easily accessible spot—loading and unloading is the matter of a minute or two. Of course, your vehicle must be equipped with a receiver hitch mount, and the bikes get in the way of the rear cargo compartment, although most receiver racks swing down or out of the way. The bikes also tend to get dirtier on the back of the vehicle than they do on the roof. So it's largely a personal choice.

For more on getting into mountain biking, see *Mountain Biking: The Ultimate Guide to the Ultimate Ride* (Ragged Mountain Press, 1998) and the *Ragged Mountain Guide to Outdoor Sports* (Ragged Mountain Press, 1997).

FOREST SERVICE AND ROAD BUILDING

The U.S. Forest Service road network is eight times the size of the interstate highway system. That's a lot of roads. Unfortunately, road building still goes on in our national forests, usually associated with logging and other extractive uses, and usually it's the taxpayer who pays for the roads. Once an unroaded area is pierced by a road, it is, by rules of legislation, ineligible for future wilderness designation. So wilderness foes often push for road building (as this book was going to press, the Clinton administration initiated a moratorium on road building in many National Forests; we're hoping the moratorium will be extended to include all of our forests).

Our remaining wilderness areas are precious. They are vastly important for wildlife—many species need unbroken tracts of land for successful breeding—and for us, as areas to get away from civilization. They are important even as areas we might never go into, for the simple satisfaction of knowing we have saved some of this country nearly as the pioneers found it. Please support wilderness. We don't need more roads.

the millions of acres under Forest Service management.

In logging country, be sure to stay alert to the presence of logging trucks. These monsters can come barreling around curves, taking up the whole road. When driving, always keep track of where the last safe pull-out was, in case you have to back up when you meet a truck. If you venture into an active logging area and visibility drops because of a storm or blowing dust, it would be best to leave the area.

BLM Roads and Driving Tips

The Bureau of Land Management publishes maps of its lands, but usually these are just overviews, with roads marked as either highways or "other." For conditions of roads in a certain area, you must contact the regional BLM office (see Appendix II or Chapter 3, page 43). Often BLM land and Forest Service land are side-by-side or enclose one or the other, so a Forest Service map will include good road signs for BLM land.

Tips for driving on Forest Service lands apply to BLM lands as well. More mining takes place on BLM lands than on Forest Service lands, so be aware of mining trucks and, if exploring on foot away from roads, of open mine shafts.

CHAPTER 3

Planning & Preparing for a Backroad Adventure

BY ROSEANN HANSON

- Finding Places to Go
- Family Trip Tips
- *Pursuits: Birdwatching*
- *Road Trip: Beyond the Arctic Circle*
- Pre-Trip Vehicle Check
- Backroad Adventure Kit

Lure of the Road

Strewn across the living room floor like the aftermath of an overturned newsstand delivery truck are half a dozen guide books, unfolded big maps (the cat's holding down a corner of one), several atlases with dog-eared corners, and a dozen pages torn from glossy magazines, tantalizing color pictorials of Places I Want to Go.

Ochre and plum slickrock canyons of Utah.
Newfoundland, violent surf pounding the shores.
Vast expanses of Arctic tundra.
Hillsides aflame as winter touches the Great Smokies.
Boojum tree and cactus sandscapes of Baja.
A tranquil, anonymous mountain meadow overflowing with wildflowers in my nearby national forest.

I love the planning part of a backroad adventure—sometimes I think it's half the fun of the whole trip. I look forward to it with hedonistic and selfish delight, like anticipating a bar of Vahlrona chocolate or a bottle of 25-year-old Macallan. I love the hours of fantasizing (nothing ever goes wrong during a mind trip, of course); the truck is troublefree, weather perfect, solitude guaranteed, the scenery sublime—and the saturation in places beautiful and wild is elixir to a soul harried by schedules and deadlines and bills. I could pore over maps for hours, gleefully avoiding all responsibility. Fortunately, Jonathan suffers the same habit, so guilt is minimal (but a dual session can wreak havoc on our work deadlines).

But in addition to the fun of planning, there's a practical side. During those hours of route finding and campground scoping and mileage calculating, you are working out important logistics for your future trip (*Can we really drive 4,000 miles in two weeks?*); you are determining if the trip is feasible or should be dropped (*Do the ice bridges across the Mackenzie River melt before April?*); and you are testing the mettle of your own ability to handle a trip (*Am I prepared for the challenges of backcountry travel in a country where English is not commonly spoken?*) In short, you are saving yourself time-consuming, expensive, and frustrating mistakes that can ruin a trip.

Finding Places to Go

Most of us already have stashes of magazine clippings or hordes of guidebooks about far-flung destinations. But while there's not usually a lack of ideas for places to go, it helps to learn about more possibilities, especially closer to home for those weekend backroad getaways.

There are a few basic ways to get ideas for and more information about backroad adventures: from land management agencies, from books, and from maps and atlases. From these sources you can narrow down many choices to a few feasible ones, based on some common-sense guidelines (see Pre-trip Test Drive box, page 54). After that, you'll want to follow some easy pre-trip maintenance chores (see page 146), load up with some essential gear (see page 112), select your camping gear if it's an overnighter, and then it's road trip time (Chapter 4 covers the art of backroad tripping and tips for comfortable car-camping).

Public Land Management Agencies

More than one-third of the land in the United States is publicly owned and open to a wide range of recreational pursuits, from hiking in unroaded wilderness to driving and camping along backcountry roads.

Five government agencies oversee the land: Bureau of Land Management, U.S. Forest Service, National Park Service, U.S. Fish and Wildlife Service, and Bureau of Reclamation. Each agency was established with a different mission for the uses of the lands under its management. With the exception of the National Park Service, those missions included management for varying degrees of extraction of resources, including minerals, forage, timber, water, and game animals (although to be completely realistic and honest, the toll taken on our national parks by the hordes of view-seeking tourists—numbering annually in the millions at our most popular parks—amounts to no small degree of impact and its own type of extrac-

BLM Back Country Byways State Offices

For information on BLM Back Country Byways, write or call the Bureau of Land Management at the following addresses:

Arizona
222 North Central Avenue
Phoenix, AZ 85004
(602) 417-9200

California
Federal Building
2800 Cottage Way, E-2841
Sacramento, CA 95825
(916) 978-4400

Colorado
2850 Youngfield Street
Lakewood, CO 80215
(303) 239-3600

Idaho
3380 Americana Terrace
Boise, ID 83706
(208) 373-4000

Montana
222 N. 32nd Street
Billings, MT 59107
(406) 255-2888
255-2742

Nevada
850 Harvard Way
Reno, NV 89520
(702) 861-6500

New Mexico
1424 Rodeo Road
Santa Fe, NM 87502
(505) 438-7400

Oregon
1300 NE 44th Avenue
Portland, OR 97208
(503) 952-6001

Utah
324 S. State Street,
    Suite 301
Salt Lake City, UT 84145
(801) 539-4001

Wyoming
2515 Warren Avenue
Cheyenne, WY 82003
(307) 775-6256

Courtesy of BLM

You can also check out the BLM at www.blm.gov.

tion). All of these public lands are laced with unpaved roads. Many were established to access extracted resources, to be sure, but today are being used by more and more families on backroad adventures. In fact, because of recent increases in nonextractive uses on government lands, land management policies are shifting away from logging and mining and ranching and more toward broad-based recreation, from hiking to backcountry driving.

The BLM, in the Department of the Interior, manages nearly 275 million acres, the largest chunk of federal land, most in the West. In the past, BLM land was managed nearly exclusively for mining and ranching—most BLM land is below the elevations where logged timber grows—although recent shifts in policy are turning management toward ecosystem protection, more recreation (including developing more campgrounds, which is relatively new for BLM), and more controlled extraction. BLM is the only agency that manages unpaved roadways specifically for scenic driving, some of it four wheel drive, called the Back Country Byway system. Although mined and grazed, it isn't hard to find BLM lands that are wild and still offer pristine scenery and solitude.

The U.S. Forest Service of the Department of Agriculture is the next largest land manager, with just fewer than 200 million acres across the country. USFS land is largely managed today the same way it was 50 years ago, for logging, ranching, and mining industries, despite intense public pressure to control those activities in certain areas. Although the USFS manages less land than does the BLM, it boasts an astounding network of roadways—in fact, the total miles of USFS roads is eight times that of the entire U.S. interstate highway system. Certainly that is more backcountry roadway mileage than our country needs. We don't need any more and could, in fact, stand to close many roads. However, there are USFS roads that provide countless wonderful backroad trips (see Chapter 2, page 21, for more on USFS road policy and this important conservation issue). Most USFS lands are in mountains and are to some degree forested. Most USFS roads are used regularly and can be dotted with campsites, timber slash piles, mine tailings, and grazing paraphernalia such as stock tanks and windmills. The Forest Service manages campgrounds with a range of amenities, from fully developed (with tables, running water, bathrooms, and sometimes electricity and ramadas) to partially developed (usually with tables and water, maybe a toilet) to primitive (parking pullouts only).

The Department of Interior's U.S. Fish and Wildlife Service manages about 100 million acres across the country, as wildlife refuges for game species, endangered species, and now whole ecosystem protection. Some of these refuges are closed to the public entirely or open only minimally, but many have hundreds of miles of backcountry roads and campsites (developed campgrounds are rare), established for hunters but increasingly used by campers, birders, and hikers. These are some of the country's most scenic lands, largely free from the scars of mining, logging, or ranching. If you are not a hunter, you can easily plan your backroad adventure around hunting seasons.

National Park Service lands add up to about 75 million acres, most of it unroaded. Public access is largely via carefully controlled, paved roads, parking lots, view points, and visitor centers. However, some of the larger national parks do maintain some unpaved backcountry roads, many of which are largely ignored and lead through some of the country's most beautiful wildlands. Campgrounds in national parks are usually of the fully developed variety and are located close to the main hub of visitation.

Bureau of Reclamation lands are those managed for power production and water diversion from dams and have limited access for backcountry driving.

For Information: See Appendix II, beginning on page 165, for phone numbers and addresses of these agencies.

State Land Management Agencies

Some state lands are maintained with backroad access, including some designated as "four wheel drive only" areas. Rules are different in each state, so refer to your local phone book for contact information for your state.

Adventure in Canada and Mexico

Not only do we have many backroads adventures awaiting us in the States, but our northern and southern neighbors are vast countries with some of the world's most adventurous backroad highways.

Canada offers us incredible backroads in Newfoundland, New Brunswick, and Nova Scotia as well as in every other province, a few highlights being the Yukon and Dempster Highways of the Yukon and Northwest Territories (now split into the NWT and Nunavut), and in the Rocky Mountains and the Banff area in Alberta. We've explored both the coast and interior of British Columbia by backroad and found the clearcutting of the forests to be too depressing to view day after day, so we recommend parts north, central, and east in Canada.

Entering Canada is easy—no need for visas or any other permits, just proof of U.S. citizenship and your car registration and insurance. There are some restrictions on what you can

(continued on page 48)

RESOURCES FOR TRAVEL IN CANADA

CANADIAN CONSULATES

Canadian Consulate, Buffalo
The Consulate General of Canada
1 Marine Midland Center, Suite 3000
Buffalo, NY 14203-2884
(716) 858-9500

Canadian Consulate, Detroit
Consulate General of Canada
Tower 600 Renaissance Center, Suite 1100
Detroit, MI 48243-1798
(313) 567-2340

Canadian Consulate, Los Angeles
Consulate General of Canada
550 South Hope Street, 9th Floor
Los Angeles, CA 90071-2627
(213) 346-2700

Canadian Consulate, New York
Consulate General of Canada
1251 Avenue of the Americas, Concourse
  Level
New York, NY 10020-1175
(212) 596-1700

Canadian Consulate, Seattle
Consulate General of Canada
412 Plaza 600, Sixth and Stewart
Seattle, WA 98101-1286
(206) 443-1372

INTERNET

Visit the official Canada website:
http://canada.gc.ca/
or try
http://xinfo.ic.gc.ca/Tourism/

RESOURCES FOR TRAVEL IN MEXICO

MEXICAN CONSULATES

Mexican Consulate, New York
8 East 41 Street
New York, NY 10017
(212) 689-0456

Mexican Consulate, San Francisco
870 Market Street, Suite 528
San Francisco, CA 94102
(415) 392-5554, 392-3604

Mexican Consulate, Chicago
300 North Michigan Avenue, 2nd Floor
Chicago, IL 60601
(312) 855-0056

Mexican Consulate, Canada
Commerce Court West
199 Bay Street, Suite 4440
Toronto, Ontario, Canada
M5L 1E9
(416) 368-2875, 368-1847

(In addition to those listed above, there are 40 smaller consulates in cities across the U.S.)

INTERNET

The official information website for Mexico is excellent: www.mexonline.com.

TOURISM OFFICES

If you would like to call the tourism offices for the Mexican border state through which you will enter the country, try the numbers or addresses below. These are helpful to obtain border crossing hours and current requirements for automobile importation.

Baja California
Blvd. Diaz Ordaz s/n, Edif. Plaza Patria
Nivel 3
CP 22400 Tijuana, B.C.
66-81-9492

Baja California Sur
Carr. al Norte Km. 5.5 Fracc. Fidepaz
CP 23090 Tijuana, B.C.S.
112-4-0100
e-mail turismo@lapaz.cromwell.com.mx

Chihuahua
Calle Libertad No. 1300- 1 Piso
CP 31000 Chihuahua, Chih.
14-16-2106

Coahuila
Blvd. Los Fundadores Km. 6.5
Centro de Convenciones, Planta Alta
CP 25000 Saltillo, Coah.
84-30-0510

Sonora
Comonfort entre Av. Cultura y Paseo
Canal 3 Piso
CP 83000 Hermosillo, Son.
62-17-0076

The phone prefix from the United States is 011-52.

BOOKS

The following are some excellent books for travel in Mexico, especially by backroad.

- *Backcountry Mexico: A Traveler's Guide and Phrase Book* by Bob Burleson and David H. Riskind (Austin: University of Texas Press, 1986). This is an excellent guide for first-time Mexico travelers, with a good section on driving, and laced throughout with appropriate phrases for day-to-day needs of backcountry travelers (*Do you fix flat tires? Where does this road lead?*)

- *The Baja Book II: A Complete New Map-Guide to Today's Baja California* by Tom Miller and Elmar Baxter (Huntington Beach: Baja Trail Publications, Inc., 1977). The *Baja Book* was the best selling guidebook ever written on the peninsula. Tom Miller is possibly the most knowledgeable "Mr. Baja," and this update is well worth its weight in premium unleaded, but unfortunately it's out of print. We used it on our very first backcountry Baja trip as a companion to the atlas listed below, and they took us easily and confidently into some fabulous country. It sold well enough that used bookstores are a good bet, or Amazon.com on the Web will search for it, free.

- *People's Guide to Mexico,* 10th Edition by Carl Franz (Santa Fe: John Muir Publications, 1995). A legendary guide, it includes everything you could want to know about traveling in Mexico, and then some. *Harper's* called it "the best guidebook to adventure in the whole world . . . outrageous."

- The best Baja atlas we've found is Topography International's *Baja Topographic Atlas Directory,* with more than 200 large-scale, detailed maps covering the whole peninsula, with excellent information on services. For mainland Mexico, Pemex (the national gas company) publishes a series of excellent atlases with some information in English; wait until you get there and then start looking in the larger Pemex stations. We have been told AAA has good Mexico maps, but we have not used them.

bring into the country, of course. Canada has strict bans on handguns, but hunting rifles are okay, and you may not bring in mace or pepper spray unless the can is specifically marked "for use on animals" (such as bear spray). Before you head into Canada, contact one of the Canadian consulates for information.

We found Canada to be very easy and fun to travel through, with friendly but not overly curious people—after all, we blend right in most every place we go, except the Arctic communities and parts of Quebec and the far northeast where the dialects are different. After traveling at length in Canada, I always come away with a hint of Canadian-English accent, eh?

Traveling practically any part of Mexico qualifies as a backroad adventure, simply because only a few Mexican highways are in really good shape—you never know what's around a turn—and some of the best villages to visit are often miles and miles down very rough "truck roads" or four-wheel-drive tracks. And everywhere you go, you will be a focus of friendly curiosity and often warm hospitality, especially the farther you wander from the tourist-beaten track.

The challenges of traveling in Mexico are greater than those in the United States and Canada: language (although French-speaking Canada can also be a challenge, English is almost always spoken there as well); gasoline shortages; lack of service and parts for newer four-wheel-drives, especially those of most Japanese or European makes (Ford, General Motors, Volkswagen, and Nissan are common brands in Mexico, but sport utilities are not as popular as they are up north, with the possible exception of Suburbans).

Different Mexican states

Jonathan Hanson

The rewards of Mexico backroad travel: a cool "coco helado," a chilled coconut, savored on the beach at the end of a long, dusty track.

(continued on page 50)

PURSUITS: BIRDWATCHING

The air hangs heavy and still at 30°F in the pre-dawn murkiness. To the east, southeastern Arizona's Dos Cabezas Mountains begin to glow from behind. Black and flat in silhouette, they look like paper cut-outs of mountains. Cold feet stamp and shuffle impatiently in the chilly dawn, virtually the only sound in the hundreds of acres of corn-field stubble except the occasional bark of a farm dog.

Then we hear it. The first call, a sound as old as time. It could be a few hundred yards away, or a mile. A clear, piercing, bugle: *CHURIUP! CHURIUP! CHURIUP!* The first of ten thousand sandhill cranes are gliding into the surrounding fields of corn stubble to feed for the morning before returning to the safety of their roosts

Jonathan Hanson

Birdwatching is a perfect companion to backroad adventuring.

on the vast and shallow rain-fed waters of the Willcox Playa.

Each winter in southeastern Arizona (in Cochise County, about two hours from Tucson), the fallow winter agricultural fields and the huge shallow lake south of the town of Willcox host tens of thousands of waterfowl, which fatten up for their long spring migration north to their breeding grounds in the Rockies, Canada, and Alaska. The sandhill crane may be the oldest migratory bird represented in the fossil record— perhaps 10 million years

(continued on page 51)

have different entrance rules and requirements. To enter Baja from the United States, you pretty much just drive across, no visas or permits required, unless you plan to take a ferry across to the mainland, in which case you will need to stop for a visa and automobile permits. With its easygoing personality, high reliance on tourist traffic for its economy, and stunning and underpopulated countryside, Baja may offer the best backcountry adventures in North America—although they are not for the ill-prepared or novice traveler.

Entering Mexico via the state of Sonora will test your patience. You will find out just how many separate waiting lines a government can require visitors to stand in for its umpteen different stamps and fees and permits. Then you'll go back to your vehicle to wait for another inspector (there seems always to be only one working the busiest port in Sonora) to check the umpteen stamps and permits against your VIN and visa (forgetting to get them before you started the process will cost you at least another wait in line). Then the inspector slaps a futuristic hologram-printed decal on your windshield and declares you are ready—to pull your truck up over there to wait for an inspection by the Army for contraband. We usually plan at least three hours for the border stop.

The states of Chihuahua, Coahuila, and Tamaulipas are marginally better. (Ironically, Sonora instituted its new complex system in part to do away with the infamous old system, which worked remarkably smoothly and quickly, well-oiled by small *mordidas*, or bribes ["little bites"], placed discreetly into the palms of the inspectors. I miss the good old days, and so, most likely, do the inspectors who used to elevate their incomes to comfortable middle-class with the old system and who now, in spite, probably delight in making us wait so long in so many lines.)

If planning a Mexican backroad adventure, lots of homework is in order. Check out the books in the box, page 47, and contact the government several times to make sure you get all the entrance rules straight; make sure you tell them you are driving, not flying. One important thing to remember is that not all ports are open all the time, and at only a few can you obtain the proper traveling permits; getting caught in Mexico without the proper permits can result in lengthy, frustrating, and sometimes expensive encounters with the customs officials. The American Automobile Association (see Appendix II, page 167) is very helpful with planning travels in Mexico, including providing good maps, as will be your Mexican auto insurance broker (see below).

You will need supplemental automobile insurance when traveling in Mexico, as most American policies won't cover you beyond just a few dozen miles from the border (also check your coverage in Canada; we once completed an 8,000-mile trip in my new Toyota truck and never checked if we were covered—luckily we had no accidents).

Never, ever, *ever* take any guns or controlled substances into Mexico. In separate instances last year, two American men were caught at the border with guns—one had a hunting rifle, the other a handgun. The rich guy who knew the governor got out of prison, but as far as I know the other guy is still there.

(continued on page 52)

old, by some accounts. Thousands of Canada geese also share the waters and fields, as do a few hundred snow geese.

We are on a backroad drive in southeastern Arizona, looping through the rutted dirt farm roads of the Sulphur Springs Valley and exploring the rugged Middlemarch Road in the Dragoon Mountains, which ends at Tombstone. In the valleys we look for the cranes and waterfowl, as well as the many species of raptors that winter there: beautiful northern harriers, rough-legged hawks, ferruginous hawks, merlins, kestrels, and prairie falcons. If we're lucky, closer to the mountains we might see a slate gray sleek form streaking through the skies: a peregrine falcon. When we cross the mountain, we'll listen for white-breasted nuthatches and Mexican jays.

Birdwatching is a perfect companion to backroad driving. Most of the best birding in the world—the kind where there aren't 30 other birders jostling elbows to see a bird— is far off the beaten track, down unpaved roads, hard to get to, and, in short, worth the effort.

Birdwatching takes a number of forms, the most conspicuous if not most numerous being the "lister" variety. Listers keep a "Life List" of the birds they've seen, and among listers there is an intense competition to make benchmarks—500 species, 700, 1,000 and more, plus annual state or regional records. There are about 700 regular species occurring in the U.S. as residents or migrants, and a passel of rare "transients" that hop across the Mexico border to tease us, so you can imagine the obsessive drive necessary to "list" 700. Because some of the most wonderful birding in the United States is in southeastern Arizona (with lots of rare species), you can also imagine we'd want to avoid the birding crowds. In one canyon a few years ago, a pair of rare gnatcatchers was building a nest and soon after word leaked out along the astonishingly organized "birding hotline" network, 100 birders in one day converged on the beleaguered nuptial site.

But usually birdwatching is a pastime of people like us, ordinary people with a deep love of wilderness and a sincere interest in the lives of its wonderful habitats and inhabitants. We don't know how many birds we've seen, but we remember fondly the place where we saw our first northern goshawk, a cloud-colored forest raptor, swift and silent as it shot through the pines above us in the Catalina Mountains. Or the brave, tough little Arctic terns that chased us away from their nest site we had inadvertently wandered past on an Arctic trip.

WHAT YOU'LL NEED

- **A pair of good binoculars.** You'll want something compact enough you won't be tempted to leave them at home but powerful and bright enough to see birds in shade or far

(continued on page 53)

Books

In a casual search of the Internet bookseller Amazon.com, which lists every book in print and a million out of print, I found 100 books with the word "backcountry" in the title just for North America (granted, some of them were for *paved* back roads, but it's a start). There is no lack of printed material on exploring North America—or the world—by truck. Nearly every public library today has a computer with free access to the Internet. Use yours to search Amazon.com or use the library's free access to *Books In Print*.

Following are some of the more broad-interest guides we have found particularly excellent as resources for finding and traveling to wonderful backroad adventures.

■ *Milepost.* Anyone thinking about driving any part of the Alaskan Highway, (which starts at Dawson Creek, B.C., and ends in Fairbanks, Alaska) or its many sister highways, should buy the latest *Milepost* from Alaska Northwest Books (Bothell, Washington), an annual bible of northern automobile travel; 1999 will mark its 50th edition. Our first experience in the Canadian Arctic and parts of Alaska and British Columbia would have been

(continued on page 54)

INTERNET ADVENTURE

Using your computer or your public library's, you can find out more than you'll ever want to know about backcountry travel around the world.

As mentioned in the Books section, above, Amazon.com is the best place for new-book searching; Bibliofind (www.bibliofind.com) and Interloc (www.interloc.com) are excellent sources for used books.

For other information, such as four-wheel-drive clubs and club-sponsored trips, I've had good luck searching Yahoo.com under the subject "Recreation and Sports: Travel: Four-Wheel-Drive" and "Recreation and Sports: Travel: Regional: U.S.," the latter for specific destination information. For example, an Internet surf through Maine got me all the information I'd need to plan a fall colors drive, with contacts for campgrounds, scenic tours, B&Bs, and sources to write for free information. Under the "four-wheel-drive" search, I waded through a lot of ads for tours and found some interesting events, including a 50th anniversary Land Rover extravaganza with expos and drive-yourself tours.

For fun I searched globally for the word "backcountry" and hit a gold mine. Among a lot of junk, I found the website for Bay Area Backroads (www.bayareabackroads.com), which is a KRON-TV production in San Francisco, hosted by Doug McConnell and sponsored by Jeep. Bay Area Backroads travels all over North America, usually by Jeep on backroads, exploring, hiking, canoeing, kayaking, rafting, fishing—you name it. The website is a treasure trove of past trips, from Baja to Georgia, with video and sound on some of them. Great information. Bay Area folks are lucky to have this great program.

PURSUITS: BIRDWATCHING, CONTINUED FROM PAGE 51

away. Binoculars come in a variety of magnifications and sizes, represented by two numbers, such as 8 x 30 (the first number refers to the magnification, the second to the diameter in millimeters of the front, or objective, lens). "Compact" binoculars are usually around 7 x 20 and are very lightweight and tiny but not great for birding (these binoculars usually have a small field of view and less light-gathering capability, which makes it hard to "spot" birds). "Mid-sized" binoculars are generally around 7 x 30 to 8 x 30 or so, and are ideal for birding because the moderate objective lens, coupled with a medium magnification, give you good light-gathering power and a good field of view. More powerful binoculars, such as 10 x 40s, can be a little harder to hold steady and have a shorter field of view (although you do see things more magnified, you see less area in the lenses), and bigger binoculars, such as 8 x 50s, will be quite heavy.

The low end for decent binoculars is around $100 for a pair that will do the job—high end is $1,000. Go for a reputable brand. U.S. and Asian companies make good optics for less money; hard-core nature nerds will usually be found with something from Germany or Austria. Many outdoor suppliers carry binoculars; so does your local Audubon Society chapter's nature shop.

Nature and outdoor shops may also carry binocular and camera mounts that attach to your car window—an excellent accessory for backroad birding.

■ **Field guides.** The best field guide for beginners is the American Bird Conservancy's *All the Birds of North America* (1997). The paintings are excellent, and most birds are represented doing something natural in their preferred habitat (instead of painted stiffly like dead specimens on a white background). Range maps—where the birds are found in winter and summer—appear right next to the description, on the same page as the pictures; this is a big improvement over the Peterson guides. The birds are arranged so that you can look them up by size and bill shape—a quick system—and there are excellent tutorial pages on behavior, physiology, conservation, and identification. Our second vote, for more serious students of ornithology, is the *National Geographic Birds of North America.*

■ **Classes.** The quickest ways to learn are to go out in the field with other birders, and to take a class. Nearly all Audubon chapters offer field trips, either free or very cheap; most offer birding classes at reasonable rates. Contact the National Audubon Society for information on the chapter nearest you; (212) 979-3000; Audubon@audubon.org; www.audubon.org.

Check your local bookseller for magazines such as *Birder's World,* (800) 446-5489, and *Bird Watcher's Digest,* (800) 879-2473.

much harder without the many maps, mile-by-mile descriptions (hence the name *Milepost*), tips, events, and ads for everything from camps and hotels to stores and craft outlets. After your trip, it becomes a kind of memoir, covered with trip stains (coffee in Whitehorse, chocolate in Dawson) and scribbled notes (fabulous camp near Skagway, horrible one at Hyder).

■ **The "*Adventuring in . . .*" series.** Sierra Club Books publishes this excellent travel guide series, covering Hawaii, Arizona, Alaska, and Florida, and regions such as the Gulf Coast, Southeast Coast, California Desert, Chesapeake Bay, Pacific Coast, Bay Area, and the Rockies (as well as Europe, Asia, South America, Africa, and the Caribbean). These guides provide excellent coverage of backcountry adventures, including drives, hikes, climbs, pad-

PRE-TRIP TEST DRIVE

Try this 10-part "test drive" to see if the trip you picked is ready to launch or if you need to go back to the planning table.

1. How much time do you have off? _____

2. About how far is your planned route (err on the longer mileage)? _____

3. How many people will be going? _____ kids? _____

4. How many vehicles? _____

5. In what condition is (are) the vehicle(s)? _____

6. What is the farthest distance you will travel from a service area (auto repair, gas, food)? _____

7. What are the worst driving conditions you are likely to encounter en route?

_____

8. What are the worst weather conditions you are likely to encounter en route?

_____

9. Do you need any permits or paperwork (for border crossings, for example)?

_____

10. Do you have enough cookies? _____

Check the answer to #1 (time off) against those of questions #2 (distance), #7 (driving conditions), and #8 (weather or season). If you've never been to an area, you won't be able to be exact about road conditions (guidebooks and articles can be very helpful, however), but in general we have found that on good quality gravel roads such as the Alaskan Highway we can travel 40 to 50 miles an hour (or 200 or more miles a day); on fair quality dirt roads with some washboarding or rocks and holes, we can plan on about 20 to 35 miles an hour (or about 100 miles in a day); and in any rougher conditions or

dles, and more, and they are updated regularly (buy the latest version you can, since access changes fairly frequently).

- *Country Roads* **series.** Country Roads Press offers tamer adventures along the country roads of nearly every state and some in Canadian provinces. There are also many other presses that publish "backcountry" series all over North America. Look for them at your bookseller.

Magazines

Most of the four-wheel-drive magazines publish stories of backroad trips. I find most of

---

bad weather, low range will drop us to 2 to 10 miles an hour (or fewer than 50 miles in a day). Obviously for roads with a variety of conditions, your speed and mileage will vary widely. Always choose the longer mileage and time, and be thankful for extra days to play, rather than dreading the call from Timbuktu to your boss to say you'll be a few days late.

Don't forget to factor in your overall state of being when figuring time off versus distance and route and weather conditions; if you've just spent two months closing a deal with the client from hell, or two of your kids just recovered from chicken pox and are stir-crazy from a week in bed, don't pick a long, difficult route (unless you really like self-punishment).

Consider questions #3 (how many people) and #4 (how many vehicles) in terms of trip complexity. The more people and vehicles, the more planning and logistical details should be worked out (although a second vehicle is good—for safety and help in a pinch—more than that usually results in the chance of a breakdown increasing and personality conflicts becoming more prevalent). If kids enter the picture, remember to cut down the in-the-car time per day; usually just half a day will max out both kids' patience and, subsequently, the parents'.

Questions #5, 6, 7, and 8 should be considered together for obvious reasons—if your rig is not in top shape (did you have that squealing fan belt replaced as you promised?), either decrease your mileage and/or your distance from a service center or be prepared for do-it-yourself wilderness repairs. If you don't want to deal with it, postpone your trip and have your rig worked on at the shop.

Question #9 (permits) is self-evident; lack of permits or documentation can end a trip in particularly annoying ways.

And Question #10 (cookies) is partly in jest, partly serious. Have you provisioned properly? We once left a campsite in the far backcountry of Baja two days early because we ran out of cookies and beer. It was brutal.

these magazines, except the British ones (which don't do much North America coverage), to be a bit, well, masculine. If you can get beyond the typical hot pink and lime covers featuring huge mud-tire-equipped trucks with skimpily clad babes caressing the hoods, you'll find good resources inside. Contact information for the magazines is listed in Appendix II, on page 164. Here's a sampling:

- *Four Wheeler.* Monthly, lots of ads, good technical information, reviews, fair number of "babes" (scantily clad women in ads and editorial photos), moderate on chrome; overall good information, plus it often features the terrific trips of Monika and Gary Wescott, of Turtle Expedition fame. This interesting duo travels the world in their highly modified Ford trucks, which are loaded with every expedition accessory known. They have just completed a trans-Russia trip that took years and years of planning. We happened to meet up with them in Tuktoyaktuk, Northwest Territories, of all places, on one of their "test drives." Nice folks, great trips.

- **Petersen's 4-Wheel & Off-Road.** Another glossy that is high on chrome and lift kits, with plenty of "babes." There is less to offer sport utility owners in this publication than in

GREAT ROAD TRIP LIST

Here are our some of our favorite books about backroad adventures—to inspire a trip or to read while on your own adventure.

- *Campfires on Desert & Lava* by William T. Hornaday (Tucson: University of Arizona Press, 1983). This edition is a photographic reproduction of the original 1908 book published by Charles Scribner's Sons, New York, and may be the very first Southwestern automobile road trip. In a four-horsepower Whitewater touring car with an automatic tonneau and a two-horsepower Callahan runabout, Hornaday and a handful of scientist friends and colleagues set out from Tucson to explore northern Mexico's Pinacate volcanic region 200 miles away. Accompanying the entourage were numerous mules and horses (which often pulled the automobiles). A great read about an incredible area.

- Any of the *Backroads series* of beautifully illustrated books by Earl Thollander (various publishers). These have lovely prose, too. His adventures include Arizona, New England, and California.

- *The Hidden West: Journeys in the American Outback* by Rob Schultheis (New York: Lyons & Burford, 1997). Despite the title, which implies some sort of guide to "secret" places, this chronicle of many years of exploring the American West is one of the best collections of writings on the state of today's West. Beautiful example of the written word.

- *Malaria Dreams* by Stuart Stevens (New York: Atlantic Monthly Press, 1989). This book is not remotely about backroad adventures in North America—it is about the author's

the others listed here, but the technical articles can be helpful for the do-it-yourselfer. Most of the featured "trips" involve either sponsored expeditions or competition trials.

- *Open Road, The 4WD Adventure Magazine from Road & Track.* Quarterly, upscale (nearly all higher-end sport utilities), great trip stories, little technical information, good reviews, no chrome, no "babes"; excellent magazine.
- *Chevy Outdoors.* Family-oriented, trucks as well as vans and RVs, good sports and trip information, all-GM products plus some smaller ads for trailers and accessories; light but useful, especially if you own a General Motors truck or sport utility.
- *Land Rover Owner International.* For Land Rover, Discovery, and Range Rover owners, excellent technical information, lots of ads (nearly all U.K.), fun to read; recommended.

Atlases & Maps

Of the many excellent atlases out there, we've found the DeLorme series of atlas-gazetteers to be the most useful guides to the states we have traveled through by backroad—

(continued on page 59)

bizarre misadventures driving an old Land Cruiser from the Central African Republic to Algiers. If not exactly an inspiration to venture off to Africa on your own, it definitely makes any part of North America seem tame by comparison. Stevens is one of our favorite travel writers, with an intelligent wit, an eye for irony, and a talent for strange adventure.

- *Vermilion Sea: A Naturalist's Journey in Baja California* by John Janovy, Jr. (New York: Houghton Mifflin Company, 1992). Janovy recounts the story of his first road trip down the peninsula in the company of other naturalists and students. Nothing breathtaking, but it is a very sincere account, with wonderful natural history and scenic details; it is an excellent accompaniment to any trip to Baja.
- *The Forgotten Peninsula* by Joseph Wood Krutch (Tucson: University of Arizona Press, 1986). More luminous than the Janovy book—Krutch was, after all, one of our great nature writers—this is the book to whet your appetite for an exploration of the land of boojums.
- *The Lost Continent: Travels in Small Town America* by Bill Bryson (New York: Harper Collins, 1990). Someone described this book as the kind you find yourself wanting to read parts of to anyone nearby—a spouse, a friend, your dog—as well as inspiring moments of uncontrollable laughter.
- *Lost World of the Kalahari* by Laurens van der Post (New York: Morrow and Morrow, 1958). This is the thrilling—and superbly told—story of one of the first Land Rover expeditions into the heart of Africa, to search for the vanishing Bushmen of the Kalahari region.

ROAD TRIP: BEYOND THE ARCTIC CIRCLE

"So, is this your idea of a *dream trip*?" the hip, twentysomething Inuit said to us with no small amount of irony dripping from her voice, when we'd told her where we'd come from and how we'd gotten there.

She was giving us a ride from the boat ramp to the only hotel in Tuktoyaktuk, a remote Arctic coast village that is accessible only by boat and float plane in summer and by ice road in winter. To reach Tuk, as locals call it, we had driven our Toyota 4x4 from our home in Tucson, Arizona, near the Mexican border, north for 4,000 miles. We crossed the border into Canada and traveled through Alberta, British Columbia, Yukon, and Northwest Territories—up the Alaskan Highway, a right turn near Dawson City onto the gravel-from-hell Dempster Highway (at the time, the northernmost-attaining public road in North America; the beginning of the Dempster is nearly the same latitude as Nome, Alaska), across the Arctic Circle, all the way to Inuvik on the Mackenzie River. There, we plopped our sea kayaks into the mighty Mackenzie and paddled 120 miles down the river, out into the Beaufort Sea and Arctic Ocean, to Tuktoyaktuk, home to several hundred mostly Inuit and Inuvialuit, where the young woman and her friends watched incredulously as we paddled up to the beach. Ironically, they had never seen sea kayaks before.

"I mean, if it were me," she volunteered, "*I'd* go to Hawaii or something. There's nothing here!"

Having grown up in this incredible, remote wilderness, in a town that, although located in a place of great value to lovers of wilderness and nature, truthfully holds nothing for the

(continued on page 60)

Jonathan Hanson

In Arctic Canada, services are few and far between and are often expensive; on the Dempster Highway, gas was about $3.20 a gallon.

hands-down. No other series of atlases has so much information of import to those who travel off the paved roads. DeLorme atlas-gazetteers are large, easy to read, and up to date. Only a few times have we found them to be "off" regarding the location or existence of a road—and that's amazing considering they cover 33 U.S. states and counting (with about three or four new ones each year).

DeLorme atlases have the best characteristics of Forest Service maps; they show land ownership categories by color, with roads marked by type (highway, urban, improved, unimproved, and trail), and lots of features such as campgrounds, wells, railroads, and, of course, towns. They also have the best features of topographic maps, showing vegetation cover and types by color, contour intervals, elevations, and benchmarks. Contours and elevations are a must if you are planning a four-wheel-drive trip and need to know how steep a hill is or through what type of terrain the road runs.

DeLorme gazetteers include listings (with map grid cross-referencing) for federal and state lands; lists of selected hiking trails and scenic drives; hunting units, fishing sites, and boat launches; campgrounds, wildlife viewing hotspots, and special sites of interest (our Arizona *Atlas & Gazetteer* includes a special guide to the Grand Canyon). All this for under $20!

If you are driving Forest Service roads, you will want to buy the latest maps available from the USFS (see Appendix II, page 165, for ordering information or visit your local outdoor retailer). These include road numbers and types; forest roads are usually well-marked on the ground (Chapter 2, page 36, will help decipher the different types and rules of forest roads). Keep in mind that on Forest Service lands, road status changes frequently. Fires and landslides can cause closures, or land managers may close roads that are badly eroded (more often than not, however, not enough roads are closed and new roads are built; see Chapter 2, page 36, for more on roads on federal lands).

U.S. Geological Survey maps are great for hiking, but since most of the maps haven't been updated for decades due to budget cuts, road information is often so far off as to be unusable. We usually take a set for our destination area, mostly to get a feel for the lay of the land and for hiking.

Family Trip Tips

With five kids to haul around, my parents always owned some version of the old International Travel-All. My dad, a great aficionado of backroad adventures, loved to pile us into the Travel-All and take off on weekend explorations all over the southwestern U.S. and northern Mexico. I don't remember a whole lot about the actual time in the truck and the scenery—I easily got car sick (the kid hierarchy always meant the youngest got the worst seat: the middle of the middle seat, close to The Parents but not a window seat) and was usually drugged-out with Dramamine so I wouldn't barf and ruin the trip for everyone. However, I do remember a few of the little tricks my mom used to keep the kids quiet and happy—or at least quiet and under control.

(continued on page 61)

future of its young people, the woman had no intention of staying in Tuk longer than necessary. It was understandable. We found it to be similar to economically depressed third-world villages the world over: small, inexpensive homes surrounded by yards full of equal parts broken-down pickups, junked boats and fishing gear, and hungry-looking dogs (and, in this case, dog sleds). Children ran in wild little groups; we were advised to leave nothing of value unlocked. Boom-era industries such as oil and the military have pulled out. Tuk was home to the last operational DEW-Line station (the Cold War's Distant-Early-Warning system); in fact, we were there during its final decommissioning and talked with older Air Force officers about their experiences watching Soviet MiGs play "chicken" with our fighters along the northern border. Now the only industry left in Tuk is a large base for the northern shipping giant NTCL and a continental shelf research station.

Most people here still hunt marine animals for subsistence; a large polar bear hide could mean many months-worth of income plus meat. We were told a story of one old Tuk hunter who saw a polar bear wander into his front yard. He got so excited at his great luck that he grabbed his rifle and squeezed off a premature shot that pierced the fridge and stove, while the second shot, this time aimed, went through the front window, which he'd forgotten to open. He got the bear, but most of the $1,000 or so from the hide and parts went to pay for the damage to his house.

We stayed in Tuk for three days, enjoying an all-Inuit Northern Games festival, a non-stop affair in the 24-hour-daylight of the northern summer. We sampled muktuk, or whale blubber, and toured a meat freezer dug into the permafrost, then negotiated a ride back to Inuvik on a float plane, kayaks strapped to one of the pontoons. Flying over the treeless, lake-pocked Arctic tundra, we could best appreciate the vastness of the North. Literally for thousands of miles all around, there was only wilderness, covered by a seemingly endless quilt of tundra and

In Tuktoyaktuk we attended the Inuit Northern Games, where we sampled local fare: muktuk, or whale blubber.

Jonathan Hanson

(continued on page 62)

First, there were the cardinal rules:

- **No fighting.** (Once, when my sister and I were bickering worse than normal, my dad threatened to turn around and go home; we kept fighting, and he did. Boy, were my brothers *mad*. From then on, we stopped fighting when we were told.)
- **No yelling.**
- **Seat belts must always be worn,** even if we wanted to nap (we learned to do it sitting up), and even when going slowly on dirt roads.

Usually about an hour into the trip, after the initial thrill of Going on a Trip wore off and the boredom of When Do We Get There? set in, mom would produce a little game or quiz booklet or puzzle for each of us. Remember those little cards filled with iron shavings that you would use to decorate a picture of a monkey or something, using a little magnetic wand? These were usually good for about an hour, maybe less, depending on the game.

There are all sorts of road trip games to play as well: Contests to see who could spot the most of a particular thing along the way—types of birds, Volkswagen bugs, green cars, and so on; license plate bingo; and many others. Check your local bookstore for some of the following books:

Donna Erickson's Travel Fun Book (Prime Time Family Series, 1997)

Enjoying Travel Games by Anne Ingram (1996)

Have Kid, Will Travel: 101 Survival Strategies for Vacationing With Babies and Young Children by Claire Tristram, Lucille Tristram (1997)

The Highlights Book of Travel Games by Liz Kauffman (1994)

Road Trip: A Travel Activity Book by Holly Kowitt (1994)

Trouble-Free Travel With Children: Helpful Hints for Parents on the Go by Vicki Lansky and Jack Lindstrom (1996)

For us, snacks were not available on an unlimited basis. They were used as bribes. My mom was a brilliant tactician. If we were quiet, we'd get more. Bickering or whining caused a delay in the snack flow—even if everyone wasn't taking part in the offending act. This may seem unfair, but peer pressure or sibling pressure is an excellent behavior-modifying tool, and besides, moms and dads are usually right in assuming they can't always be sure just who the culprits are, and it's not fair to single out one or two offenders when there are five little *bored* heathens riding behind their backs.

Although the car time sometimes seemed intolerably long, I think they must have limited the driving time to under about four hours, to keep their sanity. This seems about max to make kids sit in a car, especially if they've been in school all week, *sitting*.

Pre-Trip Vehicle Check

Regular maintenance, covered in Chapter 6, will keep your sport utility in top shape

ice, with a few nearly insignificant human footholds such as Fort Good Hope and Old Crow, accessible only by plane or boat. Again in the plane, as we had in our kayaks on the vast Mackenzie Delta, we felt very small and human.

Back at our truck we loaded up and pointed south again down the Dempster Highway. The Dempster is an unforgettable road. I had been pretty nervous about traveling by kayak in polar bear and barrenlands grizzly country. It was summer, and the great white bears usually remain on the pack ice farther north, but sometimes they do range down into the areas through which we paddled. (I was prepared with a big can of bear spray, and I kept trying to psych myself up for a bear encounter.) But nothing prepared me for the sheer terror of the huge logging trucks barreling down the Dempster. Give me a bear any day.

Yes, there are logging trucks all over North America, but the Dempster is a unique highway, if you can call it that—it's really more like a glorified gravel road. And it is the nature of the road that gave the trucks their great menace, in my mind (Jonathan, of course, enjoyed every hair-raising minute). The Dempster is built on top of the tundra, under which lies the permafrost, a layer of constantly frozen ground. Throughout the tundra in summer there are impassable boggy areas and in winter the snow is many feet thick. To make a road, the Canadian highway department built up 20 feet or so of hard-packed earth on top of the tundra, winding 460 miles from near Dawson City in the Yukon to Inuvik, a sizable Inuit political and cultural center in the Northwest Territories, on the Mackenzie River. The road is usually well maintained, fairly smooth in most areas, and topped with gravel chipped out of sharp-edged bedrock sandstone, a locally available rock. The abundant sandstone dust is dark gray, very light, and soon completely coats your truck and seeps into every nook and cranny inside and out of the vehicle. The highway department uses calcium chloride on some parts of the Dempster, as a bonding agent, so frequent vehicle washings are recommended.

It was possible to see the logging trucks coming for miles, their paths marked by enormous plumes of gray dust. We calculated the preferred speed of the trucks to be between 60 and 70, the slower speed usually reserved for blind curves. Because the highway has no verges and is just wide enough for two trucks, the only thing to do when a semi is charging down on you—its windshield and two headlights glinting menacingly through the dust-gloom—is to hold tight and scream. Well, I usually did, but Jonathan just laughed, maniacally. The aftermath of a passing logging truck was about a minute of utterly blind driving through the pall of dust; we just had to hope no one was traveling close behind the truck and on the wrong side of the road.

I was certainly glad we had installed the heavy-duty K&N air filter, the wire rock guards over the headlights, and the Lucite guard over the front of the hood. But by the end of our

(continued on page 64)

and ready-to-leave condition. But let's be honest. Life is hectic, and sometimes not everything gets done. It's a good idea to run through a checklist before every trip to make sure everything's in working order (see Chapter 6 for details on specific maintenance chores):

- Engine
  - ❑ Oil
  - ❑ Belts
  - ❑ Radiator and other fluid levels
- Electricals
  - ❑ Headlights, tail lights, turn signals
  - ❑ Spare fuses
- Running gear
  - ❑ Tire pressure (including spare)
  - ❑ Tire condition
- Backroad Adventure Kit
  - ❑ *See page 67 for list*

Before every trip, run through a "pre-trip maintenance list," which includes checking the oil.

We do enough backroad tripping that our pre-trip checks are automatic. Until you can remember everything to check, keep a list in the glove box.

Backroad Adventure Kit

On any trip into the backcountry, you should be prepared to deal with just about any situation that arises—delayed by weather, getting stuck, stopped by a breakdown—or face the alternatives: a long walk out or a cold, hungry couple of nights while someone comes looking for you. A good backroad adventure kit will have everything you need to get you unstuck and fix most minor breakdowns, plus extra food and water if your backcountry stay is extended.

You can pack your backroad adventure kit into one large box, such as a contractor's toolbox or a lockable molded polyethylene box, that is bolted or strapped into the cargo area or onto the roof rack, or into several smaller, labeled boxes. For his Land Cruiser, Jonathan crafted a beautiful matching set of varnished, marine-quality plywood boxes lined with foam; they are bolted into place and lock with brass hardware. Some people use old ammo cans, Tupperware-type boxes, or plastic milk crates. It doesn't matter as long as it's organized, you can find everything easily, and, if heavy, it's bolted or strapped down in case of a rollover. *(continued on page 67)*

Jonathan Hanson

One of the biggest hazards of traveling the Dempster Highway are the speeding trucks, which cast huge plumes of dust over the road.

960 miles on the Dempster, our windshield was pitted and chipped. The other casualty of the trip was our tires; nearly 1,000 miles of the sharp gravel took their toll, resulting in two flats and many chunks missing. By the time we reached Whitehorse on the Yukon River we had to buy a new set (we replaced the stock Bridgestone tires with much more rugged B.F. Goodrich All-Terrains. I can say I would not want to subject a new set of expensive AT's to that tortuous road, as even the best tires would lose a lot of life).

Traveling by vehicle in the Arctic has its costs for the vehicle, certainly, as well as for supplies. Gas averaged about 77 cents per liter; packaged or prepared food easily cost two or more times what it did south of 60°N; bleak hotels ran $120 a night for a double; an oil change in Inuvik cost $110, not including filter and oil (we waited until Whitehorse); and ice, ironically, was up to $8 for an 8-pound bag.

We took three days to drive the length of the Dempster, giving us plenty of time to stop for hikes and to look around the few settlements along the way. We camped in the gravel quarries, which are the only places to pull off the road. Near the beginning of the highway there is an interpretive center and a nice provincial campground, at which we had stayed on our way up. In summer resident naturalists lead hikes, and on our first foray into Arctic tundra we saw up-close the dense carpet of dwarf Arctic willow and birch that comprise the tundra, plus four Dall's sheep, a willow ptarmigan, Arctic ground squirrels, marmot droppings, and fresh grizzly signs. One animal famous in the Arctic, the caribou, wasn't around for our July/August visit; the Hart River and Porcupine River herds winter in the middle-Dempster area, but may be seen primarily when they migrate through in March/April and September/October.

ROAD TRIP: ARCTIC CIRCLE, CONTINUED FROM PAGE 64

That night's entry in my road trip journal reads: "Stunning mountains all around us—the Ogilvie Mountains are very rocky, with scree slopes, patches of snow, and no trees. Webbed rivers cross the valleys. . . . Views are awe-inspiring, and the colors and quality of light far from anything we could imagine. The scope of the earth is mind-boggling. Can't sleep. It's midnight and still light. Too excited."

At the wide and slow-moving Mackenzie River and at the smaller Peel River, there are no bridges, but free ferries work the rivers during the summer, while in winter you simply drive across the ice. During the weeks of spring thaw and fall freeze-over, however, there is no passage. Just south of the Mackenzie River crossing is the Gwich'in Dene town of Fort McPherson, where we stopped to tour the Fort McPherson Tent and Canvas Company, makers of classic northern-style cabin tents. At the factory, yet another of our tired tires went flat, the second. It was Sunday and we had a hard time finding a tire repair shop with someone in attendance. Finally, after getting detailed directions to two places we never found, we stumbled on one house with a hand-painted "tire repair" sign out front. A very grave, nearly silent Gwich'in man in his forties emerged, clearly in the midst of his Sunday supper. With surprising speed he repaired the flat, and we were pleasantly surprised that he charged us only $15 (being the only game in town, he could have asked two or three times that), so we tipped him generously.

Throughout our drive in the Arctic, we were often surprised at the similarities of the landscape and the people to our home in the Sonoran Desert, 4,000 miles south. The vast, rolling tundra and dramatic, rugged mountains seemed familiar, a greener version of the rolling deserts and rugged mountains of the desert. The large Mackenzie River Delta reminded us of our Colorado River and its delta on the Sea of Cortez. Both areas are deserts by rainfall standards—each receives about 10 inches annually—and there are strong communities of native peoples who have learned to deal with environmental extremes, either bitter cold or broiling heat. The Inuit in the north, and the Seri in the south, along the Sea of Cortez, are ancient fishing cultures as well as makers of beautiful art from local materials. Their villages look remarkably similar, and their fates in the presence of economically more powerful European "newcomers" are also identical.

By the time we were driving south again, we had become accustomed to the "midnight sun," but at first the 24-hour daylight completely fooled our biological clocks. The sun is up all the time but at a low angle. It does not move across the sky from one horizon to high overhead and down to the opposite horizon, it simply moves around the horizon 360 degrees, ever so slightly rising and falling as it goes, the light having the quality of between 8 to 9 A.M. or 4 to 6 P.M. Thus, we didn't have the usual visual clues for everyday events like lunchtime. Once, we drove past noon, and lunch, through to 8 P.M. before our stomachs really took offense and let us know we'd messed up. Sleep was hard at first; I usually woke up every hour or so, confused.

On our last night in the Arctic region, we camped at yet another gravel pit, this one in a valley facing the Tombstone Mountains in the southwest. My journal entry from the next morning reads:

"This is possibly the most beautiful place I've ever been. Tall, jagged peaks rise across the valley, snow clinging tenaciously . . . Streams and small melt ponds, ice in one, reflecting snow, a beaver lodge at one end. Clouds descend, rain and mist surround us.

"Today we reluctantly leave the Arctic . . ."

For information: With a few well-placed phone calls and letters, an impressive pile of free information on the Yukon and Northwest Territories arrived in our living room, courtesy of the provincial governments. These included superb maps, several thick glossy magazines with ads and calendars of events, pamphlets on bear safety, and excellent information booklets on flora and fauna.

For Northwest Territories information and material, call the Department of Economic Development and Tourism, Government of the Northwest Territories at (800) 661-0788, or write the department at Yellowknife, NWT, Canada X1A 2L9. Also contact the Department of Renewable Resources, P.O. Box 1320, Yellowknife, NWT X1A 2L9; the Sahtu Tourism Association, (403) 587-2054, Box 115, Norman Wells, NWT, Canada, X0E 0V0 ; and the Western Arctic Visitors Tourism Association, (403) 979-4321, Box 2600, Inuvik, NWT, Canada X0E 0T0. For the Yukon, including information on the Yukon section of the Dempster Highway, contact the Northern Frontier Visitors Association, (403) 873-3131, or write 4807 49th Street, #4, Yellowknife, NWT, Canada X1A 3T5. And, the Yukon Department of Renewable Resources (ask about the *Milepost* travelogue), Parks and Outdoor Recreation Branch, Box 2703, Whitehorse, Yukon, Canada Y1A 2C6.

You will also want to buy the most recent *Milepost* from Alaska Northwest Books (Bothell, Washington).

Jonathan Hanson

A good backroad adventure kit will include jack, flashlight, shovel, jumper cables, spare oil, flat fix-it kit, tools, at least a gallon of spare water, snatch strap, gloves, spare parts, and a first aid kit.

Keep a list of contents in the box, and check it before each trip, in case someone "borrowed" something and forgot to replace it.

- Tool kit (see Chapter 6, page 144)
- Spares (see Chapter 6, page 144)
- Jack and accessories (see Chapter 5, page 131)
- Tow strap (see Chapter 2, page 30)
- Jumper cables
- Folding shovel
- Work gloves
- Flashlight, spare fresh batteries
- First aid kit
- Toilet paper
- Can of bear spray for unwanted visitors
- Emergency water (one gallon minimum; we carry the durable five-gallon Nalgene plastic jerry cans.)

- Spare food (a few cans and an opener, or a box of energy bars; we've used our spare food more often than we would have thought, usually when out longer than we intended because the route was slower than we remembered or when weather delayed us, so we always store something durable but palatable, like canned tuna, fruit, or energy bars.)
- Blanket or old sleeping bag

CHAPTER 4

Backroad Tripping

BY ROSEANN HANSON

- On the Road
- *Sample Backroad Trip: Plan and Execution*
- Finding Campsites
- Car-Camping Equipment
- Organizing and Packing
- After-Trip Tips

Follow the Dotted Line

Remember in kindergarten when the teacher handed out crayons and a photocopied sheet with a picture outlined in faint dotted lines? Your task was to carefully trace the picture—connecting the dotted lines—until the real picture emerged; it was a lesson in patience and hand-eye coordination.

Think of backroad trips as the grown-up extension: On a map, choose a dotted-line road (the "unimproved backcountry" type) connecting points A and B; aim your truck down the two-track at point A and follow the dotted line until you find point B; it is a lesson in fun and map-reading skills. I've connected a lot of dotted lines on maps around North America, and it's still one of my favorite tasks.

Unlike your schoolroom crayon trips, backroad adventuring in your sport utility or truck takes a little extra trip planning, as we discussed in the previous chapter. This chapter offers some tips for on-the-road travel and good gear to make your trip and your camp as comfortable as possible.

On the Road

A number of things can kill a good backroad trip. One is weather. Late spring snows, early hurricanes, or El Niño have a way of turning trips into epics. At first it's fun—challenging

Roseann Hanson

Scenic, private campsites, such as this camp on Mexico's Sea of Cortez, beckon when you're exploring by backroad.

the environment and thwarting danger and all that macho stuff—but then, after digging out of three feet of snow four times and getting out six times to scrape ice off the windshield because the defogger vents are clogged with gum wrappers and dead moths, you decide this is not fun.

Another trip killer is embarking with someone who turns out to be the Passenger from Hell. A friend of ours spent eight weeks driving the backroads of Baja with a dozen other people. Passengers rotated among the vehicles for fun, but after a while, she said, it was clear everyone was avoiding giving a ride to a guy who apparently talked nonstop about his failed love lives, unsuccessful search for the meaning of life, and everyone else's faults. You know the type. Quite early on in the trip he was secretly referred to not by his name, Jon, but as "Yawn."

Two other things can kill a good road trip: miscalculating the necessary time to enjoy yourself, and making your schedule too strict.

Judging Miles-in-a-Day

It helps to be able to plan your trip within at least a day or so, to avoid disappointment or arriving back to work on Tuesday instead of Monday. The trick is calculating how many miles you can travel in a day in any given terrain.

In general, average miles per hour to plan for are (at safe speeds):

Two wheel drive

Dry, smooth gravel or well-graded dirt road, few twists and turns: 25 mph

Dry, smooth gravel or well-graded dirt road, many twists and turns: 15 mph

Dry, gravel or dirt road with washboards, few twists and turns: 15–20 mph

Dry, gravel or dirt road with washboards, many twists and turns: 10 mph

Dirt road with intermittent washouts, potholes, few twists and turns: 15 mph

Dirt road with intermittent washouts, potholes, many twists and turns:
5–10 mph

Four wheel drive

Most dirt road trips where low-range four wheel drive is necessary will average about 5 mph

So if your map says there are 100 miles ahead of road that gains and loses 1,500 feet elevation, and the legend indicates a rough, twisting two-track, plan on about 10 miles an hour average for speed. If you get started around 9 A.M., drive for three hours, take a couple hours for lunch, and drive until at least an hour before dark (time to find and set up camp), that's about six hours. Knock off about an hour from the total time to allow for potty stops, sightseeing, and munchies, so five hours × 10 is 50 miles.

Obviously these are a rough estimates, but the rule here is to always give yourself plenty of time for unforeseen road hazards, sightseeing, or just plain relaxation.

For Information: See Chapter 6, page 143, for more about on-the-road troubleshooting, repairs, and maintenance of your vehicle.

Keep the Plan Loose

The result of rigidity is often shattering. Learn to be flexible in your tripping. If you stumble on a really outstanding place in your backcountry drive, have enough extra time built into your schedule so that you can stay a day or two longer in that spot. We once found a canyon off a backroad in southern Utah that was truly spectacular: red rock gorge lined with brilliant green cottonwoods, beavers swimming in the creek and doing repairs on their lodge, swifts diving the currents above. We tossed our "schedule" out the window and lingered an extra day and a half, splitting our time between hiking up the creek and lying on a rock and watching the beavers work. It was a trip we won't forget, and an experience that a more rigid schedule would have denied.

Our usual and preferred way to travel is to rough-in our itinerary—pull out maps and plan a few solid possibilities, places and roads we definitely want to try, and others, such as interstates, we want to avoid. Then we work out the necessary days, using the average miles per hour listed above, and add at least two extra days for unplanned side trips or stopovers. If we really want to unwind and are feeling adventurous—which means we have to be *(continued on page 73)*

Sample Backroad Trip Plan and Execution

Origin and Destination: from Tucson, Arizona, to Salt Lake City, Utah, via canyon country

Time Frame: Leaving Tucson on August 12, need to be in Salt Lake City for an outdoor industry trade show on August 17

Total Interstate Miles from Origin to Destination: 850

Planned Activities: relaxation (too much work lately!), birding and other nature explorations, easy hiking, see new areas

Day One (August 12)

Leave at 8 A.M. via Interstate 10, bound for Flagstaff (we want to get as many northbound miles under our tires as possible—get close to canyon country—on the first day). Stop in Phoenix for fast, early lunch (yuck—remember to note in our trip journal that Phoenix is a rotten place to eat; pack sack lunches next time; we've only lived in Arizona all our lives, don't know why we can't remember this).

12:30 P.M.: Arrive in Flagstaff, gateway to canyon country, nestled in the pines near Arizona's highest peaks (which soar to more than 12,000 feet). Stop at Albertson's for ice, fresh vegetables, lunch meat, bread, cookies. Stop at Macy's, our favorite coffee shop in Arizona. Over hot brews we pore over the Forest Service map of Coconino National Forest to pick some likely backroads where we can camp for free, and also free from people. Around Flag this is hard to do, given how crowded it is in summer with seemingly half of Phoenix chilling out in the high country. Both of us loathe commercial campgrounds in or near urban areas and will choose federal or state "organized" campgrounds only in desperation. But we have a rough idea of some out-of-the-way woodcutting roads not far from town where we should have solitude and silence—for free.

3:00 P.M.: Turn off the highway at a likely access road 10 miles north of town. Engage four wheel drive for the loose, very deep dark-gray gravel that covers the roads; we're near the base of the northern slope of Sunset Crater, an old volcanic cone. We head in about three miles (to lose the highway noise) through ponderosa pines, piñons, and junipers, try a few side roads, and finally find a clearing where there has been recent woodcutting. We level the truck and get out to stretch and marvel in the silence and the views—from our slightly elevated position, we can see for 50 miles or more across the magenta, blue, and pink Painted Desert to the northeast and the Kaibab Plateau and Grand Canyon to the northwest. A perfect camp (mark this one on our map).

(continued on page 74)

ready to accept "failure" if we choose poorly and end up in a less-than-perfect campsite—
we even leave most of the itinerary planning up to last-minute decisions (see box, page 72).

Finding Campsites

There are three types of car-camping: fully serviced, improved, and rustic. Depending on
what type of trip you are taking and what you want to do and where, each has advantages
and disadvantages.

- **Fully serviced camping.** Full-service campgrounds are usually commercial RV parks,
although some state campgrounds, such as those in California, are so well-run with such good
services that they rival or even surpass some privately owned campgrounds we've used. Full-
service campgrounds offer electricity, water, and a sewer connection (for RVs) at each campsite and can range from around $10 a night to more than $20. For a little less money per night
(usually several to five dollars less), car campers can get water- and/or electric-only sites away
from the big rigs. If generators are not being used by the RVers, we sometimes find it's quieter
and a little nicer in the RV sites. However, if you're tenting it instead of sleeping in your vehicle, you will be better off in the "tent" camping area. Bathrooms with showers are another
plus for these camping havens. Their primary drawback is that they are usually located just
off major streets or highways and lack any natural charm (although sometimes you can find
some real jewels, such as one we found near Bosque del Apache National Wildlife Refuge in
New Mexico). Even during busy times of the year—summer, major holidays—we've found if
we stop early enough in the day, such as before 5 P.M., we can find spaces available and don't
need reservations. However, some state and federal campgrounds do require reservations.
One summer, when exploring the Oregon coast by truck, we had to drive south all the way
through the state to California before finding a campsite because all the camping spaces in
the prime coastal state-run campgrounds were reserved, and there were no nearby national
forests with open camping.

- **Improved camping.** National forests, wildlife refuges, and most national parks and
state parks operate "improved" campgrounds, which usually are parking spaces with picnic
tables and varying degrees of services at the sites. Some have a water spigot at each site, others have a central shared spigot. Some have nice gravel parking sites and leveled tent clear-
ings, others offer just packed dirt. Some have bathrooms and showers, others just
port-a-potties or a convenient bush. The settings are always beautiful, however, and the prices
range from free to a few dollars (usually less than $10) a night. Overcrowding in popular
areas, such as the Grand Canyon, can be a drawback, however.

- **Rustic camping.** Throughout our national forests and BLM lands, and even in some
parks and wildlife refuges, there are countless places to camp away from campgrounds. Usually just pullouts off backcountry and side roads, these can offer the most scenic and remote

(continued on page 75)

SAMPLE BACKROAD TRIP PLAN AND EXECUTION, CONTINUED

DAY TWO (AUGUST 13)

Up at dawn to birds and coyotes singing. Spend a couple hours drinking tea and coffee, watching the sun paint the Painted Desert, following some bridled titmice, spotted towhees, and piñon jays.

9 A.M.: Head north on Highway 89 toward Page, around the eastern edge of the Grand Canyon.

10:30 A.M.: At the turnoff to Page we pull off the road to consult our maps. Our initial plan was to head through Page, then continue on 89 up through Bryce and Zion National Parks, to St. George, Utah, then take the interstate up to Salt Lake. Or, we had tossed around the idea of heading up a backroad just northwest of Page through a place called Kodachrome Basin and take all state routes north, then cut west across the Wasatch Mountains to Salt Lake.

Then I say, What about going over to check out Tuweep? We had both talked for years about this remote overlook on the north rim of the Grand Canyon, reputed to be one of the most spectacular vistas of this utterly spectacular park.

(continued on page 76)

Jonathan Hanson

This campsite at Tuweep, on the North Rim of the Grand Canyon, is one of North America's most scenic, and scary, campsites: The drop-off to the right goes 2,000 feet straight to the mighty Colorado River.

campsites of all—the chance for solitude and encounters with wildlife improve drastically the farther you are from the beaten path. This kind of remote car-camping is the forte of sport utilities—it's why we own them in the first place. The biggest drawback to rustic camping is that you have to look for the good sites; if you don't know the area, luck is a major factor in finding a good campsite. And obviously there

Established backroad campsites sometimes have amenities such as well-built fire rings and convenient logs for tables.

are no services, but with only a zillion stars and the owls and coyotes to keep you company, who cares? When visiting a new area, we usually stop at a local outdoors or hunting store and ask a couple of the employees where there are good backroad camping areas (we've learned to be specific about "no campgrounds, no people"). Experience has taught us that calling the information numbers for most public land agencies usually puts you in touch with a front-desk person, most likely a volunteer, who often has no experience whatsoever in the backcountry, so avoid this tactic unless you can get hold of a backcountry ranger or resource person. Rustic camping is usually free, but it's always a good idea to check with the land management agency in advance to find out its policies and restrictions (such as no fires during dry months). Some, especially wildlife refuges, want you to camp only in designated sites to minimize impact, which is important. During times of the year when prescribed burning is undertaken, it's a good idea to find out the areas and to steer clear.

Happy Camping

Choosing a campsite is perhaps the most critical step for making any camp, and no less so in a car-accessible campground or campsite than in the roadless wilderness when backpacking. And the crucial elements—safety and low-impact—are often lost on most campers because scenic value is usually considered first.

Some good general tips to consider for campsite selection include:

- Use preexisting campsites.
- If there are no old campsites, look for open areas with durable ground cover only (bare soil, sand, small gravel).
- Never clear any vegetation or dig trenches or tent sites to set up camp. If you

(continued on page 77)

Why not? So we hang a left instead of a right and climb up and over the Kaibab Plateau, through Fredonia, and turn south into the Antelope Valley. A sign warns that this is a rough, nonserviced road ("travel at your own risk, unsuitable for RVs"—our favorite sign!) of some 55 miles. Miles and miles of open land roll by; the road is indeed rough, and it is after 4 P.M. when we finally pull up to the tiny ranger station to pay the fee, then drive the final eight very rough miles to the rim.

What we find is perhaps one of the most spectacular camping sites in North America. Maybe the world. Only a dozen or so pullouts and tables are set into the junipers and piñons and red canyon rocks, and of these only four are filled (it is over 100°F). And two of these sites are literally just feet from the rim—which at this remote outpost has no guardrail, no warning signs, nothing, between you and a 2,000-foot-plus drop to the mighty turquoise waters of the Colorado River below. These rimside sites are, of course, taken, and I am secretly glad because I am afraid of heights; even the proximity of such a yawning maw would leave me sleepless. We set up camp a quarter-mile away in a quiet site nestled among boulders and junipers with a lovely view of Tuckup, a side canyon. We are tired but thrilled at our find.

Day Three (August 14)

At dawn we wake not to birds or coyotes but the whir of props on the sightseeing planes out of Las Vegas; they will continue all day from dawn to dusk without cessation. Ignoring this noise pollution (which is supposed to be largely banned in the park soon), we hike to Lava Falls Overlook and sit for hours watching a couple of commercial and one private rafting trip run this infamous rapid. Even from a distance of both a linear and vertical mile, we hear the roar of this giant rinse-and-spin cycle and see the violence with which it grabs the boats.

The heat persists, the visitation remains low, and the hiking and views are so beautiful we decide to stay an extra day. We nap, write, read, hike, and eat. Perfection.

Day Four (August 15)

Repeat of Day Three. Very relaxing. Still a long way from Salt Lake City, so we decide we must leave in the morning.

Day Five (August 16)

8 A.M.: Leave the park and decide to head to St. George, Utah, where we will pick up the interstate to Salt Lake, via the rugged old Mt. Trumbull Road (more dotted lines on the

(continued on page 78)

move any rocks or logs, remember where they were so you can put them back, although for the lowest impact on an ecosystem, campers shouldn't move anything but small rocks.

- Set up camp at least a quarter mile from solitary water sources during dry periods; some animals won't come in to drink if you are too close.

- Always restore any campsite to pristine condition (as if you had never been there) after you strike camp. It takes only a few moments.

> *A thing is right when it tends to preserve the integrity, stability,*
> *and beauty of the biotic community. It is wrong when it tends otherwise.*
> —ALDO LEOPOLD, *A SAND COUNTY ALMANAC* (1949)

Certain ecosystems or areas also require some particular forethought when setting up camps:

- **Woodlands and forests.** Take care setting up camp under tall or big trees whose falling branches might pose a hazard. Check for and avoid shrubs such as poison ivy or poison oak, or fruiting berry bushes, which might attract bears.

- **Rivers, streams, lakes.** Tempting as it may be, don't camp along the banks of water sources; camp at least 200 feet away. Bankside vegetation provides critical wildlife habitat and erosion control, and camp-related activities trample seedlings and cause soil compaction. And there's the obvious flooding danger and the presence of mosquitoes around standing water (such as lake or river backwaters and ponds).

- **Deserts.** Look for durable surfaces such as rock slabs or dry wash beds (but beware of flash floods!) for campsites. In many North American deserts, steer clear of open unvegetated areas with crusty soil, which might be tracts of biologically rich and very delicate cryptobiotic (literally "hidden life") soil. Vegetation in desert areas is delicate and slow-growing, and any soil disturbance will eventually lead to erosion. In many parts of the country (not just deserts, though they seem most conspicuous there), watch for scorpions under tents or other camp structures when you move them or take them down.

- **Ocean or inland sea coasts.** In spring and summer, many species of shorebirds nest in the flotsam of the storm tide lines, so care should be taken to keep activities away. Also, rocky shores and tide lines are often full of small, hungry arthropods such as sand fleas.

- **Bear country.** In bear country, the widely held wisdom is to set up the camp kitchen as far from your tent as possible. See page 80 for more tips on bear-country camping.

Critter Control

Our ancestors huddled around the campfire, a haven from hungry wild animals. Today, the animals that wander into popular camping areas are not nearly as wild as their ancestors once were. The resident raccoons have probably been foraging in trash cans and bins since their parents taught them how to pry off the covers. Local squirrels are practically

map!) instead of back up through Fredonia and a paved road. This road accesses some of the most remote ranches in the Southwest—over the heavily logged Mt. Trumbull we wind, then down across the bleak but beautiful Shivwits Plateau, which is dotted with names like Poverty Knoll, Dry Canyon, and Last Chance Canyon. Mt. Trumbull, the town, lies in a now-barren valley of abandoned fields where tumbleweeds catch on rusty barbed wire and mark the old fence boundaries. In the middle of this nothingness stands an unlikely but lovely restored white clapboard schoolhouse from the turn of the century, a reminder of times passed.

We underestimate the time we need to cover this rugged country as well as misjudge the ease of finding a good and legal campsite, and it's dark when we finally try a tiny logging road near Wolf Hole. Tired and a little cranky from the long day, we set up camp in a not-too-ideal spot, eat dinner, and curl up with a couple of good books.

DAY SIX (AUGUST 17)

Dawn: Up and at 'em, through St. George (stop for breakfast) and then hit the interstate to Salt Lake. We have 313 long miles ahead of us but we're relaxed and happy after such a wonderful backroad exploration.

domesticated in many campgrounds. Even deer lose much of their shyness after constant exposure to people.

Despite this gradual taming (and no matter how much we might want the storybook picture of nature to be real), the truth is that these animals are not trying to be friendly, they are simply trying to take our food. Understandable though that may be, giving them food does not help them in the long term. They will become dependent on (and later, demanding of) handouts, when they should be practicing the self-sufficiency that is *their* nature. Finally, wild animals can carry and transmit diseases that also affect people. Tick-related diseases and rabies are just two of the most commonly recognized.

Regardless of how cute a forest creature may appear, don't be tempted: Ignore them or shoo them off.

General Critter Proofing

Animal-proof your campsite by leaving no food out unattended during the day and putting all of your food inside the vehicle at night, not in the tent (if you sleep in your vehicle, hang the food from a tree; see page 80 for how-tos). You don't want to attract night visitors.

RESOURCES FOR FINDING CAMPGROUNDS

Check out these resources for finding good full-service and improved campgrounds. Many more books and websites are available. For help finding rustic campsites, contact the government agencies for the area to which you are heading (see Appendix II, page 165) and talk with employees at local outdoors and hunting stores.

GUIDEBOOKS

Camp the U.S. for $5 or Less (available in Western and Eastern/Midwestern editions) by Mary Helen and Shuford Smith (Globe Pequot Press, 1994).

Don Wright's Guide to Free Campgrounds (Cottage Publications, 1997).

The Best Tent Camping series for California, Washington, and Oregon (Menasha Ridge Press, various dates).

Camper's Guide series for California, Colorado, Florida, Indiana and Ohio, Minnesota, Texas, Washington, Oregon, (Gulf Publishing Company, various dates).

Woodall's North American Campground Directory: The Complete Guide to Campgrounds, RV Parks, Service Centers & Attractions (Woodall Publishing Company, annual). Woodall also offers regional guides.

Woodall's 1996 Plan-It, Pack-It, Go . . . Great Places to Tent . . . Fun Things to Do (Woodall Publishing Company, annual).

America's Hidden Treasures: Exploring Our Little-Known National Parks—National Geographic Park Profiles (Random House, 1997).

Camping series by Foghorn Press. Includes Baja, California, Northern California, New England, Pacific Northwest, Rocky Mountain, Southwest, Utah, and Nevada.

INTERNET

Great Outdoor Recreation Pages, www.gorp.com, is the best hub for searching for campground links, including backcountry and RV-types, and books, gear, and so on.

Happy Camping offers a very complete guide to full-service campgrounds at www.happycamping.com.

Also try Camping USA at www.camping-usa.com.

And post a question about camping in an area you're headed to on a Usenet newsgroup such as rec.outdoors.camping or alt.rec.camping—you'll be amazed at the scope and helpfulness of the answers.

If your food boxes or coolers aren't well-hinged and clamped, tie them shut with a buckled utility strap, or the raccoons will be enjoying your camping food. Raccoons are *very* strong, clever, and persistent.

Rodents such as squirrels and chipmunks are eager to try people food, too, and while it's tempting to offer them some tiny morsel, remember they can, and sometimes do, bite the hands that feed them. Any rodent can be pesky; they'll chew their way into your food supply, given half a chance, which is why you don't leave any flimsy food packages around camp.

Discourage bird beggars, too. It might be fun, at first, to watch them catch food you toss, but the downside is they just become bigger pests. Crows, gulls, and jays are especially bad; they're not at all timid.

IF YOU GET SKUNKED

If a surprise encounter with a skunk results in your worst camping nightmare, be prepared with Skunk-Off, which claims to remove all traces of skunk smell (look for it at outdoor retailers). Old stand-by solutions are tomato juice, or a vinegar/water mix of about 1 to 10.

Bearing Up

When you head out to camp, check with the land agency's rangers regarding the presence of "problem bears" and ask advice on bear-avoidance tactics. Remember that bears range all up and down a mountain, so you might find them as low as the oak-covered foothills.

At night, and when you leave your camp, be prepared to bag your food and hoist it high, out of reach of a bear standing on its hind legs. First pack your fresh and dried food and secure everything in one or more heavy-duty plastic bags or stuff sacks. To hang your food bag, find a usable tree limb about 15 feet high and extending out from the trunk far enough to prevent a small bear from crawling out to it. Tie a rock or other weight to the end of a line, so you can toss the line over the limb. That done, tie the food bag onto the line, haul it up, and tie if off securely to the tree trunk.

Remove all food and toiletries—anything that smells, including bug repellent, sunscreen, lip balm, toothpaste, lotion, and so on—from your sleeping tent.

As an added precaution in bear country, locate your cooking area as far from your sleeping tent as possible, and group your sleeping tents fairly close together.

If you're fishing and consuming your catch, be prepared to attract curious and hungry bears—the smell carries for a long way. Clean your fish far from camp and wash both your dishes and yourself extremely well.

If you come across a small bear along the trail or near camp, leave as quickly and quietly as you can, before the big bear knows you're there. Mama bear stories are true.

Dealing with Insects

On the basis of numbers and ability to drive campers crazy, the smallest pests win. Biting insects—whether flying or crawling—seem the constant enemy. Don't be overly aggressive about insect killing: Try to remember that most insects pollinate flowers and food plants and are the first link in many food chains. Even the majority of the biting/stinging group are more often annoying than threatening. Only a few—fleas, ticks, and mosquitoes—actually carry diseases that are harmful to humans.

Focus on insect-deterrence rather than killing bugs. Never use "bug-bombs"—one study in a national park along the Rio Grande in Texas showed that enthusiastic campground use of bug bombs resulted in extremely high levels of pesticides accumulating in the soil, plants, and animals (as much as 38 pounds of DDT accumulation over one season in four campgrounds).

- **Citronella.** Citronella is a nonchemical repellent made from a plant commonly called lemongrass. Of all the bug-chasing preparations, citronella is easiest on the humans using it—although, unfortunately, not always hard enough on the insects. You can buy citronella oil to burn in a lamp, or you can light a bunch of citronella candles. You'll also find it as an ingredient in insect repellents applied directly to skin.
- **Mosquito coils.** Other burnable deterrents include mosquito coils, although these are treated with a repellent that sometimes bothers people as much as it does insects. With one brand, the coil sits inside a short, metal canister; holes cut into the sides allow the smoke to escape. Another holder leaves more space for smoke to exit; a fiberglass netting material over the coil keeps ashes in if the container should be knocked over.
- **Permethrin.** An insect repellent in a water-based formula, Permethrin is EPA-approved for use on clothing and tent fabric. One application will be effective for two weeks, even if it rains on the tent (or you wash the clothes).
- **Insect repellents and other insect-deterrence strategies.** If you use "bug juice," look for something natural (citronella is popular). If you buy something with the chemical DEET, be sure the product has a nonabsorbent agent (DEET used in too-high quantities and for too long can cause severe health problems).

Car-Camping Equipment

Our parents knew a heck of a lot about the art of car-camping—it was one of *the* things to do with the family of the 1950s and 1960s. They knew how to make a great camp, with folding picnic tables, awnings, comfortable chairs, kitchen ("chuck") boxes, Dutch ovens, and big tents full of cots and comfy sleeping bags with deer leaping across the linings, or even better, a Teardrop Trailer. We have an old book, copyright 1958 by Ford Motor Company, called the *Ford Treasury of Station Wagon Living.* It's full of color pictures of unbelievable car-camping setups: Cartop boxes that seemingly at the touch of a button disgorge complete cabin tents, chairs, elaborate kitchens, awnings, and screened dining tents. The book showcases the high art of '50s modern convenience in the woods as well as squeaky-clean couples and kids (no dirt in these pictures, and many of the women wear pretty floral dresses while happily flipping flapjacks on a tailgate kitchen extraordinaire). Our parents' setups weren't necessarily so perfect, but we remember them as being pretty neat.

Apparently the backpacking boom of the '70s and the adrenaline-sport crazes of the '80s diminished the art of car-camping. Good car-camping gear—folding tables and chairs, big tents, car awnings, and kitchen boxes—was pretty hard to find in those decades. But with the '90s came a surge in the popularity of sport utilities—be honest, the station wagon of our adult generation—and we have seen a renaissance in car-camping equipment availability as well as quality.

Sleeping Easy

Shelters for car-camping usually are not limited by weight or packed-up size, so the variety to choose from is broad. Although there is the option of sleeping in the back of your sport utility, we'll cover separate sleeping and dining tents here; see page 84 for more on in-truck options.

SLEEP IN OR OUT?

When setting up your car-camping rig, you will be deciding whether to sleep in the back of the vehicle or to have a separate tent. Here are some considerations:

First, check how comfortable you'll be sleeping in the back of your sport utility or pickup. Are you too tall? Do the back seats fold completely flat, or are they canted up at an angle when folded?

One of the most comfortable "outdoor beds" around is a mattress cut to fit the back of your vehicle (buy an egg-crate foam mattress pad from a bedding or department store). Heaven.

Remember that to sleep in the back of your vehicle, everything that was packed back there for traveling must be removed to lay out your sleeping pad. In bear and critter (raccoons, marmots, mice) country, everything must be secured. Roof racks can solve some of this problem, but remember that bears can climb. If the only secure place is in the front seat, that means you and your food are in the same place, so to a bear, it's one and the same.

Classic Freestanding and Hoop Tents

The most readily available tents are freestanding and hoop-style. The former set up with a metal- or fiberglass-pole framework that supports the tent without need of tie-outs to keep them pitched. (A note of caution: Although called "freestanding," these and all tents should always be secured with guy-lines, lest a gust of wind turn them into large parafoils). Free-standing tent styles include dome, modified dome, and cabin. Hoop tents are supported by several poles arranged Conestoga-style; guy-lines at either end are necessary to keep the tent pitched.

Freestanding tents are more convenient than hoop tents because once they're set up, you don't need to get the guylines set up just right to achieve tautness, and usually less open space is necessary to pitch a freestanding tent. Headroom and floor space are usually very generous. However, some freestanding tents, especially large cabin-style ones, can be complicated to set up and have more little parts to lose.

When camping from your sport utility, you can indulge in a luxurious, large-capacity tent such as this modified dome-style Mondo 5 CD tent from Sierra Designs.

Hoop tents are not complicated to set up because the poles are often all the same length or of obvious size distinction (small in back, larger in front), and their placement is pretty straightforward. The hard part is getting the guyline tension right so a 3 A.M. wind doesn't cause an infuriating flap-flap-flap and rain doesn't pool on the fly and seep through. Also, if you're in very sandy or rock-hard soil, setting stakes can be particularly fun.

Both freestanding and hoop tents usually pack into small packages if space is limited in your vehicle. Hoop tents tend to be more compact when rolled; big cabin tents, especially those with two rooms or screen porches, can be heavy and bulky. Both styles are also widely available at outdoor retailers and department stores such as Wal-Mart and Kmart. Beware of quality, however: If you don't want to fuss with broken parts, splitting floors, leaking roofs, and poorly cut walls that flap in the slightest breeze, select a name

ANATOMY OF A GOOD TENT

Look for the following features when tent shopping:

- Tempered (heat-treated) aluminum poles
- Tight, even stitching and finished/sealed seams
- Taut walls when pitched
- Full-coverage rain fly that fits well
- Heavy-duty zippers with stainless steel sliders
- Plenty of attachment points for guylines
- Fine-gauge "no-see-um" mesh panels on windows and doors
- Plenty of ventilation

brand such as Sierra Designs, Moss, Eureka, Kelty, or Marmot, among others. Mail-order companies, such as Cabela's, L.L. Bean, and REI, also have their own brands of gear. (See Appendix II, starting on page 163, for contact information for the brands listed.)

Cartop Tents

Cartop tents are nothing new—they've been used on safari-rigged sport utilities in Africa for nearly as long as there have been vehicles on the Dark Continent. Europeans have embraced them, as have Australians, but unfortunately they are not yet widely available in the United States.

Cartop tents are housed in cases made from wood or composite, such as fiberglass, that flip open flat, either to the side or to the front of the vehicle, creating a large platform out of the top and bottom of the case. Poles running to the ground or front bumper provide support. Another style opens up like a clamshell. On all styles the tent is attached to the housing and is set up via integrated poles that lock in place. A mattress is usually part of this very convenient and comfortable package.

The convenience of such a tent on top of a sport utility or truck-camper shell is unparalleled: It takes just a few minutes or even less to pop them open. Side-flipping tents also provide instant awnings—another item you won't have to rig. A cartop tent does mean you lose your roof cargo space. For long excursions, a utility trailer is a good solution (see page 85).

For years, attaching any cartop tent capable of holding the weights of occupants meant drilling holes in the roof of your vehicle. Lately, strong, *removable* rack systems have been introduced.

The nicest cartop tent made in the United States is the Top Bunk by High Gear. The Top Bunk opens like a hatchback door with the aid of two gas struts. The upper half of the

Courtesy of High Gear, Inc.

shell is propped upright with two telescoping poles that lock with a twisting motion. The 50-by-80-inch foam mattress is encased in a nylon cover for protection, and the side tent walls are made from nylon fabric that is breathable, water repellent, fire retardant, and UV resistant. These side walls can be completely unzipped from the fiberglass shell in order to convert it to a 30-cubic-foot cargo carrier once the mattress is removed. The ladder is stored inside on

The Top Bunk is a versatile solution for camping in your sport utility. Take out the mattress, and the shell doubles as a storage pad.

top of the mattress while traveling and is removed and attached to the vehicle's rack with Quick Clips.

The Top Bunk by High Gear is high quality and high price: around $2,000. See Appendix II, beginning on page 163, for contact information.

"Caboose" Style Tents

A few manufacturers—and the list is getting shorter, unfortunately—make tents that attach to the back of a sport utility or pickup with a camper shell, creating an extra room that is big enough to stand or sleep in. Most of these attach to the back of the truck with straps and an elastic sleeve. Some are freestanding and can be detached from the truck and remain pitched while you take the truck for a day of exploration. Others rely on the body of the truck to provide structural framework, so to leave the campsite you must take down the caboose.

Good places to look for these tents are in catalogs such as Cabela's and Campmor (see Appendix II, starting on page 163, for contact information).

If you can't find a true caboose tent (they are getting very hard to find), look at a traditional Baker tent such as that made by Duluth Tent & Awning (they call theirs Campfire tents). A versatile tent made from tough cotton canvas, it can be pitched so that the large front flap forms an awning. Back your sport utility or truck up to the awning, and you have a wonderful ready-made camp. The four-person size has a $7' \times 7'$ sleeping room and a $6\frac{1}{4}' \times 7'$ porch.

Truck and Trailer Tents

In addition to the freestanding and caboose tents that can be used as a "room addition" to your truck, there are several specialty tents just for pickups without camper shells, and a very nice four-wheel-drive–capable trailer tent.

Sportz makes a tent that pitches over the open bed of the truck, a sort of collapsible pickup bedroom (for sleeping only—you don't drive with these on!). They're not widely distributed; Cabela's and Campmor offer them through their mail-order catalogs.

The TrailBlazer Camper from USA VenturCraft is a small pop-out camper that is light enough and rugged enough to tow, even on rough

Courtesy of USA VenturCraft

You can save or even add a lot of cargo space with a special four-wheel-drive camping trailer such as this USA VenturCraft Trailblazer Camper, which has a bed and space for dressing and gear storage.

four-wheel-drive roads. In addition to sleeping space for two and a full-headroom changing area, there is also plenty of cargo room. This is a great alternative to cartop or separate tents.

Shelter from the Storm (and Sun)

Although an awning may seem like a luxury, I'd venture out on a limb and say that, to complete the perfect car-camping setup, you need an awning. In the event of rain, you won't have to cram into the back of your rig with the food, stove, fuel, and one or more other grumpy people. And don't expect all campgrounds or campsites to have perfect trees for shade; lack of shelter from sun can ruin a perfectly great camp if you can't find respite from its glare.

Lest you think an awning is a bother, some truly ingenious roll-out shade and rain shelters attach to your roof rack—a great solution if you choose a small dome tent or a cartop tent that does not have a built-in awning. Encased in aluminum or other light metal, the fabric rolls out under tension, and side poles attach to the truck or ground for support. Check out the eight-foot-wide sport rack awning by Jetrak and sold through Performance Products. (See Appendix II, starting on page 162, for contact information.) If you're handy, you can also modify a lightweight pullout awning made for pop-up trailers (the kind pulled by sedans and widely sold at RV dealers) to fit your own roof rack or camper shell. If you can't locate one through your local RV dealer, try Camping World, a huge mail-order and retail store business that caters to big RVers but also has a smaller catalog for camper accessories.

With a little more bother and a lot less cost, you can also rig a useful awning from a well-cut nylon tarp and adjustable poles (see photo, page 70). The best such tarps, Parawings from Moss, come in several different sizes. Make sure to attach plenty of guylines and rig it sloped to shed rain away from the truck.

Let There Be Light

Endlessly black skies dotted with diamondlike stars surely are one of the great joys of camping. It's often surprising how bright just plain starlight can be. Alas, you will want some artificial lighting to avoid cooking up too many bugs or bumbling over logs, into bears, or over a drop-off. There are many different gas or electric lanterns from which to choose, as well as candle lanterns and headlamps.

Classic Camp Lanterns

The classic camping lantern has been updated and upgraded and made for use with various fuels, but it still looks at least semi-old-fashioned, with its traditional shape, glass globe, and flame glow.

The kerosene model is the only one that still requires preheating (done by pouring denatured alcohol into the burner cup and lighting it). Kerosene is economical, readily available (often from gasoline stations), and, unquestionably, the safest fuel to use. A minor disadvantage is carrying the alcohol as well as the kerosene. Also, some people object to the smell of kerosene, especially if it's not burning properly.

Many camping lanterns burn white gas (also described as "Coleman fuel"). Some are "dual-fuel," with ordinary unleaded gasoline as the second choice. These lanterns need no preheating or priming. Just pump up the pressure, turn the knob, and light with a match or butane lighter. Fuel for these lanterns is easily found, but highly flammable, so it must be handled and stored with care.

Propane lanterns can be used with disposable cylinders or connected to a larger, refillable tank via handy poles that also elevate the lantern above work areas (a stove and heater can also be attached to this tank system; see page 91 for more on propane systems). Familiar, convenient, and clean-burning, propane might be the lantern of choice.

Because gas lanterns work by pressure, they emit a constant, characteristic hiss. Some people find the noise annoying, disrupting the sought-after quiet of nature. If you can live with less light, but more quiet, use a hurricane lamp instead. Small (about 10 inches high) and practical, with the charm of form-and-function, hurricane lamps burn quietly, using a wick to carry the fuel. They'll burn kerosene, lamp oil (your choice of scent), or citronella oil (an insect repellent). Few things can go wrong: Fill it, lift the globe, and light. They're even reasonably priced. You can find them in basic black- or red-painted metal or a gleaming brass finish.

Alternatives

- **Candle lanterns.** At camping stores you can find a number of different mini-lanterns, about six inches tall. Some burn lamp oil, some use candles. A glass globe brightens the flame and keeps it out of the wind.

- **Do-it-yourself candle lights.** Punch some holes in the side of a juice can (or other small can that is tall rather than squatty), and set a candle in it. Melt a bit of wax onto the can bottom to hold the candle—just like a Halloween pumpkin. Loop a wire handle into the top rim (but handle it cautiously when the candle's lit). Never use in a tent.

- **Fluorescent lanterns.** Battery-operated (either 12-volt or flashlight-sized batteries) or rechargeable fluorescent lanterns are efficient, although replacement bulbs can be hard to find.

- **Flashlights and head lamps.** Flashlights have come a long way from the basic beam-pointer. They've stretched out in both length and diameter. The same flashlight can give you a focused spot or a wide-angle circle of light. They may be waterproof (some float) or PVC coated for bump and drop protection. You can find one with a clip-on handle, a stand-and-tilt base, or a wrist-tie strap. Some flashlights have two sides, with a choice of fluorescent and incandescent beams. One small flashlight becomes a head lamp when inserted into a loop on a headband. A real head light is much more useful than an ordinary flashlight; hands are free to put up the tent, fix dinner, or hold the map you're trying to unfold

PRIMAL LIGHT: CAMPFIRES

Our love of the campfire is strongly atavistic, going back to the times when it provided our only warmth, cooked food, and much-needed security.

Alas, in many areas campfires are completely banned or severely restricted during certain seasons. And it has become in many respects politically incorrect to build a campfire; with so many millions of people venturing into North America's wildernesses each year, important forest resources such as deadwood are quickly disappearing and fire rings in the backcountry are a real eyesore. Certainly in some ecosystems, such as above-timberline, canyonlands, and deserts, fires have no place at all (at least not fires burning wood found locally).

But campfires are among the joys of camping. What are some ways to still enjoy campfires while minimizing impact?

- **Car campers should bring their own wood.** Better yet, the wood should be waste-wood, such as lumber from construction sites or from renewable sources such as pruning remains.
- **Never create a new fire ring.** If your campsite has a preexisting fire ring, use it and leave it for the next party (it's tempting to sanctimoniously destroy existing fire rings, but if each backcountry party on popular routes used the same campsites and fire rings instead of creating new ones at every hill and dale, wilderness impact would be greatly reduced). If there are no fire rings at your campsite, follow the following formula for a low-impact "Zen fire," courtesy of the National Outdoor Leadership School's Leave No Trace program: *Do not use rocks to make a fire ring; instead, make the fire on a mound of mineral soil that you have built up on a tarp or fire pan (to keep the heat from sterilizing the soil). Use only dead and downed wood, and compromise with a small fire. The last morning, crush and widely scatter the cold ashes with your hands and sweep away signs of the fire site with branches or disguise with debris. Pack out any fire remains that can't be crushed and scattered.*

and read. We keep at least one head lamp in the truck full-time as both a backup for the lantern and for night hikes or potty excursions.

Kitchen Gear

You *could* stick to cold cereal, sandwiches, and finger-food dinners from the grill; then you don't need pots, pans, or plates. That's actually fun for a couple of weekends, but eventually you'll want to fix other foods—really *cooking* outdoors becomes part of the fun. Car campers can bring almost as much kitchen stuff as they'd like—within reason, of course—initially taken straight from cabinet to car.

With the exception of cooking over a campfire, cooking outdoors is really not much different from cooking at home—you just have one or two burners instead of four, and your baking might be done in a Dutch oven or a special outdoor baking oven instead of a big, standard convection oven. And, of course, the views are better.

So at first, raid your pantry for gear, but when camping becomes a regular thing, it's practical to have a "camping only" inventory of pots, utensils, and dishes. Keep these packed and ready to go in their own "chuck box." To outfit your own box (see page 98 for tips on buying or building your own), head for the camping store, browse the garage sales, or shop a local flea market. Look for:

- Pots with bucket-type bail handles if you want to hang them over a campfire. Camping pots are often sold in sets of graduated sizes; handles either come off or fold in, so pots nest completely into one another for the most compact storage.
- Pots whose lids become frying pans—you just invert them and attach a handle or use a pot lifter.
- Nonstick-coated aluminum cooksets—for easy cleanup.
- One or two medium-to-large frying pans (covers aren't essential; you can always use aluminum foil) and/or a long griddle.
- A cast iron or nonstick-coated aluminum "sandwich cooker" (sometimes called pie irons), to cook single burgers, meat pies, or dessert mini-pies.
- Don't forget the "fire sticks"—one giant fork holds six hot dogs at once, or choose smaller forks or skewers for traditional marshmallow toasting.
- Long-handled spoons, forks, tongs, and spatulas—look for those with non–heat-conducting handles, and keep a pair of thermal quilted elbow-length mitts for insurance.
- Mismatched stainless flatware found at garage sales makes excellent campware, as do plastic or metal plates, and old (thick) ceramic or plastic insulated mugs. (Many campers use paper plates, but the cost in the long run is much higher than buying reusables, and if weather or forest conditions preclude a fire at camp, you're stuck with a bunch of smelly garbage.)

Other essentials: a good Lexan cutting board (thinner, lighter-weight, easier to sanitize than wood), plastic table cloth, several sharp knives, plenty of paper towels for napkins as well as mop-up, assorted plastic bags (zip-top and garbage-sized), matches, mechanical can opener, can and bottle opener, and corkscrew.

Cooking Up a Storm

Most car campers use a two-burner camp stove. When folded for transport, the stove is about the size of an attaché case and is similarly equipped with a convenient carrying handle. When set up to use, the lid stands at a 90-degree angle to the cooking surface, to provide a back-wall wind block. Side panels pop into position to keep side-drafts from threatening the flame. Camp stoves sit conveniently on a picnic table, tailgate, or level rock or log. Single-burner backpacking stoves are often used as backup to larger stoves, but some people do use them for their primary stove for car-camping.

Regardless of their fuel source, all two-burner camp stoves have a similar compact shape. Those that burn liquid fuel (kerosene, unleaded gas, or white gas) have an attached, cylindrical fuel tank. Those that burn propane use disposable propane bottles or are connected to a larger, refillable propane tank.

- **Propane.** Propane stoves are clean and efficient, and they are the easiest camp stoves to use because they are most familiar, especially if you are used to a gas stove or grill at home. While you may need to use a match or other spark to light the burner, from then on it is cooking as usual. The knob adjusts for high or low heat, and cooking times will be fairly close to what you expect on a home stove. (Some models do have a built-in sparkmaker, eliminating the step of lighting the burner, but these have a way of breaking.) A few campers shy away from carrying pressurized fuel because of the potential hazards, and disposable fuel bottles are quite expensive (however, propane in refillable cylinders is extremely cheap and efficient). See page 91 for more on propane systems for car-camping.

- **Liquid fuel.** Most popular liquid fuel stoves burn white gas (also sold as "Coleman fuel"). Some dual-fuel models accept either white gas or plain, readily available automobile unleaded gasoline. These stoves are just as easy to cook over once they're burning, but they are not quite as easy to start as the propane stoves (keep in mind that while white gas is relatively "clean," automotive fuel is smelly). While propane is already pressurized in the cylinder, liquid fuel must be pressurized. This is accomplished with a simple pumping mechanism built into the tank. If you've followed the manufacturer's instructions carefully, you simply pump up pressure, turn the knob, and light the burner with a match. (A common problem with lighting these stoves stems from overfilling—if the tank's too full, you can't get enough pressure into it to vaporize the fuel for combustion). Once you become comfortable with using a liquid-fuel stove, you'll find they provide the best heat.

Propane, white gas, and automobile fuel are all commonly available. As with all combustion appliances, use common sense when operating them: Follow the manufacturer's directions carefully, especially regarding the fuel type and source; don't use stoves inside a tent or in any unventilated place, such as the back of your vehicle (all fire uses oxygen and produces odorless and deadly carbon monoxide).

Be wary of the advertised amounts to determine how much fuel you should take. On your first trips, take a lot; then keep track of what you actually use in a typical weekend. Some people drink lots of coffee or cook long, complex meals, while others use stoves a lot less and thus burn less fuel. We use a five-gallon propane tank for a two-burner stove and a lantern; our experience has been that it lasts much longer than we anticipate. With average use being a couple of three-day weekends a month, we generally fill our tank twice a year, with each fill

CAMP COOKSTOVE TIPS

Jonathan Hanson

A two-burner white gas stove is convenient and relatively simple to use when camping.

- Folding stands are made to hold camp stoves. While not a necessity, you might like the convenience of cooking at a familiar standing level. (Some stands have a pot-or-food-holding shelf about midway between base and stove platform.)

- Propane is also known as LPG or liquefied petroleum gas.

- When pouring liquid fuels, use a funnel for less chance of spillage. Coleman sells a filter/funnel that helps keep impurities out of the stove.

- Don't store liquid fuel for any length of time (not in the can and especially not in the stove), or it may get gummy. If you use the stove every week or two, there's no problem, but burn out all fuel before seasonal storage.

- Liquid-fuel stoves sometimes need help. Carry spare parts and whatever tools you'd need to put in the parts. (Kit could include gasket and/or O-ring, spare jet, cleaning pad, and jet-cleaning needle.) The pressure-pump plunger should be lubricated regularly with a light-grade machine oil. Reread stove instructions and maintenance tips before each trip, and bring troubleshooting instructions with you.

- Carry an inexpensive backpacker's one-burner stove with you as a backup in case your big stove goes on the blink and a campfire is not possible or practical. For example, the Scorpion stove folds up into a small bag and costs less than $25 with a fuel cartridge,

costing less than $6 (the tank almost always has at least a quarter tank of gas remaining when we fill it).

Propane Tank Systems

Our favorite camping system is a five-gallon refillable propane cylinder for running a two-burner camp stove and a lantern. We don't have one, but a radiant heater is also available. The cylinder sits on the ground with the lantern suspended above it via a four-foot gas line that is a pole (the lantern screws on top). A twin connector allows us to attach, along with

A propane tank system is a step up in convenience from white gas–powered appliances, since you don't have to worry about messy liquid fuel. This setup shows the tank feeding a two-burner stove on a special stand, and a lantern on a pole that attaches to the tank. Heaters are also available for these systems.

the lantern pole line, a flexible gas line from the tank to the stove (if we wanted to attach a heater, a tri-connection would be necessary). The stove sits at waist-level on a collapsible stove stand (available from the manufacturer; ours is Coleman). Our custom-made chuck box (see page 98), which holds all our kitchen utensils and spices, sits on another stove stand next to the stove. Our roll-up table sits nearby, for food prep and dining. With this incredibly compact system, which takes up less than six square feet in the cargo area, we don't need to rely on the presence of picnic tables at our campsite, and cooking is a delight rather than a chore.

Campfires for Cooking

Once you have the desired hot coals in your Zen fire (see page 88), you can use the fire to cook directly (as in hot dogs on sticks, kabobs on skewers, or steaks on a grill) or indirectly (as the heat source for Dutch oven stewing, frying, baking, or steaming).

Look for cooking kettles with lids as well as handles in camping stores; Dutch ovens, hung from a tripod, work great as regular pots. Good campfire cooking accessories include:

BACKROAD ADVENTURE TIP

Keep a notebook handy during your trips and use it to jot down wished-for gear, truck or gear modifications, better packing or preparation ideas, and so on, as the trip progresses. When you get home, use it as a guide for buying new gear and modifying your camp setup.

You can also expand the notebook into a trip journal. I use mine to record daily mileages, information about good or bad campsites, food, thoughts, ideas, sketches— just about anything related to the trip. I also stash in an envelope all the receipts and other paper items that accumulate on any trip: business cards, menus, clippings from local papers, postcards. Many times I have dug up my old trip journals to access information about a place for friends and relatives (a great campground on the Alaskan Highway; a wonderful restaurant in Moab) or for future trip planning.

■ **Cooking platform.** Buy or make a simple grill—recycle a grill from a burned-out barbecue, for example. Bend some V-shaped metal legs to hold it up, or prop it up on rocks. Then cook directly, by broiling (grilling); or indirectly, with frying pans, pots, or by heating the food right in the can. Adjustable legs rather than rigid ones are very handy for uneven or rocky ground.

■ **Tripod.** The classic camp "bean pot" hangs from a tripod. To make a tripod, use three lengths of half-inch or three-quarter-inch electrical conduit for the legs, each about four feet long. Clamp them together at the top; an electrical-fitting J-clamp works well. Use an appropriate length

HEALTHY HELP FOR CHARCOAL FIRES

Charcoal lighter fuel works, but it's unhealthy for people and the environment. (Self-starting charcoal is just presoaked with starter fluid, so it doesn't count as a reasonable alternative.) However, alternative fire starters exist; they just require a little more effort than standing in the checkout lane. One way is to make a reusable chimney from a large can.

Using tin snips, cut away the bottom as well as the lid, and scallop the bottom edge to allow air to flow through. Place the chimney on the fire mound or in the barbecue, then rumple up some sheets of newspaper and put them into the bottom of the chimney. Put briquettes on top; light the newspaper, and it ignites the charcoal. Later, remove the chimney with tongs or pliers, and spread out the coals.

You can also buy commercial chimney-type starters at barbecue and stove shops.

of lightweight chain to hang the bean pot, with an S-hook at each end. You can also add a grill to the tripod—square or round, whichever you find first. Attach pieces of chain to the corners of the grill, if square; or to the north, east, south, and west marks on a round grill. Connect the chain ends with one S-hook, and use another piece of chain and a second S-hook to hang the grill.

Dutch Ovens

The cast-iron Dutch oven could be your ticket to one-pot cooking for car-camping. For entrees you have the option of stewing, roasting, or frying. You can cook meats and vegetables together in a sauce or in one pot but separated by foil wraps. Use the Dutch oven for baking, too: Prop cake or muffin tins on a few small rocks placed in the bottom of the oven (or on an upside-down cake pan) for even baking without bottom-burning.

Cooking in a Dutch oven takes a little practice—try it at home a few times for a fun change—to master the temperature control (charcoal briquettes offer more reliable, even heat than do wood coals). If you've never savored steaming dumplings over sumptuous stew, or hot and spicy apple cobbler, you are missing out on some of life's greater pleasures.

Some tips on Dutch ovens and cooking in them:

- Don't be tempted by lighter aluminum varieties, which burn food more easily.
- A true Dutch oven will have legs and a slightly domed, lipped lid with a handle.
- Dutch ovens are sold by inches-in-diameter. Common sizes are 10 (4 quarts), 12 (6 quarts), 14 (8 quarts) and 16 (12 quarts). Twelve- and 14-inch ovens are most useful.
- Save the box your oven comes in and use it for storage and transportation in the truck. You can also buy padded nylon oven cases.
- Season a new oven (after washing with soap) by coating the interior with vegetable shortening or bacon fat and heating it in a 400-degree conventional oven for about an hour. Wipe down, cool, and repeat.

A Dutch oven makes a great backroad adventure kitchen addition. Besides roasting or frying, these large pots can be used for baking breads or dumplings.

- Never use soap or harsh scouring pads on your oven again (it takes the seasoning off); just wipe down while still warm. A properly seasoned and cared-for Dutch oven will last nearly forever.
- Start learning to cook with a Dutch oven by using charcoal briquettes; they provide even, easy-to-manage heat. A rough guideline for guestimating temperature in a 12-inch oven is: For 350 degrees, use 8 coals under, 16 on the lid; for 450 degrees, use 10 coals under, 20 on the lid. (Dutch oven recipe books tell you how many to use; once you get the hang of it, you can adapt your home recipes in the field.)
- Every time you remove the lid during cooking, extend cooking time by five to ten minutes.
- Useful accessories: a "gonch" hook to lift the oven and lid (a pair of sturdy pliers will do); a lid stand, to keep it out of the dirt when checking on dinner (try a ring cut from a coffee can); and a pair of tongs for handling coals.
- A few good Dutch oven cookbooks: *The Outdoor Dutch Oven Cookbook* by Sheila Mills (Ragged Mountain Press, 1997) and *The Old-Fashioned Dutch Oven Cookbook* by Don Holm (Caldwell, Idaho: The Caxton Printers, 1970).

Other Camping Ovens

Camp baking takes a bit more practice than grilling a slab of steak over the coals, but the effort is worth the gastronomic pleasure.

Most camping stores sell square, folding ovens that sit on top of a camp stove or next to a fire. The oven collapses into a flat package for transport. The advantage of commercial camp ovens is that they are large-volume; the biggest drawback is their high price and bulk, even when folded. If you've got the room and inclination to bake a lot while on the road, you won't regret an investment in one of these. If you want something a little less bulky and costly, read on.

The Outback Oven includes a portable baking hood that fits over cook-pot sets, or a nonstick pan with lid.

Smaller and less expensive are the BakePacker and Outback Oven units, available at backpacking specialty stores. A single unit produces enough for two people but skimpy amounts for a growing family or group of hungry boaters (the obvious solution would be to take several bakers).

Experiment with baking in your large Dutch oven (see page 94), in a large coffee can converted to an oven (see the instructions for a great one in Don Jacobson's *The One Pan Gourmet*), in a converted heavy-gauge aluminum ring-style bake pan (see the August 1996 issue of *Canoe & Kayak* magazine for instructions and recipes), or try an even easier and more portable creative alternative—a large roasting bag, or a length of roasting wrap or aluminum foil, placed over any makeshift framework to confine heat.

Keeping Your Kitchen Organized

■ **Bag it up.** For easy, no-rattle carrying and convenient use, put cooking utensils in their own "bedroll"—make one from a rectangle of canvas with cloth pockets sewn to the one side (one pocket for each of your cooking utensils). When cooking, untie and unroll the holder so everything is within reach; you can hang it from your awning or the side of your chuck box or stove stand.

■ **Chuck box.** Anything that helps organize the kitchen area is good, whether it's a basic packing box, a few plastic milk crates, or a chuck box—a counter-and-cabinet arrangement that folds up and out to hold a whole miniature kitchen (see page 98). Whichever you choose, it's most helpful when things are visible (at least, after lifting one lid), so no searching or rummaging is necessary. Visibility not only prevents the constant "where" queries, but helps your camping companions help themselves.

■ **Other keepers.** Organize your food in plastic bins, cardboard boxes (heavy-duty

GOOD ROAD FOOD

When we enjoy a backcountry road trip, we tend to take along foods that are similar to what we eat at home. This is both for comfort and convenience: It's easier to organize what you already know, rather than try to learn all-new recipes or make a bunch of stuff ahead of time. (Although virtually every outdoor cookbook has a section on drying your own fruit and jerky, do any of us really know anyone with that much free time?)

The only differences between the food we take car-camping and our home food is that meats will be canned or frozen (the latter to be used the first day or two; see page 100 for more on prefreezing and using dry ice); we choose vegetables and other items for "durability" (firm flesh) first; and we use a few more prepared or "packaged" foods. We prefer cans to other packaging because we can clean, flatten, and recycle them; too much plastic wrap and inside packaging is environmentally unsound.

Here is a sampling of fare from a typical weeklong backroad trip in Baja (with little or no chance of resupply). Note that we try to fix one-pot meals.

DINNER MAIN DISHES

- Soft tacos (medium-sized flour tortillas, canned chicken, fresh garlic, cheese, Roma tomatoes, shredded cabbage, limes, jarred salsa)
- Green bean casserole (canned French-cut green beans, cream of mushroom soup, canned fried-breaded onions)
- Pasta and jarred red sauce with bread toasted with butter and garlic
- Fettuccine Alfredo (a packaged product)
- Pasta with tuna sauce (canned tuna and peas with fresh garlic, butter, and canned milk; or good-old-fashioned Tuna Helper)
- Black bean stew (canned beans, steamed or canned vegetables)
- Chicken in hunter sauce over rice (canned chicken and a package of sauce mix made with butter and milk; instant brown rice)

moving boxes are great), or other handy containers. As much as possible remove cardboard-packaged food, especially baking or stovetop mixes, from the original packages and put in freezer-quality zip-top bags (cut off the cooking instructions and place in the bags). It saves space and garbage volume at the campsite. Some campers like to have separate bins for breakfast, lunch, dinner, and snacks, while others like to organize by food type, such as baking items, canned food, cereals, and so on. Just keep it consistent and labeled to help yourself and to guide kitchen helpers.

DINNER SIDE DISHES

- Salads made from fruit, shredded cabbage, and carrots with slaw-style dressing; iceberg lettuce with Roma tomatoes, carrots, celery, and parmesan cheese
- Raw vegetables with dip
- Fresh or frozen vegetables (first few days) such as green beans, zucchini, eggplant, and others with firm flesh
- Instant brown and white rice

LUNCHES

- Sandwiches are our favorite road lunch (as well as at home). We take durable wheat bread, iceberg lettuce, lunch meats and cheeses, and condiments. Sometimes we take hummus and tortillas, and pita bread and bean filling. If we are lunching at camp, we might make grilled cheese, quesadillas (tortillas and cheese, grilled, with salsa), or refried bean burritos.

BREAKFASTS

- Cereal with milk is our mainstay in late spring and summer when it's 85 degrees right after dawn in the deserts.
- Pancakes (from a mix such as Krusteaz)
- Biscuits and honey (also from a mix, such as Bisquick)

SNACKS AND DESSERTS

- We always take plenty of cookies, pretzels, crackers, and cheeses. My big indulgence here is Pringles potato chips—a wicked processed food that I'd never eat at home but can justify on the road because "they travel so well!"

See page 100 for tips on keeping items cool and page 106 for storage tips.

Sinks and Sumps

So-called wilderness camping areas have different levels of amenities. Some have water available at a few central sites. Some have no improvements; your water source is either your own supply or the nearest stream, river, or lake.

For those places where you'll be ferrying water, whether from a tap at the bathhouse or from a natural water source, bring easily carried jugs, preferably three-gallon square or rectangular bottles (the five-gallon size, when full, is too heavy for most people). If you don't

MAKE YOUR OWN CHUCK BOX

You can buy ready-made aluminum chuck boxes, or you can make your own from half-inch plywood or even solid hardwood. The beauty of do-it-yourself is that you can custom design to fit not only your own needs and desires but also the shape and size of your van, car, or truck storage area. Usually chuck boxes hold your pots, pans, utensils, gadgets, towels, and a few condiments; food goes in other containers. Use your imagination, but here are some ideas from some great custom-made chuck boxes:

- Don't make it too big to carry easily—about 24 inches wide by 15 inches deep by 15 inches tall seems good for exterior dimensions. Don't forget carrying handles.
- Sand and varnish well inside and out, so it can withstand some weather and spills.
- Make the door fold-down style, attached at the bottom with a piano hinge and with retainer-chains at the sides to hold the lid horizontally.
- Line the inside of the lid (the "kitchen counter") with a Lexan cutting board or Formica. You could do the same with the top of the box, thus doubling your counter space.
- Line the shelves with thin cork to cut down on rattles and slippage.
- Split the box into two sides—one unshelved, to store pots, pans, and plates (get creative with nesting), and paper towels, and the other divided into shelves for mugs and bowls, spices, and a drawer for silverware (size it for a plastic silverware divider).
- Include a way to hang your large-utensil roll from one side.

Jonathan Hanson

A chuck box organizes your kitchen utensils and accessories and provides a flip-down work surface.

have room to pack these, look for soft, collapsible containers at camping stores, though you'll have to treat them carefully because they do puncture.

Once upon a time, you could dip water from most streams and drink it safely, but those times and places are mostly gone. In most places, if you're using found water for drinking, cooking, or dishes, you must first treat it in some way to make it safe. Without some kind of water treatment—boiling, purification tablets, or filter—you risk severe stomach cramps, vomiting, and diarrhea that can lead to dehydration and long-term illness. For a discussion of different types of water purification systems for camp use, see a book such as *The Ragged Mountain Guide to Outdoor Sports* (Ragged Mountain Press, 1997).

When bringing your own water, five-gallon containers are the most convenient. Use these to fill small one- to two-and-one-half-gallon containers for camp use. We have several reasonably priced, hard-plastic "jerry cans" that we've used for a number of years, but our favorite containers are five-gallon Nalgene cans. These are pricey ($30 or more) but Nalgene makes containers for industrial use, including chemistry labs, and they guarantee their products for life against leaking and splitting.

Kitchen chores require some special attention to water usage and disposal. First rule: Dirty dishwater (gray water) does not drain onto the ground at camp; use a bucket to collect it. At some campgrounds, you'll be asked to empty the bucket into the appropriately named "slop sink," usually outside the bathhouse. In the backcountry, scatter it far from the tent site, where it can filter naturally through sand or soil. You can also dig a "sump" pit in which you can pour your gray water. Remember that animals will be attracted by the smell, so make sure it's far away.

The key to efficient camp cleanup is to wash dishes as quickly as possible with a simple substitute sink/drainer/drain arrangement. Make up a container (pot or plastic tub) of soapy water, scrub up your dishes and set them on towels or plastic, then rinse with hot water (for sterilization) from a teapot or pot, pouring over a bucket, other pan, or your sump to collect the gray water. Inflatable sinks and plastic sinks that incorporate a reservoir of water, a pump and spigot, and a drain, are also available.

In backcountry areas, it's especially important to use the right soaps. Buy the mildest, natural, nonpolluting, biodegradable products you can find, to prevent contami-

CLEANUP TIP FOR CUTTING THE CARBON

To ease cleanup when cooking over a fire, pre-coat the outside of your pots with liquid dish soap, or a paste of bar soap and water. Black soot will wash off more easily.

nants from reaching ground or stream water. And for easy rinsing, greatly dilute your soap. For a whole catalog of "green" products, call Seventh Generation at (800) 456-1177 or look in natural foods markets. You can also follow Jacques Cousteau's lead and use Shaklee products; look in the white pages of your local phone directory for a distributor in your area.

Chilling Out: Ice Chests & 12V Coolers

Keeping the food cold is basic to a good camp kitchen. Choices include traditional hard-sided coolers, ranging in size from a few gallons to 20 to 100 gallons for longer trips, to electric cooler/freezers that run off a car battery.

If you use a traditional cooler, here are some good tips:

- Block ice lasts the longest.
- Use frozen foods to augment the cooling power of the ice.
- At camp, keep the cooler in the shade and leave melted water inside as long as it stays cold; a filled cooler retains cold better than empty air space.
- If space permits, use two coolers, one for beverages and snacks (this will be opened often) and one for the food to be kept cold for mealtime (less opening, longer cold-keeping).
- Pre-cool your cooler the night before your trip with some ice cubes, and pre-cool everything that goes into it.
- Freeze water (or lemonade or other fruit drinks) in plastic bottles to use as "ice"; you'll have ice to start the camping trip, and cool drinks as it melts. Don't fill containers completely—allow space for expansion.
- For the cooling benefit and to save at-camp cooking time, prepare and pre-freeze food items: chili, meat loaf, pasta sauces, and so on.
- Experiment with dry ice, especially if you take along frozen meat. Wrap the dry ice in layers of newspaper and then plastic (taped up well) and place it on top of your prefrozen food. Don't let bare dry ice come into direct contact with the cooler, or it could warp the plastic. Most full-service grocery stores sell dry ice (you will need to ask).

At campgrounds with electric outlets at each tent site, car campers can enjoy another way to keep food cold. Cooler-sized portable refrigerators can be operated on 12-volt DC or 120-volt AC. As you drive to camp, connect it to the car's 12-volt system (cigarette lighter plug-in); at camp, switch to the 120-volt cord. You won't have a separate freezer compartment, and it may not hold as much food as a comparable-size cooler, since some interior space is taken by the cooling mechanism and the walls are thicker for insulating. Still, it is definitely a more consistent cold than ice provides. (Tip: These coolers are designed to chill only a certain number of degrees—usually about 40—below outside air temperature; if it's 95 degrees, your cooler may not get below 55.)

Tables and Chairs

Although we remember with great nostalgia our parents' metal folding tables with four integrated seats, our favorite camping table rolls up to a three-foot-long tube that is six inches in diameter and has a convenient carrying handle. The table top is made from two-inch slats of soft-plastic-encased wood that lock together when opened flat. Two aluminum cross-members and four legs screw easily into fittings in the bottom. Setup takes just a minute, and the table is sturdy enough to hold our heavy chuck box and seats four comfortably. We've seen them for sale at specialty outdoor stores and through mail-order companies that specialize in whitewater rafting supplies since these tables are well-loved by boaters (try Northwest River Supplies, 800-243-1677).

Part of the reason we don't use the folding integrated-chair tables today is that they are heavy and bulky, and they're made from wobbly plastic rather than the bombproof steel of earlier generations. Friends who have tried the newer plastic tables all report with disgust at how short-lived and wasteful they are.

Our current chairs are compact, lightweight folders from the French company Lafuma. They are expensive (about $45 each) but extremely durable and comfortable. We especially like the fact that the strong, heat-treated aluminum frames are smooth, so we can pack them in the cargo area without worrying about tearing upholstery or carpet. We use ours heavily and unmercifully, and they're going strong at seven years of age (Jonathan is an incurable chair-tipper, and any furniture that can withstand this cruel treatment is worthy of note). Compare with buying a new set of cheapo chairs at $30 for two each year, and you see how much cheaper good equipment really is.

Other camp furniture options include some great wooden folding chairs and tables, including "cocktail" tables, from companies such as Byer of Maine. These are pure American craftsmanship, and lovely to boot. We use one of Byer's cocktail tables, and if we had the space, we'd get a couple of the company's lounge chairs as well.

Sleeping Soundly

Nothing is fun if you haven't slept well. No matter how much you may want to

Jonathan Hanson

Durability and compactness are two desirable features in camping tables and chairs. This Roll-a-Table rolls up to an easily stashed 3-foot-long, 6-inch-diameter tube, while the two hardened aluminum La Fuma chairs fold flat.

enjoy the pleasures of sun rising, wood fire smoking, coffee steaming, and bacon sizzling, you won't even recognize them if you're still in sleep mode. All the jokes about grumpy-in-the-morning can't change the way you feel.

Beds

You can help ensure a great night's sleep while camping with a number of great bed products, from cots to air mattresses to foam pads. Remember that besides providing comfort, one of the things a bed should do is help keep you warm when the nights turn chilly. Some thoughts on each:

- **Cots.** If you have plenty of space, you can go for the luxury of camp cots, which will work only in a tent with sufficient headroom and near-vertical walls, or if you're not using a tent. Also, they are best in temperate weather (cold air circulates all around you). Before buying, check the way the cot is made. Bent, rounded tubing for legs is easiest on the tent floor, although other styles could be cushioned to protect the fabric. At the very least the cot should fold in half for carrying and packing, but roll-ups are more space-efficient. Look for sturdy, mildew-resistant fabrics and consider the convenience of removable covers.

- **Standard air mattresses.** Most air mattresses are variations on two styles: the full-length, tubular-shaped I-beam construction, or the nonchambered fake-button-quilt look in a square-cornered, flat design. They're made in an assortment of materials, but the rubberized canvas seems most favored; even though it may be heavier, it has a softer touch. (The heavier weight also means heavier-duty, as it lasts longer.) Air mattresses are a perfect solution for maximum comfort for minimum size. Deflated, they are small and light. When filled, they provide a large, fairly thick mat. If you've got weak lungs, take along a foot or hand pump.

- **Self-inflating air mattresses/pads.** Self-inflating foam pads cushion using both foam and air and are the most efficient heat-insulators of all the bed types. Several variations are available, but Therm-a-Rest is the most popular mattress for good reason. Its open-cell foam compresses to a smaller package—the choice for backpackers but also good for car campers who need to save space. Therm-a-Rests are made in full and three-quarter length and in several thicknesses. Two can be connected for a double bed.

- **Foam pads.** There are two types of foam pads—dense, efficient (keeps you warmer) closed-cell foam, and thicker, softer, and more airy open-cell foam. The former is more water-resistant (actually, open-cell foam is essentially a sponge). A full-length pad is very comfortable, but it makes a big bundle to pack and carry, so many campers settle for a three-quarter length. A thickness of ⅜-inch is the minimum, and it is truly minimal for comfort. You'll find maximum comfort with two-inch-thick egg-crate foam mattress pads cut to fit the floor of your tent or the back of your pickup truck. Buy pads as thick as you can pack and carry.

Don't forget the pillows—it's surprising how much better you sleep with a good pillow. Take your home pillows or look around camping stores for a variety of creative outdoor pillows: down- or polyester-filled; inflatable; or pile-covered stuff sacks that you fill with clothing.

Sleeping Bags

Bags are most practical for camp bedding. They're cozy for sleeping and more convenient than messing with sheets and blankets.

Sleeping bags are made in two basic shapes, each with a modified version.

- **Rectangular** is the roomiest, so you have the most freedom of movement. They sleep the coldest, but that's not a problem for summer campers.
- **Semi-rectangular,** or **barrel,** shape tapers at the feet and a bit at shoulders. With less space inside, it warms up faster than a rectangular bag.
- Shaped and tapered, a **mummy bag** has the least space to heat. Made for cold-weather camping, it also has a head-covering hood. If you move around a lot when you sleep, you won't like the confinement of a mummy bag.
- A **modified mummy** shape tries to ease the claustrophobia without sacrificing too much heat-keeping ability.

Most sleeping bags are made for an average-size adult, but if you're above average in height, look for extra-long. If you're otherwise oversized, or simply like more room to move, look for extra-wide or jumbo. A few bags are made in children's sizes, too.

Sleeping bags are given temperature ratings to indicate a range within they are likely to keep you warm. Unfortunately,

DOUBLE-BAGGING

Two of the same model rectangular bags can often zip together into a double-bed bag; this also works with barrel-shaped bags. You can use two of the same length or put a longer bag on the bottom.

HAMMOCK HAVEN

A hang-anywhere bed lets you loaf in the nicest places. Beach-front is a favorite; the cooling touch of a steady sea breeze, the lullaby of endless waves, and the gentle swing of your private cocoon put your world on hold—*and* give you something to call on for future stress management.

A cotton woven hammock is probably the most comfortable, though eventually it will mildew and rot. You can also find hammocks in nylon or polyester twine or a solid canvas fabric. Wooden spreader bars at the ends of some hammocks hold the shape, but they must be well padded or they destroy the feeling of unhampered freedom.

You could forget the tent if you sleep in a jungle hammock. With mesh net sides, a fabric top, and a cotton canvas floor, you have a self-contained, functional, elevated shelter with all the fun of a hammock. Look for them at military surplus and supply stores.

there is no industry standard for these ratings, so use them as a guideline only. In general, a bag rated at 20 degrees will be the most versatile for the generalist spring-summer-fall camper. A better way to judge a bag's warmth-keeping ability is its loft—how thick the insulation is (this is particularly true with down; newer synthetic insulations can offer more warmth for less loft). For example, a down sleeping bag with four-inch loft is generally considered a spring-summer bag, while one with eight-inch loft is a full wintertime bag. Talk with salespeople who have used the type of bag you're looking at and be sure to read manufacturer's information carefully.

For practical reasons, frequent car campers, especially families, should get sleeping bags with an easy care fabric and synthetic insulation, so they can throw them into a washing machine when necessary.

The Bathroom

Most commercial and many public campgrounds have nice toilet and shower facilities, so you don't have to worry about a bathroom. However, backcountry campgrounds and campsites won't have such amenities, so here's how to set them up yourself.

Jonathan Hanson

SunShower products, such as this shower enclosure and 2½-gallon shower, can add a lot of home comforts to your camp.

Showers

Weekend campers seldom worry about showering. Some might use a lot of moist towelettes, but a full shower is hardly a necessity in a back-to-nature experience. When you set up camp for a week or two, however, part of the setup should include a way to bathe. Whatever method you choose, don't use the nearby lake or stream for a bathtub. No soap degrades instantly. And make sure your shower is at least 70 adult paces from any water source or does not drain off into one.

- **SunShower.** Pour water into the black, heavy-duty plastic bag, leave it out in the sun till the water's warm, then hang the bag so gravity feeds the sprayer hose attached to the bottom of the bag. You control water flow by the foolproof hose-up or hose-down method. (Hurry the warming with stove-heated, but not boiling, water.) Look for SunShowers at camping or boating stores.

- **People sprayer.** If you have enough storage space, another portable shower setup uses a two-gallon garden bug sprayer (buy a new one that hasn't had chemicals in it). Fill it partway with cool water and add heated water; pump up the pressure and shower away. (If you replace the attached spray hose with a kitchen sink sprayer hose, you'll get a better water flow.)

- **Engine-powered hot water.** R & M Specialty Products in California produces a hot water system that draws water from a reservoir (installed in your truck, a bucket, or even a stream) and heats it via a simple heat exchanger installed in the engine compartment, then pumps it to a showerhead for as much hot water as your container holds. The cost will set you back more than $200, and you need to run your engine for it to work, but, oh, the luxury! I've kept R & M's information in my truck's "wished-for" file for half a dozen years, hoping some day to take the plunge, when the "need-to-do" file is empty (which it never is, of course).

- **Dry shower.** When camping in places where water is hard to get or unavailable, you can still wash your hair and your body with products that don't need to be rinsed away. Appropriately called "No Rinse," both shampoo and body-bath make washing suds using only a small amount of water. You wash with a cloth or sponge, but after washing, you don't rinse; just towel yourself dry. It may sound strange, but it has worked for NASA astronauts as well as for more down-to-earth expeditionists. (You'll find other specialty products, too, like liquid soaps that work in hot or cold water, fresh or salt; or dry shampoos that you brush in, then brush dirt out. Sailing supply stores are good places to look for these products.)

For information on products mentioned: See Appendix II, starting on page 162.

Toilet

There are a few schools of thought for how to best deal with backcountry toilet duty. The currently accepted method is to dig a shallow "cat hole" (about five inches deep), at least 70 adult paces from any water source, in an area that gets maximum sun exposure. Pack out your toilet paper in zip-top bags (because of fire danger, burning is no longer recommended, and burying it is not ideal because critters almost always dig it up). Likewise, pack out all toiletries associated with menstruation. Re-cover the cat hole with soil.

> **TIP**
>
> Put together a toilet kit to hang in a handy spot in camp and include a trowel, toilet paper, plastic bags, antibacterial soap, and a small bottle of water.

Organizing & Packing

It's 11 o'clock on Friday night. You blasted out of work late, rushed over to the outdoors shop to pick up a new stove generator, stopped at the health food store to buy granola and dried fruit, scarfed some Chinese takeout, and now you're frantically stuffing gear and provisions into the back of the truck. Tempers flare as you discover . . . you can't find your flashlight and you forgot to buy batteries, your tent fly ripped on the last trip and you forgot to fix it, and you let your best friend borrow your favorite sleeping pad. Is there some way to avoid all this hassle of *having fun in the outdoors?*

Aside from the initial planning, packing for a trip is one of the more important aspects of adventuring—certainly one that if done too haphazardly can derail even the best-planned trip.

The keys to good packing are (1) lists and (2) organization. For tips on lists, see page 112.

To help make backroad adventuring as simple as load-and-go, keep all your camping gear organized and labeled in storage bins that can go from shelf to car.

Jonathan Hanson

Organizing

Packing for trips can be greatly simplified if you store your trip gear in boxes that can go directly from closet to car and if you followed the outdoor adventurer's cardinal rule: Always clean, repair, and resupply your trip gear after each trip and store it in ready-to-go condition (see page 107).

The box-to-car system works very well for backcountry adventuring. Medium-sized, heavyweight cardboard packing boxes from moving companies are very inexpensive, durable, and recyclable. Or look at hardware stores and home improvement centers for plastic boxes with hinged or snap-on lids (keep the sizes down, so one person can easily handle them). Try to get different colors, or label them on all four sides if you plan to separate your gear by category: food, kitchen gear, sleeping gear, bathroom gear, and clothing.

Try to keep your camping gear in the same closet, grouped together, so that you can get to it easily when packing for a trip. We won't stand for any "we don't have the space" excuses for organizing camping gear at home—for nearly a decade we've lived in a 700-square-foot house without any outside storage buildings. All our camping gear lived in one closet, on three shelves, and in the bins we use in the truck. Packing for a trip has been as easy as opening a door, unloading what is needed from the shelves, and carrying it out to the vehicle. Recently we added a 100-square-foot storage building, and it feels huge (although it's already full).

Another important rule to remember to help keep all your organization running smoothly: When you use something out of your gear shelves and boxes, make sure you return it where it belongs or replace it.

Packing

We used to just toss our camping stuff in the back of our old four-door Land Cruiser and take off. Once at camp, it took some time to unload the pile and find first the ground cloth, then the tent, then—*where did you put the stakes? I thought you packed them!* and *Have you seen the sleeping bags—?!* Often it was after dark when we got around to rooting through ripped grocery bags trying to find dinner or parts of dinner that had fallen out of the bags and were rolling around the back of the truck.

Over the last 15 years of car camping we have developed a system of storage for our gear that not only keeps it organized and well-protected on rough roads and long trips, but serves as storage in the closets at home, too. And because we've never had too much free time on our hands—too busy out camping, hiking, birding, and having fun—our system comprises only one custom-made box (the chuck box), the rest being free or cheap boxes, including the boxes some of the gear came in and a couple of purchased specialty cases.

Early on we used two 24-inch-square, heavy-duty cardboard moving boxes, plus two, foot-wide, 30-inch-long cardboard boxes with the lid flaps folded in to add more rigidity. These fit strategically into the back of the Land Cruiser to provide the basic structure for organizing the gear. Later we "graduated" to three or four of the Rubbermaid-style boxes with two folding, interlocking lid flaps. These are great for in-house storage, and you can't beat the stacking ease, but I do miss the ability to over-stuff the open boxes.

> **Box One** held, standing on end, the tent, rolled up awning, stove and chuck box stands (packed in their own long, two-inch-square cardboard boxes), the lantern in its own plastic carrying case, and two down sleeping bags in small stuff sacks (these helped pack the box full and keep it rattle-free).
>
> **Box Two** held miscellaneous camp items such as the toilet kit in a small stuff sack, the first aid kit in its Pelican case, the spare parts and small tool boxes (made of Lexan), several filled one-liter water bottles, a nonstick griddle stored in its shipping box for protection, and other small items that always need a home.

Boxes Three and Four (the long skinny ones) held the food, divided as dinner and breakfast stuff in one box, lunches and snacks in the other. For trips shorter than a week we used only one food box. On trips longer than a week, we stored extra food cans and bags (only noncrushable items) in small boxes under other gear boxes.

These four boxes fit into the cargo area of the Land Cruiser (back seat folded down) and created "corrals" for the heavy and/or bulkier items such as the Dutch oven, rolled-up table, chairs, propane tank, and one or more five-gallon water jugs. The chuck box and lunch-snacks food box were always packed at the rear so we could fold down the tailgate and pull them out for instant fixings. We always placed the cooler at one of the side doors to ease access and allow us to pull it out partway en route to drain water/replace ice. We put other heavy items, such as water and the propane tank, on the opposite side to balance the weight (you could also invest in two smaller coolers, one for drinks and lunch, the other to hold dry ice and items such as cheese, meats, fruits, and vegetables). We packed long skinny gear, such as awning poles and lantern stands, along the sides on the floor. Our clothes and personal items went in duffels stowed on top of other gear.

Jonathan Hanson

Pack your cargo area carefully, placing heavy items such as water and propane at the sides and making sure they are well secured. Place the chuck box at the rear, so it is accessible from the tailgate; position your cooler on one side, with the drain hole toward the door.

When we sold our Land Cruiser and bought a four-wheel-drive pickup with a camper shell, we invested in a carpeted insert for the back. This works wonders for organization and is wonderfully comfortable to sleep on. We modified the above system only slightly, adding some nylon straps with Fastex buckles to secure the chuck box and other boxes along the sides of the insert, so the middle two platforms could be taken out and the boxes wouldn't fall into the resulting maw. You could customize any rear cargo area with straps and cargo nets, but you have to be willing to drill into your sport utility's body—a stressful endeavor for some. We have seen a few advertisements for cargo inserts for sport utilities, but most are high-end products designed for vehicles like Range Rovers and intended for shopping or for shooting parties with expensive shotguns rather than for rugged backcountry

POWER UP

A very nice accessory for your vehicle is a portable refrigerator—essentially an ice chest with its own 12-volt cooling unit. It frees you from visiting convenience stores for ice every day or two, and you're less likely to wind up with soaked food. But electric coolers use a fair amount of electricity—too much draw to add to your vehicle's starting battery, which is not designed for constant loads.

What you need is a separate deep-cycle battery. A deep-cycle battery is designed to be used continuously and can be drained and recharged many times with no harm—treatment that would quickly destroy a standard battery.

In the camper on our truck, we have not only a built-in refrigerator that can be run off battery power or propane but also an inverter that converts 12-volt battery power to 120-volt AC current—just like the electricity in your home. We use the inverter to power our laptop computers when we are on the road. To handle the load, I installed a deep-cycle battery in the camper, and a device called a battery isolator in the engine compartment. The isolator takes the charge from the alternator and distributes it as needed between the vehicle's starting battery and the deep-cycle battery, so both stay fully charged. If the deep-cycle battery is drained, it does not affect the main battery.

To further strengthen this system, I added to the roof of the camper a solar panel, which also charges the deep-cycle battery. That way, if we are camped for several days, we don't have to periodically run the engine to keep the battery charged.

You can easily add a deep-cycle battery and isolator to a sport utility vehicle (as well as an inverter and even a solar charger if you choose). The extra battery will probably fit in the engine compartment, and you can run a wire with a socket for an electric cooler to the cargo area (most coolers use a cigarette lighter plug). Make sure you have a qualified electrician do the job, because 12-volt wiring is tricky—the wire has to be the correct size to avoid losing voltage, and it should include a fuse of proper amperage.

camping. (Truckvault is one maker; see Appendix II, starting on page 162, for contact information.)

We have never developed a rooftop storage system since most of the time when we travel backroads with our four-wheel-drives we have either sea kayaks or mountain bikes on the top, and it's always just the two of us. But there are excellent carriers for rooftops that free up your cargo area for sleeping and more gear or that allow you to use your back seats for passengers. Yakima, Thule, and Packasport all make high quality fiberglass and plastic (not the cheap kind) pods of varying sizes that lock securely, and are weatherproof and very durable. Each of these pods works with the integrated rack systems of either Yakima or Thule (see the section on roof racks, Chapter 5, beginning on page 135). There is also a very nice combo cartop tent and cargo pod called the Top Bunk; see page 84 for details. Several companies make soft-sided cargo carriers (for a good selection, check out some of the accessory catalogs listed in Appendix II).

We don't recommend trying to save money by buying one of those cheap discount store cargo carriers that lash onto your existing luggage rack; we have seen more than one wobbling precariously at highway speeds and one that flew off and shattered, spilling gear all over an interstate.

Incidentally, Packasport (see photo, page 137) and High Gear (see page 84) make especially good boxes that can be custom-matched to your paint job. Chapter 5 also covers other types of more rugged cargo-hauling roof racks, to which you can strap cargo boxes and other gear.

Some things to remember when packing your vehicle:

- Store items you need access to during the day—lunch, snacks, cooler, drinking water, first aid—next to a door or tailgate, or immediately behind the front seat.
- Keep the weight balanced side to side, and keep the heaviest items—fuel tank, water, coolers—over or in front of the rear axle.
- Tie down all heavy items that could become airborne in an accident or emergency stop. Most sport utilities will have at least a couple of tie-down points in the floor; you may have to cut through the carpet to access them. They are easy to install if you don't have them. A bungee net that secures your whole cargo area is perfect, and unhooks easily for access. Make sure the net, or any other tie-down, is not tied to a nonstructural part of the vehicle, such as side paneling.
- Pay attention to the drain stopper on your cooler(s). Orient the cooler so you can slide it partway out of the vehicle to empty the water when you add new ice. Also, always double-check that the stopper is stopped up. We once left ours open, and two bags of ice melted slowly into the interior of the car over the course of a day, soaking the boxes and some of the food via capillary action.
- Keep a small whisk broom and a 12-volt mini-vacuum handy for occasional cleanup during longer trips. Keeping your equipment and vehicle cleaner cuts down on excessive wear and makes back-home cleanup easier (see also page 111, for tips on post-trip chores).

After-Camping Chores

To make your next trip as easy as buying food, checking lists, and loading the truck, make sure you clean, inspect, and repair your gear—whether for car-camping, backpacking, biking, or boating—after every trip. Then stow the gear in a cool (but not cold), dry place where you can get to it easily (keep it all in one place so there'll be no last-minute treasure hunting). Of course, the same goes for your vehicle; see Chapter 6, beginning on page 151, for tips on post-trip vehicle maintenance.

Tents and Tarps

If you weren't able to clean and dry the tent at camp before packing up, set it up in the yard. If it needs cleaning, hose it down or use a sponge to get rid of mud and leaves, taking special care to remove spots from bird droppings or tree drippings. Use warm water and a mild soap, such as Ivory flakes, Dr. Bronner's soap, or the liquid hand soap you buy in pump bottles. Don't use detergents or bleach; they may damage the fabric or waterproof coating (when in doubt, refer to the care label of your tent).

It is most important that the tent be completely dry before packing, so mildew doesn't have a chance to form.

Store your tent in its carry bags, or accordion-fold it loosely and hang it over a padded hanger or lay it on a shelf.

When zippers don't work smoothly, the first step is to wash with warm, soapy water to get rid of any grit. Also try rubbing them with trusty old bar soap or a wax candle. Spray lubricants might help a stubborn zipper, but they can also stain the fabric.

Not surprisingly, major repairs (on tents, sleeping bags, and packs) are done at shops that specialize in outdoor gear.

Sleeping Bags

After each use, air the bags inside out, out of direct sunlight, for a few hours, or tumble them one at a time in the dryer on very low heat.

When sleeping bags need washing, it's easiest to take a trip to the nearest coin-operated laundry (make sure the washers are front-loaders).

Down bags can be washed—carefully—in a large washer with mild soap on a gentle cycle (check label instructions). Hand washing is also suggested, but to call that tedious is an understatement. Dry the bag at a low-heat setting for as long as it takes. Or take your bag to your local outdoor retailer—they can send it to a down cleaning service. Don't dry-clean down.

For storage, roll or fold the bag loosely and keep it in a laundry bag or a big pillow sham.

Mattresses

Sponge-wash with mild soap and warm water, then rinse with a hose and leave outside to dry thoroughly, out of direct sun. Partially inflate and store on a cool shelf. *(continued on page 114)*

LISTS

The following list is broken down into categories and should give you a good start on compiling your own lists. Once you've settled on those items applicable to your activities and your camping, cooking, and travel needs, make copies of the lists (one set for each trip).

Tack the master list to a bulletin board in your "camping closet" or keep it on the family computer, so you can update it after each trip (lists are never "done"—they will evolve continuously). Families can make copies of the individual "Campers' Needs" list for each person, so everyone can do his or her own packing and checking.

CAMP SETUP

- ❑ Tent
- ❑ Awning
  - – Poles
  - – Stakes and spares
  - – Guylines and 100 feet of extra quarter-inch nylon line
- ❑ Groundcloth
- ❑ Sleeping bags
- ❑ Sleep pads or air mattresses
  - – Foot pump (for inflating air mattresses)
- ❑ Cots
- ❑ Pillows
- ❑ 1 or 2 tarps
- ❑ Repair kit (nylon tape, duct tape, length of pipe for tent pole sleeve, snap fastener kit or grommet kit, small sewing kit with safety pins, scissors
- ❑ Table
- ❑ Folding chairs
- ❑ Lantern
  - – Extra mantles, generator (if applicable)
  - – Fuel (liquid gas or propane cylinder)
  - – Gas lighter, matches

- ❑ Battery-operated lamp
  - – Extra batteries and bulb
- ❑ Flashlight(s) or headlamp(s)
  - – Extra batteries and bulb(s)
- ❑ Candles and holders
- ❑ Water hose (for serviced campgrounds)
- ❑ Water bottles (for ferrying and for hiking)
- ❑ Water filter or tablets
- ❑ Mosquito coils
- ❑ Dishwashing
  - – Dish pan
  - – Bucket
  - – Dish soap
  - – Kitchen cleanser
  - – Scrubbing pads/sponge
  - – Dish towel
- ❑ Clothesline and clothespins
- ❑ Small shovel or trowel (for fire, latrine)
- ❑ Work gloves
- ❑ Pocket knife/multi-tool
- ❑ Utility straps
- ❑ Short shock (bungee) cords
- ❑ Block and tackle (if desired, for hanging food bag)

FOOD PREPARATION AND STORAGE

- ❑ Camp stove and fuel
  - Repair kit/spares
- ❑ Firepan
- ❑ Firewood
- ❑ Propane or charcoal grill and fuel
- ❑ Fire-starting aids: newspaper, kindling, paraffin fire starters, gas lighter, matches
- ❑ Grill platform
- ❑ Pots
  - 1 large frying pan
  - 1 small frying pan
  - 2 or 3 saucepans, preferably with lids (*or* cook set of nesting pots and pans)
    Foil baking pans
- ❑ Coffee funnel and filters
- ❑ Cooking utensils
  - Aluminum foil
  - Heat diffuser
  - Pliers or pot lifter

MISCELLANEOUS

- Stove and chuck box stands
- Lantern stand
- Nonstick cooking spray
- Paper towels (use as napkins, too)
- Spices and condiments
- Plastic food bags
- Zip-top bags
- Garbage bags
- Bean-pot tripod
- "Spit" cooking setup
- Wood chips for smoke flavor
- Long griddle for camp stove

- Oven mitts (pot holders)
- Spatula
- Tongs
- Skewers
- Large stirring spoon
- Ladle
- 2 sharp knives
- Mechanical can opener
- Bottle opener
- Potato peeler
- Cheese grater
- Cutting board
- Fish-filleting board and knife
- ❑ Dining
  - Dinner plates
  - Soup/salad/cereal bowls
  - Mugs
  - Plastic glasses
  - Silverware
  - Tablecloth

(Many of the above items stow in your chuck box)

- Measuring cup
- Mixing bowl
- Dutch oven
- Reflector oven or stove-top oven
- Hanging bean pot
- Grilled-sandwich maker/pie iron
- Ice pick
- Corkscrew
- Tablecloth clamps
- ❑ Cooler
  - Small jars for ketchup, mayo, mustard, relish, jams

(continued on page 114)

LISTS, CONTINUED

MISCELLANEOUS, CONTINUED

- Ice supplements (block ice, dry ice, or blue coolant freezer packs)
- Covered plastic containers or zip-top bags for leftovers

- Egg holder
- Juice mixer/pitcher
- ❏ Food list and menus

CAMPERS' NEEDS

- ❏ Duffel or pack with clothes and personals
- ❏ Toilet kit (tissue, trowel, antibacterial soap)

- ❏ Moist towelettes
- ❏ First aid kit

OTHER GEAR

- ❏ Bicycles and panniers
- ❏ Canoe or kayaks
- ❏ Binoculars
- ❏ Compass
- ❏ Topographic maps, nautical/ river charts
- ❏ Sport watch with alarm
- ❏ Water bottles
- ❏ Daypacks/fanny packs
- ❏ Reference books
  - Birds, animals, plants, stars

- ❏ Writing notebook
- ❏ Musical instruments
- ❏ Games and puzzles
- ❏ Fishing gear
- ❏ Books for reading
- ❏ Camera(s) and manual(s)
  - Film
- ❏ Video camera and manual
  - Blank tapes

See Chapter 6, beginning page 144, for lists for vehicle spares and tools.

If your inflatable mattress springs a leak, buy an appropriate sealer to plug the pinhole. Manufacturers usually offer repair products and kits.

Stoves

The orifices on liquid-fuel stove burners get clogged after a while and need to be cleaned out with the tiny wire device in your maintenance kit. (Kerosene is a quick clogger.)

Some liquid-fuel stoves are made to be self-cleaning. If this doesn't seem to be working, and it's possible to take the burner apart, soak the jet in some of the fuel the stove burns. When all cleaning attempts fail, replace the burner.

The O-ring or gasket on the pressure pumping handle eventually will need to be replaced.

(continued on page 117)

BRING ALONG THE POOCH

One of the sport utility manufacturers a few years back was featuring print ads of dogs dreaming about trucks—a perfect combination. Most dogs love to go on backroad adventures, but rather than just tossing 'em in and taking off, it's better to prepare ahead. Here are some tips on taking dogs on backroad adventures.

- **Car travel.** Don't forget your pooch needs "rest stops" to pee and stretch as often as you do on your backcountry explorations. Provide a secure bed for her to curl up on when underway; and please don't let her ride while hanging out of an open window (many dogs break bones or die when they fall from moving cars, or their eyes may be injured by airborne road debris), even if it is "cute."

- **Permits.** Before you haul Fido off into the backcountry for a weekend of fun, check with the land management agency for its rules on dogs. In some places, such as wildlife refuges, they may be banned entirely, and everywhere on other public lands dogs must be leashed. There are many, many good reasons for this. See below.

- **Leash.** Your dog is much safer leashed. Running free can lead to encounters with skunks, porcupines, bears (which might just get *you* into some serious trouble), or snakes. Cuts, scrapes, and broken bones can also be avoided. Also, many studies show that dogs are very disruptive to wildlife, most especially in roadless backcountry. One study in the Rocky Mountains showed that during lambing season, bighorn sheep experienced extremely elevated stress levels when a dog approached, surprisingly much higher than when a natural predator such as a fox or coyote approached.

- **Water.** We religiously filter our own drinking water in the backcountry, but we often mistakenly let our pets drink directly from streams or ponds, even in cattle country. Dogs are just as susceptible to the giardia parasite as humans, and they suffer the same symptoms: intermittent diarrhea, vomiting, and loss of appetite. Treatment is difficult, but there is an easy solution: Keep your dog on a leash. It's hard to do—they have so much fun blasting over hill and dale—but you can avoid all sorts of problems, including diseases from water-borne parasites, if Fido stays with you.

- **Dehydration, heat stroke.** Dogs can also suffer dehydration and heat stroke, so make sure they drink water as often as you do, and don't overdo sun exposure. If your dog shows signs of dehydration or heat stroke—weakness, eyes rolling back, tissues dry—immerse him in water if possible or pour water over his chest and throat.

- **Doggie doo.** If it's practical, carry out your dog's stools. Otherwise, bury it well.

- **Vaccinations.** It goes without saying, but your dog should have all the proper vaccinations before venturing outdoors: rabies, distemper, parvo, corona, and others. Con-

(continued on page 116)

BRING ALONG THE POOCH, CONTINUED

sult your veterinarian about proper vaccines, as well as the need to guard against heartworm at your destination.

- **Skunked.** A full hit of skunk spray will have an immediate and painful effect on your dog. If hit in the face, your dog will probably be temporarily blind and will foam at the mouth. Get him washed up as soon as possible. Traditional stench removal attempts involve tomato juice, diluted lemon juice, or vinegar (mix 1 to 10 with water, and wash, always being careful of the dog's eyes). There is also a product called Skunk Off, an odor eliminator/neutralizer. It's nontoxic, biodegradable, and it reportedly works "in minutes." Look for it at camping stores.

- **Doggie gear.** There is some really useful outdoor gear for dogs out there, but it can be hard to find. Some great dog gear includes packs (fit the pack so the weight—never very much—is supported on the dog's sides, not on his backbone), booties for snow, fleece jackets, personal flotation devices (PFDs), fluorescent collars and vests for hunting season, portable kennels and crates, and field canteens and bowls. For the best selection of gear, check out the hunting catalogs, such as Cabela's (800-237-4444). Another excellent source of pet products is Doctors Foster & Smith (800-826-7206).

For more on pets in the outdoors, see *Simple Tent Camping,* by Zora and David Aiken (Ragged Mountain Press, 1996), and the *Dog Lover's Companion* travel series by Foghorn Press, whose lineup currently includes Atlanta, the Bay Area, Boston, California, Florida, Seattle, Washington D.C., and Texas. For good health information, see *Emergency First Aid for Your Dog,* by Tamara S. Shearer (Columbus: Ohio Distinctive Publishing, 1996).

DOG CAMPING CHECKLIST

- ❑ Dishes
- ❑ Food
- ❑ Harness/leash
- ❑ Identification/health certificate
- ❑ Brush
- ❑ Pooper scooper/bags
- ❑ Bedding
- ❑ Toys
- ❑ Doggy pack
- ❑ Booties, jacket, other safety items

Dogs are not the only pets out there, of course: We've seen camping cats (on leashes, of course, just like all dogs should be) and even ferrets. Most of the above health and safety concerns apply across the board.

Lanterns

Treat liquid-gas lantern burners the same as stove burners. Also, burn out liquid fuel rather than let it sit for any length of time. Check your supply of spare mantles and add to the "buy" list when needed.

Other Items

Go through your chuck box and fill up any condiment bottles that are low, replace any spoiled oil or other supplies, refill paper towels, foil, plastic bags, and the like. Also check your utensil and dish inventory and replace any missing items. Wipe down the box, inside and out.

Empty your cooler as soon as possible and clean it out with dish soap. After a final rinse with mild bleach solution, let it dry completely out of direct sun. Store it with the lid partially cracked and the drain hole open.

Check and resupply as necessary your first aid kit, toilet kit, personal kit, repair and spares kits.

Every camper should have a copy of Annie Getchell's *Essential Outdoor Gear Manual* (Ragged Mountain Press, 1995), which is full of excellent do-it-yourself tips for tents, bags, stoves, boats, climbing gear, boots, and more.

CHAPTER 5

Modifications & Accessories

BY JONATHAN HANSON

Equipping for Performance and Utility

Let's be honest: You don't really *need* anything we're about to discuss to have fun with your vehicle. You can drive it right off the showroom floor, throw in some camping gear and explore the world.

However, it's easy to significantly improve the performance and practicality of any stock vehicle with a few well-chosen accessories and modifications. These can be designed to enhance backroad ability (tires, suspension, and so on), utility (roof racks and other accessories), or recovery capabilities (winches, jacks, and so forth). Besides, it's fun to give your vehicle its own personality.

Everything we're going to discuss in this chapter is useful. In fact, you won't find a single reference to a chrome tail-lamp brush guard.

Tires

A simple switch in tires will do more than any other modification to improve your vehicle's backroad performance.

Most sport utilities come from the factory with tires designed to provide a smooth and quiet ride on pavement (which is where most test drives occur), to offer maximum fuel economy, and, most importantly, to not cost the manufacturer too much money. Rough-road traction is well down on the list.

If you'll be doing all your driving on pavement or good dirt roads, the stock tires will work just fine. Once you venture farther out and start dealing with steep hills, loose sand, or mud, you'll benefit hugely

Through an accessories provider such as Performance Products, you can outfit your sport utility "to the nines," with brush guards, auxiliary lights, safari roof rack, winch, snorkel, and more.

from a more aggressive tread design. Even paved roads covered with snow and ice can be more safely negotiated with better tires.

Tread Design

Street tires, or tires designed for mostly street use, feature small, closely spaced tread blocks, which offer better traction on smooth surfaces and less rolling resistance (which in turn increases fuel economy). Tires designed for off-pavement use have larger, deeper tread blocks, which dig into loose surfaces better. Theoretically, the gnarlier the tread, the better the traction—but you eventually reach a point of diminishing returns. The really aggressive "mudder"

designs work just fine in deep muck, but they're miserable to drive on the road. The big tread blocks howl incessantly on pavement and offer a lumpy ride. Also, a too-aggressive tread won't work well in sand or other soft, dry surfaces, since it tends to dig down and bury itself rather than float on top.

The best compromise for a mixture of on- and off-pavement driving is an "all-terrain" (AT) design. Such tires are comfortable and quiet on the road and give fine traction in most backroad situations. If

The tire tread on the left is a street-oriented truck tire, common as stock equipment on sport utilities. The center tire is a typical "all terrain" tread, good for both street and dirt. The tire on the right is a mud tread, great for traction off-pavement but loud on-pavement.

your backroad travels take you across lots of muddy or very rough country, you might consider a slightly more aggressive tread, a "mud-terrain" (MT) design. Mud tires are designed to prevent thick mud from clogging the tread as it does on all-terrain tires. The tread blocks have what is called a self-cleaning feature: They fling the goop free of the tire (and all over the vehicle instead). Most tire manufacturers offer several different tread designs, and the AT and MT designations are common throughout the industry.

One other useful design is the snow tire. While it looks like a fairly mild-patterned backroad tire, a snow tire is made with very sharp-edged tread blocks, the better to bite into snow and ice. In certain sections of the country, it's worth it to have a separate set of snow tires mounted on an extra set of rims, to be installed when winter clamps down.

Size

Look at 4x4 show trucks with $2,000 worth of chrome accessories: They'll be sporting enormous tires. Likewise, the monster trucks crushing mini-vans during half-time on the professional wrestling channel.

Now look at pictures of real expedition vehicles in Africa, South America, and Australia. They'll be wearing heavy-duty tires of very modest size, which are expected to perform in a wide range of conditions.

You don't need big tires to explore backroads. In fact, tires that are too large for the vehicle can cause numerous problems. First, big tires are heavy, and the extra weight combined with their larger diameter acts as a powerful fulcrum, stressing wheel bearings, differentials, axles, brakes, steering gear, and suspension. Oversized tires can cause clearance problems with the vehicle's bodywork, contacting the wheel wells as the suspension rebounds over a bump, damaging both tire and sheet metal. If you jack up the vehicle with tall suspension to clear the tires, the center of gravity is raised, ruining on-road handling and making the vehicle unsafe on side slopes in the backcountry. Large-diameter tires throw off the overall gearing of the vehicle, reducing power. And, finally, 100 pounds or so worth of giant flat tire is a real pain to change!

That said, a slightly larger tire than the base tire size for your vehicle can offer a couple advantages. You'll gain a little bit of ground clearance, the extra width can result in more traction in some situations, and a larger tire rolls over small rocks and ridges with less felt impact.

How large a tire do you want? A good upper limit is the biggest tire size available as a factory option for your vehicle. You can be sure anything specified by the factory will have enough clearance and be within the design capabilities of the running gear. Keep in mind, however, that going up in tire size will also raise the effective gearing of the vehicle, meaning the engine has to work harder. The manufacturer compensates for this by installing different ratio gears in the differential. You can do the same thing, but it's very expensive to change gears after the fact. If the difference between your base tire size and the maximum stock size is more than one or two sizes, consider going up just one size, which will result in minimal gear-

ing effect. For example, one of
our Toyota trucks came with
235/75 tires. We switched to a
235/85—same width, slightly
larger diameter—which gained
us a half-inch of ground clearance but was unnoticeable in
terms of power loss.

TIP

If your vehicle is still under warranty when you
buy new tires, check to make sure the warranty isn't
voided if you install different-sized tires.

Tire size designations can be confusing, especially since a couple different measuring systems are used by the industry. The simple 10 × 15 designation refers to a tire with a tread
ten inches wide, made to fit a 15-inch diameter wheel. A 12.50 × 15 tire fits the same diameter wheel, but has a 12½-inch wide tread. This measurement gives no clue as to the diameter
of the tire itself, although as tread width goes up, overall diameter usually does, too. Some
tires do specify diameter as well: 33 × 12.50 x 15 signifies a 33-inch diameter tire.

Metric is becoming the more common measurement of tire size. A 235/75 × 15 tire has a
tread width of 235 millimeters (about nine inches). The 75 refers to the ratio of the height of
the sidewall to the tread width, as a percentage. A 75 series tire has a sidewall that is 75 percent as tall as the tread is wide. A 235/85 × 15 tire has the same width tread, but a sidewall
that is 85 percent as tall as the tread width. So a 235/85 × 15 tire is taller than a 235/75 ×
15 tire, even though they both are the same width and both fit a 15-inch wheel. For comparison, high-performance street tires for sports cars are sometimes 45 or even 35 series, indicating a tire that is extremely wide in relation to its sidewall height.

Wheels

Automotive engineers call the weight of everything under the springs on your vehicle—
the wheels, tires, and axles—"unsprung weight." The less of that weight there is, the easier
job the suspension has in reacting to bumps, rocks, and ruts. In addition, the weight of the
wheels and tires is referred to as "rotating mass." This is weight that has to be turned by the
engine to accelerate and slowed by the brakes to stop. Again, the less of that weight there is,
the better. Virtually all high-performance street cars wear lightweight wheels to reduce both
unsprung weight and rotating mass, and sport utility vehicles benefit from them, too. In fact,
the advantages in both performance and looks are so great that many manufacturers offer
aluminum wheels as a factory option.

If your vehicle came with steel wheels, you can gain a noticeable improvement in ride
quality by switching to aluminum wheels. If you are considering installing larger tires on your
stock vehicle, you might need slightly wider wheels than those that came from the factory. If
so, this is a perfect opportunity to move up to aluminum wheels. Your tire store will be able
to tell you what width you need for the tire you want (they should also have a chart listing
what tires will fit your vehicle).

If you go shopping for replacement wheels for your vehicle, ask about the *offset* of the new ones. If the salesperson gives you a blank look, leave quickly and find another store. Offset refers to the placement of the wheel's rim in relation to the vehicle's hub (to which the wheel attaches). A wheel with extreme *negative* offset will stick out of the wheel well, like those goofy, lowered minitrucks. A wheel with *positive* offset extends farther under the vehicle.

Too much negative offset places strain on the vehicle's wheel bearings and suspension and increases the likelihood of tire clearance problems with the fender. Too much positive offset reduces the vehicle's turning ability and can cause the tire to contact parts of the suspension or the inside of the wheel well. What you want is a wheel with the same offset as the stock wheel, or *very* close to it.

The only downside to aluminum wheels is that they are less resistant to impact damage than steel equivalents. If you whack a steel wheel really hard, you might dent the edge of the rim, but a big hammer will put things right. Do the same thing to an aluminum wheel, and it will probably crack, ruining the wheel. However, we're talking about really massive whacks, far beyond any resulting from normal use. If you're planning on driving through Africa, stick to steel wheels; otherwise, aluminum is perfectly strong.

The exception to the aluminum versus steel comparison is a cold-forged aluminum wheel, such as those available from Mickey Thompson (see page 162 for contact information). Cold-forged aluminum wheels are immensely strong and can be bent back to true just as a steel wheel can. They are, however, very expensive (more than $150 each).

Most sport utility vehicles are equipped with 15-inch-diameter wheels. Some carry larger 16- or even 17-inch wheels, and a few compact vehicles carry 14-inchers. It's almost always best to stay with the same diameter your vehicle came with, since you can vary tire diameter at will. If you are moving up in tire width as well as diameter, you might need slightly wider wheels—perhaps an inch wider than standard. Again, it's better to stay close to the stock configuration.

Suspension

The comparison I made in the tire section between show and working vehicles (page 120) holds true regarding suspension as well. Your vehicle will perform best in a majority of situations with the suspension left as close as possible to the stock settings.

A four-wheel-drive vehicle with its suspension raised by five or six inches—or more—gains one or two benefits. It can probably ford deeper water than it could with the stock suspension, and it has less chance of hanging up the undercarriage on rocks.

But think of the downsides. First, the on-road handling of the vehicle is greatly diminished because the higher center of gravity makes it roll more side to side. Even equipping the vehicle with wider tires can compensate for this effect only up to a point—and, as we've already discussed, big tires create their own problems.

Raising a vehicle's suspension almost invariably puts stress on the steering gear because of the angles at which tie rods and drag links have to operate. In addition, the vehicle will pitch back and forth under acceleration and braking.

On the backroads, things are little better. A higher center of gravity makes the vehicle more susceptible to rolling over on side slopes, and it is harder for the driver to "place" the vehicle accurately among rocks. And the angles in the driveshafts and axles are increased, putting more strain on U-joints and CV-joints.

The best setup for a backroad suspension doesn't involve lift, it involves *compliance*. The more a suspension can flex up and down, the better it can mold itself to the contours of the terrain. When traversing extremely rough trails, vehicles with stiff suspension or limited travel often lose contact with the ground with one or even two wheels—and a wheel that's off the ground obviously isn't getting very much traction. That's why more manufacturers are installing all-coil-spring suspensions in their vehicles, as Land Rover pioneered (at least in the sport utility market) in the Range Rover way back in 1970. Coil springs have much less internal friction than leaf springs, so it's easier to make them very compliant while retaining good load-carrying characteristics.

If you decide to install an aftermarket suspension system on your vehicle, stick with a very mild lift—say two inches for a compact sport utility, three or four for a "full-size" vehicle. Make sure the replacement springs have the same rate as your stock springs so compliance won't be affected. The only exception would be if you plan to tow heavy loads, in which case you might want heavy-duty springs in the rear.

Shock Absorbers

A vehicle's suspension consists of essentially two working parts: the springs and the shock absorbers. Springs provide the flex to allow the wheels to bounce over obstructions or drop into ruts; shock absorbers keep the springs from continuing to bounce after the obstruction is passed, which is why shock absorbers are more properly called "dampers." If you shove down hard on the front or rear of a vehicle with worn shock absorbers, it will bounce up and down three or four times before coming to rest. If the shocks are in good shape the vehicle will bounce once and quickly stop.

A change of shock absorbers offers an easy way to improve most suspensions. Just as with tires, most manufacturers lean toward low cost when specifying original equipment shocks (there are exceptions, such as the excellent Bilsteins available optionally on some General Motors and Toyota trucks). While the stock shocks work fine when new and when rough backroad use is minimized, they quickly lose their effectiveness with mileage, and can "fade" if overexerted, as the damping oil heats up and loses viscosity.

High-quality aftermarket shock absorbers are built to perform in all conditions and will outlast most original equipment by thousands of miles. They are also more resistant to sudden failure by breakage or leaking fluid on rough roads. An aftermarket shock that is properly matched to your vehicle will not affect compliance but will improve handling and ride on both paved and unpaved roads.

ROAD TRIPS: FOUR MORE GREAT BACKROAD TRIPS

In addition to the great North American backroad trips to Baja (Chapter 1, page 4) and the Arctic (Chapter 3, page 58), there are, of course, dozens of classic trips throughout the continent. Here is a sampling of four more.

ALPINE LOOP BACK COUNTRY BYWAY, SAN JUAN MOUNTAINS, COLORADO

This 65-mile "Jeep trail," one of the BLM's first Back Country Byways, was built in the late 1800s for mule-drawn wagons taking ore across the mountains between Ouray, Silverton, and Lake City. Take two or three days to explore its history and natural beauty. The route is marked by columbine-decorated signs, and four wheel drive is necessary to navigate many of the side trails (four-wheel-drive routes are signed as well) and several of the high passes. The best time to go is late July and early August, when wildflowers peak, and in mid-September, when fall colors blaze. Plan to camp and hike some of the 100-plus miles of backcountry trails in the Big Blue and Weminuche Wilderness Areas. The summits of five of Colorado's famous "fourteeners" (peaks at or over 14,000 feet) are gained via trails off the Alpine Loop: Redcloud, Sunshine, Handies, Uncompahgre, and Wetterhorn. There is excellent fishing for brook, rainbow, and cutthroat trout. For maps and further information about vehicle use, contact BLM offices in Montrose (970-240-5300) or Durango (970-247-4082).

DEATH VALLEY NATIONAL PARK, CALIFORNIA

With summer temperatures reaching 120 degrees F in this largest national park in the lower 48 states, a backcountry trip here is best done October through April. Death Valley National Park protects a harsh and beautiful swath of the Mojave Desert in east-central California. In spring (February through mid-April) the wildflowers offer colorful displays, and unusual cacti, shrubs, reptiles, and birds are abundant despite the harsh conditions. More than 200 miles of back roads—much of them four-wheel-drive—cross the stunning park. A 400-foot-deep canyon at Hole-in-the-Wall and a spring near Gold Valley are just two highlights of the dozens of four-wheel-drive routes. There are nine campgrounds in the park; backcountry camping is restricted in some areas. All backcountry explorers must check in at the headquarters at Furnace Creek Visitor Center to obtain permits, current road conditions, and camping regulations. Needless to say, you should carry extra water, spare parts, and food on all backcountry drives in the desert. For information, contact Death Valley National Park at (760) 786-2331.

(continued on page 126)

Virtually all high-performance shock absorbers are "gas" shocks, meaning they are pressurized with nitrogen gas or incorporate a gas cell. The gas helps prevent the shock's oil, which provides the actual damping action, from foaming and losing its effectiveness. Opinion (and marketing) varies on the superiority of high-pressure or low-pressure gas designs. I have used both and, frankly, felt no difference in performance. A top-quality model of either design should work well.

Whatever you do, don't be tempted by multiple shock setups that incorporate two (or more) shock absorbers at each wheel. One good shock absorber per corner is plenty. Multiple shock setups are fashionable copies of race suspensions, but racers face far different conditions than you or I ever will, and their shocks are specially valved to reduce the load on the individual units.

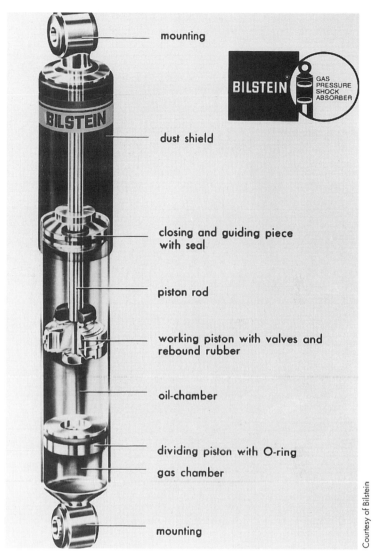

High-pressure mono-tube shocks, as in Bilstein's design, incorporate a separated gas and hydraulic oil chamber, which completely eliminates shock fade and foaming.

Another option for shock absorbers is an adjustable design, such as the RS9000 made by Rancho. The driver can vary the stiffness of these units, according to road conditions or the load in the vehicle. The RS9000s have a knob on the shock body with five settings; an optional kit includes a compressor and an interior switch and gauge that lets you adjust the shocks from inside the cab, even while the vehicle is moving.

Adjustable shocks are worth considering if you routinely carry heavy loads in your vehicle and would like to be able to vary the suspension behavior.

ROAD TRIP: FOUR MORE GREAT BACKROAD TRIPS,
CONTINUED FROM PAGE 124

BAXTER STATE PARK, MAINE

More than 200,000 acres of North Woods full of wildlife and wild places are the highlight of this largest swath of protected land in New England, just outside the northern town of Millinocket. The park was donated to the state by two-time governor of Maine Percival Baxter; its centerpiece is 5,267-foot Mt. Katahdin. Baxter stipulated that wildlife always came first in the park, recreation second. Today his wishes are honored with limited access (rough dirt roads), only 1,000 campers a night, and no pets, motorcycles, motor homes, trailers, or TVs allowed. The park is best visited mid-May through mid-October. Maine residents have free access; the rest of us pay an entrance fee. The Baxter State Park Scenic Drive winds 94 miles across the western and northern edge of the park, mostly via Park Tote Road, a narrow and very rough dirt track (four wheel drive is not necessary, but high clearance is best—perfect sport utility country). Those venturing into the park will find quiet campsites, burbling brooks, cascading waterfalls, and abundant wildlife, including moose and deer. Plan one or several overnights and hiking around or up to Mt. Katahdin. Rock climbing, mountaineering, canoeing, and fishing are also excellent. For information contact Baxter State Park at (207) 723-5140.

SNOW-BLIND EXPEDITION, MICHIGAN

For something a little different, try a trip on the snow-bound forest trails near West Branch, Michigan. Each year the Great Lakes Four Wheel Drive Association sanctions a club drive in February. Mileages are not far—these are day trips—but the driving is very difficult, and fun. Your sport utility is best equipped with snow or mud tires and chains, and you should have good snow-driving skills. At the Snow-Blind Expedition banquet, participants swap expedition stories and tell tall tales. For more information, contact the Great Lakes Four Wheel Drive Association via the United Four Wheel Drive Associations at (800) 44-UFWDA.

Engine Performance

Modern fuel-injected engines with computer controls have restored the performance of the legendary muscle cars of the 1960s, while increasing gas mileage and drastically reducing emissions.

Still, some people are never quite satisfied with the power bestowed on them by the factory—and, particularly when towing or hauling heavy loads, a few extra horses can be practical as well as fun.

Unfortunately, the sophistication of today's power plants means that it is much more

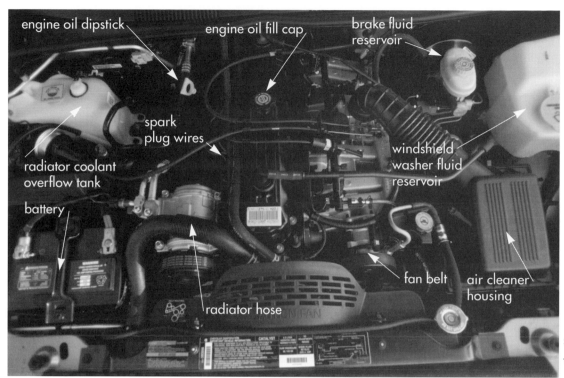

Major components of a typical inline six-cylinder engine. (Component placement varies from engine to engine.)

difficult to increase performance above the stock level than it was in the days when we could just slap on a four-barrel carb and a set of headers. But a couple of areas still have room for improvement, without compromising important emissions laws.

One area where manufacturers save money is on the exhaust system. A properly designed aftermarket exhaust can result in a power gain of up to 10 percent. We added a Borla exhaust to our truck and were impressed at the improvement in power. A bonus is that the Borla is made entirely from stainless steel and so should last the life of the vehicle.

Our Borla was a simple bolt-on unit called a "cat-back" system (so called because it connects to the stock exhaust behind the catalytic converter and consists solely of a new tailpipe and muffler designed to reduce the back pressure inherent in a stock muffler). We might have gained a bit more power by installing a set of headers as well. A header replaces the cast exhaust manifold on the engine with a precisely engineered set of individual tubes, further reducing back pressure and ensuring that the exhaust pulses coming from the engine are optimally timed.

Another way to increase power is with a replacement chip for the engine computer. These chips essentially reprogram the stock engine operating parameters to increase horsepower while not affecting emissions. They can, however, reduce fuel economy. Ask a mechanic at your service center about what is available for your vehicle.

Be cautious when investigating performance upgrades. Many modifications might work on a test dynamometer under optimal lab conditions but disappoint in the real world. An example is a replacement air cleaner assembly I once almost bought for our truck. This unit replaced the whole stock air cleaner canister (not just the filter) with a new, open filter assembly. The stock air filter breathes through a single inlet in the fender (where it is well-protected from ingesting water but is somewhat restricted). The so-called "performance filter" promised greatly increased breathing. However, I found the results of an independent test that showed how the open filter ingested hot air from inside the engine compartment, while the stock air intake sucked in cool outside air. Since the hotter air is less dense, the "performance filter" not only raised operating temperatures but didn't increase power at all. The advertised power increases had been calculated with the engine on a dynamometer—that is, in a *room* instead of inside a vehicle.

For contact information on manufacturers: See Appendix II, beginning on page 162.

Lights

Headlights

Archaic laws regulating motor vehicle lighting—implemented in the 1930s—kept American headlight design in the Dark Ages, so to speak, for decades. Things are better now, although we are still behind the Europeans. At least manufacturers have started equipping many of their vehicles with Halogen headlights.

Halogen is a gas (actually it's a group of five gaseous elements) that, when used inside a headlamp bulb, allows the filament to burn hotter, thus producing more light. Halogen lights also produce a more natural white light compared to the feeble yellowish beams of old-fashioned tungsten sealed-beam headlights.

The only problem remaining is the old one of economics. You can make an adequate halogen headlight with a cheap reflector and a molded glass lens, or you can use a high-quality, free-form reflector and a lead-crystal lens designed to precisely focus the light. The difference to vehicle manufacturers would probably be about $10 per car—but their accountants multiply that by two million vehicles. So we get the cheaper versions.

If your vehicle has standard seven-inch round or seven-by-six-inch rectangular head-

Courtesy of Hella

Auxiliary driving lights, such as the excellent Hella Rallye series, significantly enhance visibility on dark back roads.

lights, or dual headlights, it's easy to replace them with a high-quality lighting system from a company such as Hella. The difference will be immediately apparent—more light and a much more evenly distributed pattern. Yet the finely focused low beams will not blind on-coming drivers (as long as your headlights are properly aligned). Many of these aftermarket lights are now legal in all 50 states.

Want even more? Headlights such as the Hellas allow you to change the bulb without replacing the whole lamp assembly. The standard H-4 bulb has a 55-watt low beam and a 60-watt high beam. You can install a bulb with the same low beam wattage, but a full 100-watt high beam. These really light up the night—but, despite the polite low beam rating, they are illegal due to their retina-scorching capability on high. You wouldn't want to forget to dim your lights with these and find out it's a highway patrol officer coming your way.

Some vehicles come with headlights specially designed for the particular model. These normally cannot be upgraded as a whole, but in some you can still upgrade the bulb to a more powerful rating.

Driving and Fog Lights

Sometimes even good headlights don't provide all the light you want. On deserted back-roads where animals can run across your path or where steep drop-offs or washouts threaten, the more light you can throw, the safer you'll be. This is when auxiliary lights are invaluable.

Auxiliary lights come in essentially three designs:

■ **Fog lamps** throw a very broad, flat pattern designed to increase visibility in fog, snow, and rain. They are also useful for any low-speed driving situation. These should be mounted low on the vehicle to reduce glare; under the bumper is ideal as long as they don't decrease the approach angle (for a discussion of approach angle, see page 19). The effectiveness of such lights in fog or rain depends on the beam pattern's being below your line of sight so re-flected glare from the conditions is minimized.

■ **Driving lamps** produce a fairly broad but long-range beam similar to that of a very powerful high-beam headlight. These can be mounted above the bumper, at headlight level, or on the roof, although glare on the hood is sometimes a problem in the latter case.

■ **Pencil beams** throw a tightly focused cone of light to an immense distance and are par-ticularly suited to high-speed racing applications.

The ideal lighting setup for all-around, on- and off-pavement use would comprise a good set of H4 headlights, a pair of fog lamps, and a pair of driving lamps. The only problem I've ever found using good lights is that whenever I drive someone else's vehicle, the ordinary headlights on it seem downright dangerously dim.

Generally speaking, the larger the reflector behind the bulb, the more light it will put on the road. So, all else being equal, a seven-inch round driving light with a 100-watt bulb will be brighter than a five-inch light with the same bulb. The exceptions are the new projector-style lights, which put out a great deal of light from a very small unit. I note, however, that all the racers seem to still be using full-size lights, so I suspect the brightness of the projector lights is relative only to their compactness.

Light technology is advancing rapidly. Many new lights incorporate what are known as free-form reflectors, which use thousands of individual reflecting surfaces at the back of the light to precisely control and aim the beam. Lights with free-form reflectors don't need cuts in the lens to properly direct the light, so the lenses are just clear crystal.

Recently a new type of auxiliary light has hit the market. Called HID (High Intensity Discharge), these lights eclipse everything else available, making even halogen lamps appear meek in comparison. Instead of a glowing filament, they utilize an arc of high-voltage electricity through a gas field. A separate ballast bumps up the vehicle's 12 volts to the 25 *thousand* volts required by the lamp. Yet overall power consumption of an HID light is about half that of a standard halogen unit. And the HID light should be more resistant to shock, since the thin filament of a standard bulb is usually what breaks during rough usage. The obvious question is: Does all this HID performance have a downside? Well, there is the minor issue of price—currently about $500 *each* (although that will surely come down as the technology becomes more common).

Theoretically, a round light is slightly more efficient than a rectangular model with the same overall reflector area. But the difference is small enough that you shouldn't hesitate to choose a rectangular lamp if it fits better on your vehicle.

Unfortunately, adding auxiliary lights isn't as simple as just bolting them to the bumper. You need to make sure your vehicle's electrical system is up to the task of providing 200 or more extra watts of power. The alternator is what generates electrical power when the engine is running and most can handle at least one set of auxiliary lights with no trouble. However, if you plan on adding more, or if you also run a powerful stereo or a dual battery setup (see Chapter 4, page 109), you should check with your mechanic, who can test the output of the alternator and quickly determine how much excess draw it can handle. It's possible to replace virtually any alternator with a high-output substitute; many vehicles offer them as factory options.

To properly install your auxiliary lights, you'll need to run them through a relay. A relay is nothing more than a

BACKING UP IS HARD TO DO

The back-up lights on most sport utilities are adequate for reversing out of the garage, but they're worthless for retreating from a dicey situation in the backcountry. Here are two solutions:

■ Replacement halogen bulbs are available for your stock back-up lights, which will increase their effectiveness markedly.

■ For even more light, you can mount a set of fog lamps to the rear bumper, either hooked in to come on with your stock back-up lights, or controlled by a separate switch.

heavy-duty switch controlled by a smaller switch at the dashboard. The power wire for the lights runs through the relay. Flipping on the dashboard switch activates a magnetic switch in the relay, sending power straight to the light without having to detour it all the way around through the dashboard (unlike the AC current in your house, DC power drops off rapidly the farther away from the power source the load is). If you have an automotive electrician install your lights, he or she will use properly sized wire for the light and will run the power through a relay for peak performance.

Other Lights

If you have a safari-style rack on your vehicle, a very useful addition is a swiveling work light mounted on it at the rear, to light your way as you unload gear in the dark. Also, I really like the interior gooseneck map lights made by Hella, which produce a focused cone of light for reading. They come in two styles: one that plugs into the cigarette lighter, and one that must be wired into the vehicle (but which can be mounted where you like). Finally, a trouble light that plugs into the cigarette lighter and extends, via a long cord, to the engine compartment (or anywhere else you need it) is a great accessory, either for working on the engine or changing a tire.

Jacks and Winches

If you drive with enough caution—or timidity, depending on your point of view—you might never get stuck. But to maintain such a flawless record, you'd have to pass up a lot of interesting routes. And sometimes a mud pit or sand trap can catch you unaware, even on a seemingly innocuous road.

The trick to getting stuck is to not think of it as a disaster but as just another facet of exploring. With the proper equipment you can usually be on your way in little time, albeit perhaps a little dirtier than you were.

Hi-Lift Jacks

If tires are the single best way to improve the backroad capability of your vehicle, a Hi-Lift jack is the single best tool to have if you ever exceed the capabilities of those tires. Not

In an emergency, a Hi-Lift jack can be used as a manual winch.

Courtesy of Hi-Lift Jack Company, a division of Bloomfield Mfg. Co., Inc.

only that, a Hi-Lift jack will make tire changes relatively effortless compared with the hassle of dealing with even the best standard jacks.

Like "Kleenex," the name "Hi-Lift" jack is a registered trademark applicable only to jacks made by the Bloomfield Manufacturing Company. Several companies make close copies of the Hi-Lift, but they are careful to use their own names.

The only real downside to the Hi-Lift jack is that it is a pain to carry in a vehicle. One solution is a lockable bracket, made especially for carrying the jack. The bracket can be mounted on a bumper or roof rack. See Chapter 2, page 32, for tips on using a Hi-Lift jack.

Winches

Archimedes said, "Give me a lever and a place to stand, and I can move the world." Being a somewhat more modest man than he, my own motto is, "Give me a winch and something to hook it to, and I can move the vehicle." With a winch properly sized to your sport utility, and a secure anchor to which to hook the cable, you can get yourself out of, well, *virtually* any situation (see Chapter 2, page 34).

Winches fall into three categories:

■ **Power take-off (PTO) winches** run off a driveshaft from the vehicle's transmission or transfer case and are powered by the engine itself. A lever inside the vehicle engages the take-off gear to start the winch turning. The speed of the engine then regulates the speed at which the winch retrieves cable.

A PTO winch can run all day long without running down the battery, making it popular for industrial and agricultural applications. The biggest disadvantage is that a PTO winch will work only when the engine is running, rendering it useless if, for example, the vehicle stalls in a river. PTO winches are also extremely expensive.

PTO winches are becoming scarce. Very few new vehicles include a power take-off point on the transmission. You'll still find these winches now and then on older Land Rovers and Land Cruisers.

■ **Electric winches** make up the vast majority of winches sold today. They are very powerful and reasonably priced and can work even if the engine of the vehicle is stalled—even if the winch is submerged—for a short time, anyway. But an electric winch draws an enormous amount of power from the vehicle's electrical system. A proper installation includes a separate, deep-cycle battery to feed the winch, separated from the starting battery by an isolator, which allows the alternator to charge both batteries but keeps their working circuits isolated. A heavy-duty alternator is also a must. Even so, an electric winch can normally be run only intermittently without completely draining its power source.

Inexpensive electric winches are powered by permanent magnet motors. If a permanent magnet motor is worked to overheating, it can be destroyed, necessitating replacement. Better electric winches use series-wound motors which, while not immune to burnout, are considerably more resistant. They are worth the extra money.

■ **Hydraulic winches** are experiencing a renaissance. Like a PTO winch, a hydraulic winch runs off the power of the engine, but instead of a direct driveshaft coupling, the hydraulic winch is powered by hydraulic fluid from the power steering pump. Hydraulic winches can be very powerful yet lightweight, and the cost is comparable to or less than an electric equivalent, especially when you consider that the vehicle's electrical system needs no modifying.

Like a PTO winch, a hydraulic winch works only when the engine is running, and it is susceptible to fluid leaks in the power steering system (your vehicle must have a power steering pump to run the winch). But, also like a PTO, a hydraulic winch is capable of working all day.

Winches are rated by their pulling power—4,000 lbs., 8,000 lbs., and so on. You might think that a winch with a capacity equal to the weight of your vehicle would be plenty; after all, such a rating should be able to pull the whole vehicle off the ground, right? But things aren't so simple. Winch ratings are often optimistic and are always figured with only one layer of cable on the winch drum—with more cable on the drum, its diameter expands, reducing the leverage of the winch. In addition, the resistance of a vehicle that is really buried in thick mud or sand can sometimes exceed the static weight of the vehicle.

BUT CAN SHE CHANGE A TIRE?

Roseann found this ad in our local paper and has kept it ever since: "85 Toyota 4x4, 22R engine 150K miles recent rebuild, new clutch, lift kit, mudder tires, aluminum wheels, Hi-Lift jack, wench, $5000."

As a general rule, your winch should have a capacity equal to one-and-one-half to two times the curb weight of your vehicle. A typical sport utility of around 4,300 pounds would be well-equipped with an 8,000- or 9,000-pound–rated winch.

Just as important as the winch itself is how it is mounted on the vehicle. As you can imagine, a winch puts a tremendous strain on the vehicle, and substandard mounts are dangerous, particularly when pulling from any angle other than straight ahead. Mounting kits are available that bolt to the frame around the existing bumper, but even better are heavy-duty replacement bumpers designed to take the strain of winching from any angle. A bumper mount usually places the winch in tighter to the vehicle's body as well.

Probably the best winch bumpers are those from ARB, an Australian company that got its start making really heavy-duty accessories for Toyota Land Cruisers working the Outback. The ARB bumpers bolt solidly to the frame of the vehicle and can take the strain of a powerful winch pulling from any angle. They also withstand the stress of stout bumper jacks such as the Hi-Lift. In fact, the ARB bumper is available with a special fitting to solidly anchor the lifting tongue on a Hi-Lift. Several other companies are now making high-quality bumpers similar to the ARB.

Also available for winches are quick-mount systems that let you mount a winch to a standard receiver hitch on the rear of the vehicle or to a similar mount bolted to the front. It can be advantageous to be able to choose which end of the vehicle to winch from, but the security is obviously less than with a solidly mounted winch. And you have to find a place to carry the winch inside the car.

Traction Aids

As was discussed in Chapter 1 (page 2), the same mechanism in your vehicle's differentials that allows the tires to rotate at different speeds around turns also ensures that, in a low-traction situation, power will go to the wheel with the *least* grip. This can effectively render your four-wheel-drive vehicle a three- or even two-wheel-drive vehicle, with one front and one rear tire spinning helplessly while you go nowhere.

The solution is a modification of the differential that allows the tires to rotate at different speeds around turns but, if one tire begins to spin, reduces or eliminates the slippage, equalizing power to both wheels. These devices come in several types:

- **Limited-slip units** do just what their name implies—they reduce, but don't totally eliminate, the loss of power to the nonspinning wheel. Still, the gain in traction is significant and limited slip differentials are virtually undetectable in operation, make no noise, and don't negatively affect handling on pavement.

- **Automatic locking differentials** completely eliminate slippage by locking the axles together if one wheel begins to spin, resulting in vastly improved traction. The downside is that automatic lockers can be noisy on pavement in certain

TRACTION TIPS

The best time to equip your vehicle with a traction device is when you buy it.

Factory-optional limited slips are much less expensive than aftermarket units, since they can be installed right on the assembly line. Some vehicles are now available with manual locking differentials as well. Toyota trucks and Land Cruisers, for example, can be equipped with factory lockers on the rear axle.

If you decide to add an aftermarket traction aid, look closely at your needs. If most of your driving is on paved roads, with very little or no rough backcountry use, a single, limited-slip unit in the rear differential would be perfectly adequate. If you want to do some serious exploring, an automatic locker in the rear will add significant levels of grip. And if nothing but the ultimate will suffice, one or two manual locking units will endow your vehicle with capabilities far beyond its original limits.

situations; some produce a faint ratcheting sound around low-speed turns. It's generally inadvisable to use automatic lockers in the front axle because a front locker greatly increases steering effort and the sudden transition from unlocked to locked could cause problems. Also, in icy conditions on pavement, even just a rear locker can be more of a hindrance than a help. If one tire starts to spin on ice, when the locker kicks in, the likely result will be both tires' spinning, actually *decreasing* control. Still, automatic lockers are the most economical way to add traction. Some units start at less than $250 and can be installed in less than two hours.

■ **Manual-locking differentials** are, in many ways, the ultimate choice in vehicles that will be used frequently in rough conditions. A switch on the dashboard allows the driver to engage the locker when needed; at all other times the differential acts as a standard open unit. On-pavement handling is completely unaffected, but with one or both axles locked, traction is available that is unapproachable by any other system. Engaging a front locker will stiffen the steering considerably, but since the driver controls the activation, he or she can use it only when absolutely necessary.

Sport Racks and Luggage Carriers

Roof Racks

Many sport utility vehicles come from the factory with roof racks, but these are generally adequate for tying on suitcases and not much more. A tower rack system, such as those available from Yakima and Thule, is much more versatile.

In the old days, when all vehicles had rain gutters, fitting racks was easy. Now rain gutters have all but disappeared in the quest for aerodynamic efficiency, so rack makers must design many different towers to ensure a proper fit on different vehicles. Most consist of some sort of padded base that rides on the roof, with a flat hook that grips the door frame to anchor the rack.

I confess to an early, deep distrust of gutterless rack mounts, but an experience in a Toyota 4Runner changed my mind. We were coming over the notoriously windy Tecate Divide outside of San Diego, on a day when many semi-trucks were pulled off the road because of the gusts. We had two long sea kayaks mounted to the rack, and the wind kept punching us around while I peered up nervously at the bows of the boats. Finally one immense blast flung our vehicle clear out of its lane into the emergency strip. We stopped, shaken, and got out to assess the damage. Incredibly, the whole rack had shifted to the rear about an inch—but everything was still tight and secure.

So a top-quality rack system will withstand tremendous abuse. You can equip it with numerous accessories: bicycle carriers, canoe and kayak saddles, ski racks, or enclosed luggage carriers (further discussion of various rack accessories follows this section).

Another type of roof rack is the classic safari-style—a simple, heavy-duty frame of square steel tubing, to which a floor can be added if needed. I've used one of these racks on my old

A sturdy safari-style roof rack can be loaded up with a surprising amount of gear. Just make sure everything is well-secured.

Land Cruiser for 20 years, often with several hundred pounds of gear on it. Such a load obviously does no good for the vehicle's center of gravity, but it illustrates the strength of the product.

The stamped-steel mounting brackets furnished with safari racks are adequate, but a far better alternative is a product called a Quick-N-Easy, a stout, cast-aluminum bracket with a cammed clamping system. The steel brackets that came with my rack developed stress cracks within a year; the Quick-N-Easy replacements have weathered the succeeding 18 years with no problems. They work only on vehicles with rain gutters, however.

Hitch-Mounted Bicycle Racks

If your vehicle has a receiver hitch (a square tube below the bumper into which a hitch mount slides), you can mount a swing-down carrier for up to three bicycles or several pairs of skis. The advantage to the hitch-mount carrier is the easy access compared to a roof-mounted

For easy access, bikes can go on special racks, like this Supreme GetAway from Yakima, that slide into a receiver hitch. Lycra bike covers will keep your seat and shifters clean.

rack—although it does complicate getting into the cargo area of the vehicle. The disadvantages are that the bicycles are more accessible to thieves as well as you, and more exposed to traffic damage, especially rear-enders.

Luggage Carriers

It's inevitable: No matter how much space we have, our possessions expand to fill it. Nowhere is this more obvious than in our vehicles. It seems that, like nature, humans abhor a vacuum and must pack and pack until the vehicle—whether it's a Corolla or a Suburban—is stuffed to the gills.

And so what? Part of the fun of car-camping is being able to bring the luxuries (see Chapter 4, beginning on page 81, for more on car-camping). I do enough backpacking and sea kayaking to feel no guilt when lounging in a full-size folding chair under a big shade awning, with a glass (real glass) of Bass ale sitting on the folding table next to me.

However, it is good, for both safety and style, to avoid the Beverly Hillbillies look. An enclosed luggage carrier that fastens to the roof rack is the answer.

Yakima and Thule both make good-quality luggage carriers, constructed from molded ABS plastic. They are weatherproof and come in several sizes and configurations—the long, skinny ones are good for skis; the short, fat ones swallow folding chairs and other awkward items.

The best-quality enclosed carrier I've seen is made by Packasport. Instead of molded plastic, the Packasport is constructed of hand-laid fiberglass with aluminum reinforcements, immensely

Courtesy of Packasport

A hard-shell luggage case, such as the Packasport, gives you more room inside your sport utility, a real plus for families.

strong and virtually immune to ultraviolet deterioration. Packasport carriers are available in custom colors to match any vehicle and boast top-quality hardware and a beautiful finish.

Towing

A simple bumper hitch, common on sport utilities, is perfectly strong for light towing duties—say a compact tent trailer or the equivalent. The bumper will be stamped with a rating. For example, "3,500 pounds gross trailer weight; 350 pounds tongue weight" means that the total weight of the trailer and its contents can't exceed 3,500 pounds, and that the weight on the hitch ball itself can't exceed 350 pounds.

Note, however, that just because the hitch can handle 3,500 pounds doesn't mean your vehicle will behave properly towing the load. A heavy trailer exerts a pendulum effect at the hitch, making the vehicle's rear sway back and forth and bob up and down. For regular towing of trailers over 1,500 pounds or so, you should consider a more heavy-duty installation.

A frame-mounted receiver hitch is the first step up. This is the style of hitch with the square tube into which the hitch ball mount slides. Solidly bolted or welded to the vehicle's frame at

OPTIMA BATTERIES

One of the most common causes of vehicle breakdowns is the battery. It doesn't matter if you've bought the most reliable vehicle in the world, the battery is subject to its own weaknesses. Dead battery = dead vehicle.

I used to go through batteries about once every two years. I always bought the top-of-the-line models from a nationwide auto store, usually guaranteed for five years (prorated). Still, with the use I subjected them to, they invariably failed years early. It was irrelevant to me that the warranty meant the replacement would cost only half the full price; I wanted a fail-safe battery.

Finally I discovered the Optima. This is a completely sealed battery that uses gel instead of liquid inside. It can be mounted upside-down if you feel like it—the battery doesn't care. My original Optima is now nearing five years of age and is still in perfect condition.

The ultimate fail-safe battery setup would be two Optimas, with a manual switch so you could chose which one you wanted. In the unlikely even that one failed (and *all* batteries must fail eventually), you could switch to the backup. This would also protect you from discharges after accidentally leaving the lights on.

For Information: See Chapter 4, page 109, for a discussion of dual-battery systems. For contact information for Optima batteries, see Appendix II, page 162.

PURSUITS: SEA KAYAKING

It was a cool and misty morning in Johnstone Strait, an island-strewn channel off the northeast coast of Canada's Vancouver Island. The water was glass-smooth, steel-gray in color; we could hear the drips from our paddles as we stroked out of the cove where our tents stood. We paddled offshore about a half-mile, until all signs of land had disappeared in the fog and only our compasses showed us the way back. Then we waited—talking quietly and listening to the calls of birds and the lapping of the water at our hulls.

Then we heard it, far off in the mist—a single *poosh*, then several more in succession. We pointed our bows toward the sound and soon, at the edge of our vision, a group of dorsal fins solidified out of the mist, gliding toward us. The orcas were cruising lazily at less than a knot; it took the group several minutes to pass around and, once, between our kayaks. The giant, vertical fin of a large male passed by my boat, its tip a good two feet above my head, then slowly submerged into the dark water. When the animals had gone, we sat in awe listening to the receding sounds of their blowing, then paddled silently back to camp.

I can't think of any other sport that encompasses the breadth of adventure possible with sea kayaking. With the help of a competent guide, it's possible to learn enough in an afternoon of instruction to embark on a weeklong trip, carrying everything you need to camp in comfort. With experience, you can take on some of the most challenging wilderness left on the planet: the Arctic Ocean, Tierra del Fuego, Tasmania. Yet it's still fun to plop a kayak in the harbor and spend an afternoon watching sailboats. And your sport utility is perfect for transporting your boats (see the section on racks, page 135).

With their long, wide rooflines, sport utilities are perfect kayak-transporters.

(continued on page 141)

several points, it is significantly stronger than a bumper hitch. You can also vary the height of the ball by buying different mounts so a low-riding tent trailer won't sit with its nose in the air behind your high-clearance vehicle. When you're not pulling anything, the hitch mount can be removed from the receiver, minimizing clearance losses for backcountry exploring.

But the sway problem encountered with a heavier trailer is still unaddressed. Fortunately, a receiver hitch can accept something called an equalizing hitch. This hitch incorporates two spring steel bars that swivel at the hitch and are connected to the trailer's tongue, usually with chain. The bars are tensioned under load, which actually distributes the forces normally concentrated at the hitch throughout the frames of both the vehicle and the trailer. This greatly reduces bobbing at the hitch under braking, acceleration, and over rough roads. It also helps to reduce back-and-forth swaying, although an additional sway-control device, like a giant shock absorber, is sometimes added to further reduce wind- and cornering-generated weaving.

Miscellaneous Accessories

The amount of *stuff* you can add to your vehicle is limited only by your imagination. However, there are a few odds and ends you might find really useful.

Compass

No, I am *not* talking about the little toys you see on the dashboards of retirees' Cadillacs. A real compass designed for vehicle use is a serious piece of gear. A model such as the Airguide 120 has a big, easily read dial and a strong, gimbaled mount, and, most importantly, can be adjusted to compensate for the metal in the vehicle, so the needle reads accurately.

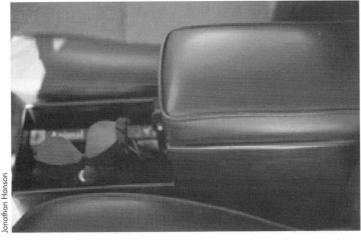

Jonathan Hanson

If your sport utility does not already have a center console or built-in storage bins, you can have them custom made. This steel set was made by a blacksmith in Tucson; the authors then had them powder coated (heat-treated paint) and professionally upholstered.

Security Center Consoles and Lockers

Sport utilities with bucket seats often are equipped with semi-useful plastic center consoles. Much better are custom steel units, built to offer a serious amount of lockable storage space. I drew up a plan and had a blacksmith make one for me; it features one open and one lockable compartment, and has an arm rest on top. The whole project, including a black, powder-coat finish, cost about $150. Ready-made versions are avail-

PURSUITS: SEA KAYAKING, CONTINUED FROM PAGE 139

There are two essential varieties of sea kayak: open-cockpit and closed-cockpit. The former are popular with beginners because they are easy to master; if you fall out you can just climb back on. They're great for warm climates and water since you get wet a lot sitting right out on the deck.

Traditional closed-cockpit sea kayaks take more practice to master but are more suited for serious trips since you are enclosed in the cockpit and have more cargo space. While most traditional sea kayaks are very stable (much more so than their river counterparts), you do need to learn self-righting skills in the event of a capsize.

The best way to learn about sea kayaking is to sign up for an introductory day trip, offered by dozens of shops in seafront communities. If you want to take the plunge, so to speak, many tour companies offer multiday trips requiring no experience. Contact the Trade Association of Sea Kayaks and North American Paddlesports Association, both at (414) 242-5228, for information about outfitters and the industry. Or check out *Complete Sea Kayak Touring* and *The Essential Sea Kayaker* (both Ragged Mountain Press) as well as *Sea Kayaker* Magazine; call (206) 789-1326 if you can't find the magazine

able for many vehicles and can include drink holders and brackets for radios.

I also had a safe welded up from 12-gauge steel, with a reinforced door locked by a stout hasp, sized to take up the considerable space available under the driver's seat of older Land Cruisers. It would be easy to have something comparable made to fit in the rear cargo area of any vehicle. Truckvault (see page 163) makes custom-fitted inserts that line your sport utility's rear cargo area; the eight-inch high drawers are lockable, and the top is carpeted to match your interior.

In a similar vein, our Toyota extracab truck came with clever storage compartments beneath the jump seats. I used some heavy aluminum bar and two big U-bolts to fabricate a locking bar that clamps down over the larger compartment with a padlock. Although not bombproof, it would significantly slow anyone trying to get inside. I intend to replace the fiberboard compartment lid with a sheet of steel—that would significantly enhance the security.

Not security-oriented, but definitely convenient, are plastic storage boxes designed to fit in the wasted space behind the wheel well in the cargo area. These usually incorporate an extension over the wheel well. They're great for camping gear, tools, or spare parts. Cabela's and Performance Products (see page 162) sell a variety of these boxes.

Air Pump

A portable air pump can be a lifesaver if you discover a slow leak 20 miles from the nearest paved road. It's also vital if you air down the tires for extra traction in sand (see Chapter 2, page 17).

Stay away from the $29.95 pumps that claim to put out 200 psi (pounds per square inch). They will put out enough pressure to inflate a tire, but they can take what seems like decades to do it. Look for pumps that list how long they take to inflate a tire—a much more realistic measure of their usefulness.

OVER-THE-TOP CUSTOMIZING

So, you've bolted on everything you could find, and you still think your vehicle blends rather annoyingly into the crowd? What you need is a custom shop. How about a 400-horsepower Chevy Suburban with satellite navigation and a full roll cage—covered in leather. Or a supercharged Ford Explorer, a bullet-proof Toyota Land Cruiser (I mean *really* bulletproof), or any number of other permutations. For a price, usually a very large one, you can get anything you want.

True custom shops can be hard to find. Check hot rod magazines and those devoted to show cars and trucks. Some starters:

Kenny Brown Performance
286 Gasoline Alley
Indianapolis, IN 46222
(317) 247-5320

Canepa Design
1191 Water Street
Santa Cruz, CA 95062

Hennessey Motorsports
18000 Groeschke Road
Hangar C1
Houston, TX 77084

Stillen/Steve Millen Sportparts
3176 Airway Avenue
Costa Mesa, CA 92626
(714) 755-6670

CHAPTER 6

Maintenance & Repairs

BY JONATHAN HANSON

- Tools and Spare Parts
- Basic Maintenance
- Post-Trip Maintenance and Cleaning
- On-the-(Back)Road Troubleshooting and Repairs

From Carburetors to Computers

Today's vehicles are a different species from those of just a generation ago. In those days, anyone with a little skill could learn to do almost anything on a vehicle, from tune-ups to engine rebuilds. A single box full of hand tools and a couple of hand meters sufficed for nearly any operation imaginable.

Now our vehicles are as much computers as mechanicals. The microchips that control our engines and transmissions have given us drastically lower emissions, better fuel economy, and more power all at once—a combination considered impossible 20 years ago.

The only "victim" of this new technology has been the home mechanic. No more hand meters—engines now include connectors to hook directly into the dealer's diagnostic computer, so the two can talk to each other and tell the mecha— . . . er, *technician* what is wrong. No more adjusting or rebuilding carburetors—the fuel injection that replaced the carburetor needs no maintenance and has its own bit-map to compute optimum performance. But the result is a far more reliable vehicle, one less likely to need repairs in the first place.

What does this mean for the owner of a sport utility vehicle at the turn of the century? It means that anyone—*anyone*—can learn the few simple maintenance and repair procedures that are all your vehicle is likely to need for thousands of miles at a time. This chapter will guide you through, first, the things you should do before and during each trip to keep everything in working order, and second, a few easy troubleshooting and repair procedures that might get you back on the road quickly in the unlikely event of some sort of failure.

Tools and Spare Parts

Even if you have no concept of mechanical things, wouldn't dream of looking inside your engine compartment, and are planning to ignore every other word in this chapter, you should carry a basic set of tools in your vehicle. At least then if something breaks and you're stranded somewhere, a chance exists that someone who *does* study this chapter will come along and be able to use your tools to rescue you.

You don't need one of those 1,500-piece mechanic's sets. You should, however, buy good-quality tools. Avoid the discount store tools—the 50-piece socket sets for $9.95 and the like. Buy Craftsman tools from Sears or the premium tools available in most good hardware stores.

The number of spare parts and repair items you should keep in the vehicle depends on its use. At a minimum I would include:

- Fan belt (one for each belt the vehicle has)

A GOOD SET OF TOOLS

- **Socket set.** This should be either metric or standard, depending on your vehicle (check your owner's manual). Buy a ⅜-inch set (this number refers to the diameter of the square male stud on the handle on which the sockets fit) with a ratcheting handle; a longer, nonratcheting handle; two or three extensions; and sockets from around 8mm to 19mm (metric), or ¼-inch to ¾-inch (standard). A broader range—up to 24mm or 1-inch—is even better, but you should be able to handle almost anything with the basic set. Most sets include a spark plug socket; if yours doesn't, buy one.

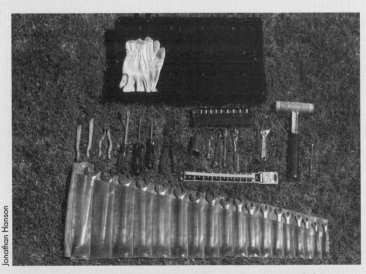

Jonathan Hanson

Your sport utility tool set will include a sturdy box, leather gloves, and (from top row left) Channellock pliers, needle-nosed pliers, standard and Phillip's screwdrivers, wire cutters/crimpers, battery terminal cleaner, socket set with extensions, six-inch crescent wrench, No-Bounce hammer, tire gauge; (bottom row) set of combination wrenches in a roll pouch, 6 to 24mm.

- Roll of radiator hose repair tape
- Fuses
- Quart of engine oil
- Turn signal and brake light bulbs

For a long trip or for extended explorations on backroads, I would add:

- Spark plug (or even a whole set)
- Distributor cap and rotor
- Fuel filter (if applicable to the vehicle—some fuel filters are now incorporated into the fuel pump)
- Can of radiator stop-leak

- **Wrenches.** Combination wrenches are the most versatile, with one open end and one box (closed) end. Get the same range as the socket set, and buy long-handled models, which give you more leverage.
- **Channellock pliers.** One small and one medium, useful for many situations when wrenches just won't work.
- **Screwdrivers.** Buy a set that includes several sizes of both standard and Phillips heads.
- **Six-inch crescent (adjustable) wrench.** I find these little things handy for a multitude of small tasks where I really don't need the whole wrench set.
- **No-bounce hammer.** This is a plastic-headed hammer filled with lead shot, which dampens the blow. It's incredibly versatile for numerous whacking jobs, with little risk of damage to the whacked part.
- **Tire gauge.**
- **Battery terminal cleaner.** This is a little wire brush designed to clean off the battery post and the inside of the cable terminal.
- **Jumper cables.** Get good ones, with clamps that are completely insulated so only the teeth that grip the terminal are exposed.
- **Tool roll or box** *kept in the vehicle.* Never, *ever* use your auto tools to fix the living room lamp or the bathroom faucet. Next thing you know, they'll be lost forever in that drawer in the kitchen. You know which one.

Basic Maintenance

You owe it to your vehicle to make sure it gets proper care. The minimal attention required by a modern automobile will pay you back in several ways—ensuring continued reliability, enhancing the resale value of the vehicle, and maximizing fuel economy while minimizing pollutants.

Such care is especially important to a vehicle that might be used well off the routes frequented by AAA tow trucks. From my experience helping stranded motorists over the years, I would guess that half of all breakdowns could be prevented with proper preventive maintenance.

The best place to start learning basic maintenance is with the owner's manual for the vehicle, which will guide you through procedures such as checking the engine oil and coolant levels. If you want to learn more, buy a more detailed maintenance and repair guide for your make and model. The factory manuals (available through your dealer)

CHECK THESE BEFORE EVERY TRIP OR EVERY 500 MILES

- ✓ Engine oil level
- ✓ Coolant level
- ✓ Power steering fluid level
- ✓ Belts for condition and tightness
- ✓ Brake and clutch fluid levels
- ✓ Tire pressures, including the spare
- ✓ Operation of all lights and turn signals
- ✓ For signs of oil or coolant leakage
- ✓ All bulbs, headlights, and turn signals

These checks can seem like drudgery on a reliable vehicle, but they are the best way to stay on top of potential problems and to familiarize yourself with the basic workings of your vehicle. Once you've become comfortable with checking the oil and so forth, you might try doing some simple maintenance procedures such as changing the oil or coolant or replacing worn belts.

are excellent but very detailed and very expensive. Better for more general information are aftermarket guides such as the Haynes manuals, sold at auto supply stores.

Performing Basic Checks

There's a story—apparently true—about a student in an auto shop class learning to check the oil on his car. He pulled the dipstick out of the engine and turned it upside down to read it. As the oil slowly ran down the stick from the ADD mark toward the FULL line, he said: "This looks a little low—oh, no, wait . . . now it's okay."

I think Auto Shop should be a required course for every high school student. Automobiles

(continued on page 148)

OILS

Nothing will ensure the long-term durability of your engine and running gear like frequent oil and fluid changes. Even if you trade vehicles every two years, receipts for regular oil changes will go a long way toward maximizing your trade-in value.

Change your engine oil, transmission oil or fluid, and differential oil at least as often as recommended by the owner's manual. Use the "heavy service" schedule if there is one.

Oil comes in grades or "weights," which refer to the thickness or viscosity of the oil, denoted by a number such as 30-weight in the case of single-weight oils, or a hyphenated number such as 20-50 for the much more common multi-grade oils. A low number signifies a thin oil; a higher number a heavier oil. In the old days of single-weight oils, we sometimes had to put lower-weight oil in during the winter and switch to higher-weight oil for the hot months. The reason is that oil thickens when it gets cold, so a too-thick oil in winter would take on the consistency of grease. Today, multi-weight oils can function in a wide range of temperatures.

Use the weight range recommended by your manufacturer for the conditions in which you drive. Remember, however, that oil weight is not critical. If you need to add oil in some backwater town, and they've only got 20-50 oil when your manual says to use 10-40, don't worry—it will work fine. Just make sure it's a name-brand oil.

Should you use natural or synthetic oils? There is evidence that synthetic oil can make a small difference in engine and gear protection, especially in very hot or cold climates and with heavy service, such as trailer-pulling. The problem is the cost of synthetics, usually three to four times more than a top-quality natural (petroleum-based) oil.

If you plan to keep your vehicle for several years, I recommend using synthetic fluids in the differentials and gearbox (if you have a manual transmission). Since these fluids need changing only every two years or so, the cost difference is not so painful. As for the engine, if you want the ultimate edge in protection and can afford it, by all means use synthetic oil there, too. However, you'd be better off using a high-quality petroleum-based oil and changing it frequently than using synthetic and procrastinating on changing it because of the expense.

An important point: Most manufacturers (of vehicles as well as oil) don't recommend installing synthetic oil until the vehicle has traveled 10,000 to 12,000 miles. Until that much mileage has accumulated, the running gear is still in the process of breaking in and seating the parts together. Synthetic oil, with its high lubricity, apparently can hinder this process by making everything *too* slick.

Another point: Clean oil does little good if it has to go through a dirty oil filter. Make sure you change the filter with every oil change.

are an intrinsic part of life in this country, and everyone who drives one should be familiar with the basic engineering behind its operation. If nothing else, it would help keep innocent consumers from being defrauded by unscrupulous mechanics who exploit customers' woeful ignorance: "Yeah buddy—you need a new sensing capacitor for your oil thruster manifold."

Herewith are some essential tips on basic vehicle maintenance. I'm going to start at the beginning for those completely new to this—if you're beyond that, skip to the next section (where I discuss replacing your own sensing capacitors).

Checking the Oil

The oil that circulates through your engine is vital to keep hundreds of moving parts sliding freely next to each other, in conditions of extreme heat. The oil is stored in the oil pan at the bottom of the engine. From there, an oil pump pushes it through the oil filter, which strains out dirt and other minute impurities, before circulating it at high pressure through the engine—into the crankshaft, rod, and cam bearings, through the valve gear, and so forth. The oil then returns by gravity to the pan.

If the level of oil in the pan falls too low, the oil pump can't circulate it and the engine will destroy itself within minutes. On the other hand, putting in too much oil is bad as well—it can cause leaks, and if the spinning crankshaft hits the oil in the pan, it will whip it into a foam, drastically reducing its lubricity.

This all sounds very apocalyptic, but keeping the oil at the proper level is simplicity itself. Your owner's manual will give you the location of the dipstick. The engine must be off; if it's been running, let it sit for a couple of minutes to allow all the oil to return to the pan. With a rag or wadded paper towel in one hand, pull out the dipstick and wipe it clean, then push it *all the way* back into its tube. Pull it out again and hold it horizontally over the rag so you can see the graduated markings on the end. There will be an upper mark signifying full, a lower mark indicating the need to add oil, and a space in between the two. The oil should be at or near the full mark. If it's down near the add line, find the oil filler cap (check owner's manual again), and add about a half-quart of the proper oil (see sidebar, page 147). Wait a few minutes for the new oil to run down into the pan, then check the level again. If it's still not where it should be, add a little at a time until the oil reaches the full mark.

Incidentally, the oil in a manual transmission and transfer case should normally not need checking between replacement, unless you notice a puddle forming under the vehicle. Checking the transmission oil level usually means climbing way under the vehicle anyway. Automatic transmissions, on the other hand, normally have a dipstick just like the engine does and should be checked every month. Follow the owner's manual recommendations if the transmission needs topping up.

Checking Coolant

Your engine produces very high temperatures in the cylinders as the fuel is burned. This heat must be dissipated quickly and continuously or the engine will destroy itself. The coolant in the vehicle circulates through passages in the engine block and head, absorbing heat from the cylinder walls and combustion chambers. The hot coolant is circulated through the radiator, which has alternating rows of narrow tubes and air passages. Air is pulled through the radiator by the engine fan at low speeds and pushed through at higher speeds by the simple force of the vehicle's moving through the atmosphere. A water pump, driven by a belt off the crankshaft, moves the coolant and also, on most vehicles, turns the cooling fan—so if you look at the base of your fan, you can find your water pump. However, some vehicles (although not many 4x4s) use an electric fan, which is not driven by the pump.

In an emergency, plain water will work as coolant, but a 50/50 mix of water and antifreeze is the proper solution. Antifreeze serves two apparently opposite functions—it keeps the water in the mixture from freezing, and it raises the boiling temperature. It also helps prevent corrosion and provides lubrication to the water pump. Traditional antifreeze was nasty stuff for the environment, but newer compounds are not quite as toxic—insist on the more benign product when you have your coolant replaced; it's just as effective as the old.

If possible, always use distilled water in your coolant mixture, unless you know your tap water to be extremely soft. Most service centers use tap water, so if you have someone else do the job for you, buy the correct amount of distilled water and ask him or her to use it.

In times past, checking the coolant level in the radiator meant waiting until the engine cooled off, then removing the radiator cap to see how high the level looked. Today, most vehicles have a separate overflow tank made of plastic. Since this tank is not pressurized, it can be checked even when the engine is hot. Read the owner's manual to see where your tank is mounted (you don't want to confuse it with the tank for windshield washer fluid). The manual will tell you how to read the level in the tank.

If the coolant needs topping up while you're on a trip, don't worry about antifreeze or even distilled water—ordinary tap water will work just fine. Only if there appears to be a problem with the cooling system, and you are losing a great deal of fluid, would you need to add antifreeze.

The rubber hoses that connect the radiator to the engine should be a regular part of your maintenance inspection. The hoses should feel fairly soft and pliable when squeezed between thumb and forefinger.

DON'T SLAM THE HOOD!

This is one of my pet peeves. Most owners, most mechanics, most everyone I know closes the hood on a vehicle by dropping it from about a foot high—sometimes two. Aagh! This is not only not necessary, it can damage the hood sheet metal.

The proper way to close the hood is to lower it all the way so the safety catch clicks. Then use both palms to give a short, firm push down until the main latch closes. Only if the hood absolutely will not latch this way should you try the gorilla approach—and then take the vehicle to your mechanic to have the latch adjusted.

Jonathan Hanson

Periodically check your air filter and clean it if necessary.

When they become stiff or brittle, it's a sign they are deteriorating and should be replaced.

Air Filter

The air filter cleans the air ingested by the engine, before it is mixed with the fuel. Without a filter, minute bits of dirt and dust could score the piston walls and erode the valve seats, wearing out the engine within a few thousand miles. A filter does restrict somewhat the amount of air that gets into the engine, so keeping the filter clean is important (racing cars rarely use air filters; since their engines must usually be rebuilt after every race anyway, the wear factor is irrelevant—they need as much air as possible crammed into the intake).

Most stock air filters are disposable units made of pleated paper, designed to be used for 15,000 to 25,000 miles and then thrown away. But the filter should be checked every time the oil is changed and replaced if it is seriously dirty. For normal dirt, most manufacturers say to blow compressed air through the filter, *from the inside out* so as not to force dirt farther into the element (and being cautious not to blow a hole in the paper). You can also tap the filter against a hard surface to dislodge dirt.

Something to consider, especially on a vehicle that sees a lot of dirt roads, is a permanent, cleanable filter such as those made by K&N (see page 162). These have a special element that can be washed out in soapy water, then treated with a special spray oil. K&N claims its filters are superior to any stock filter in effectiveness, are cheaper in the long run, and produce less landfill waste.

Checking the Tires

Proper tire pressure contributes to safe handling, better gas mileage, good ride quality, and optimum load-hauling capability.

I've found that vehicle manufacturers tend to recommend fairly soft tire pressures, probably to enhance ride quality. Going a little higher will increase gas mileage just a smidgen. Look at the recommendations for tire pressure in the owner's manual, then look at the recommended maximum pressure listed on the side of the tire itself. I usually inflate the tire to about 20 percent less than the listed maximum (for example, I put 40 pounds in a tire listed for a maximum of 50), which usually works out to around five pounds higher than what the owner's manual says. If you're carrying extra weight in the cargo area, or the bed of a pickup, add another five pounds in the rear tires.

It's better, but not vital, to check the tire pressure after the tire has warmed up with a few miles of driving, since the air inside expands and raises the pressure just a bit as the tire heats.

Make sure the valve caps are in place on the valve stems; they keep grit from clogging the valve.

Tune-ups

The current rage among manufacturers is to see who can come up with the longest interval between recommended tune-ups. Some are up to 100,000 miles already, and I'll be surprised if someone doesn't soon come up with a spark plug designed to last the life of the engine, eliminating the tune-up altogether!

However, it's important to realize that a lot of this marketing hoopla is . . . marketing hoopla. Sure, it's possible to get an engine to run acceptably for prodigious distances without any

Proper tire pressure contributes to safe handling, better gas mileage, good ride, and optimum load-hauling capability, but it's one of the most-overlooked maintenance duties.

maintenance except oil changes—as long as every environmental variable is well-controlled. In the real world of less-than-perfect fuel, smoggy air (not to mention dusty air if you're traveling backroads) and stop-and-go traffic, such extended service intervals are rarely practical. So pay attention to your vehicle and how it runs. If it feels as if it needs a tune-up, give it a tune-up.

Lubrication

At numerous points around your vehicle are grease fittings or "nipples," one-way valves where a grease gun attaches to lubricate moving parts such as driveshaft spiders and sliding yokes, and ball joints in the steering gear. These points should be lubed at the intervals specified by the owner's manual.

Post-Trip Maintenance and Cleaning

Taking care of the vehicle after a trip is just as important as the preparation beforehand. First, go through the standard maintenance list—oil level, and so on—to determine how the vehicle performed on the road and whether it needs any topping up. Then give it a good cleaning.

A clean vehicle benefits from much, much more than just looking good. Most importantly, grime and mud left on the body and frame trap moisture, which causes rust. Grit that works its way into suspension bushings will accelerate their deterioration. And a film of dirt on the exterior surface abrades the paint every time something brushes against it.

Commercial car washes—especially those that use brushes—are hard on your vehicle's finish. You can do a much better job at home.

First, use a high-powered nozzle on the hose to blast away all the mud and dirt from the undercarriage. Hit every nook and cranny you can see, and those you can't as well.

Concentrate especially on the wheel wells and inside the fenders, where the tires throw up a lot of crud. Blast the wheels themselves, too. Then widen the spray a little and sluice down the body of the vehicle, starting with the roof and working down. The idea is to get off the big pieces before you start scrubbing.

Fill a pail with lukewarm water mixed with a commercial car wash solution. These are designed not to strip wax off the car, as ordinary detergents will. Use a big sponge to *gently* swirl off the bodywork, again starting on the roof and working down. Dip the sponge continuously to keep a constant stream of soapy water carrying away the dirt. Rinse a section at a time so the soap doesn't dry on the paint, and rinse out the sponge frequently to keep it clean. Once you have finished with the painted parts and glass, wash the grille, bumpers, and trim. Finally, use a separate sponge or rag to wash the wheels and other grimy parts near the bottom. If your water is very soft, you can let everything air dry; otherwise use a soft cotton or chamois towel to dry.

A twice-yearly wax job will keep your paint looking new for years. But skip the "easy" liquid waxes—the only ones that work well take some elbow grease. I like the two-step products, which start with a paint cleaner that strips old wax, oxidized paint, and road tar, and finish with a paste carnauba wax. I kept the white paint on my 1973 Land Cruiser looking pristine for 20 years with regular waxing—and this on a vehicle that never saw a carport or garage, but sat out year-round in the southern Arizona sun. People who saw it refused to believe it hadn't been repainted.

Pay attention to the interior as well. Here the best maintenance is prevention. Buy a good set of floor mats, which will prevent mud and dirt from being ground into the carpet. I like the Husky mats, which are thick, molded rubber, shaped to fit the entire footwell and dished so they can trap and contain an amazing amount of sludge. Husky also makes liners for the cargo area.

To help prevent ultraviolet deterioration of the dashboard and other plastic or vinyl surfaces, look for a product called 303 Protectant. 303 keeps the dash looking good, but also forms a partial barrier to harmful wavelengths of light that can dry out and crack the surface.

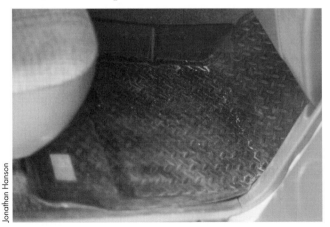

Heavy-duty floor covers, such as these Husky mats, help protect your carpet from mud, rocks, and sand when you're out exploring backroads.

On-the-(Back)Road Troubleshooting and Repairs

An engine needs several essentials to run properly:

- Fuel
- Air
- Electricity (a spark at the spark plugs)

- Coolant
- Oil for lubrication
- Belts to run the auxiliary components such as the alternator

If any one of these is interrupted, the engine will stop running. The corollary to this forms the groundwork for all troubleshooting: If the engine stops running, you can be pretty sure it's because one of the above needs has been interrupted. By using a simple process of deduction, you can usually determine the general cause of the problem. Let's look at a few situations and see how to proceed.

Engine Won't Start

A nonstarting engine will manifest itself in one of two ways: Either the starter will turn over the engine normally, but the engine won't fire, or the engine turns over very slowly or not at all.

HOW AN ENGINE WORKS

A gasoline engine works by burning a mixture of air and fuel to produce power. The air is pulled in through the air cleaner, a minute but carefully calculated quantity of fuel is injected into the air stream, and the mixture enters the cylinders through an intake valve. Inside each cylinder is a piston that moves up and down. On the intake stroke, the piston moves down and sucks in the air-fuel mixture. When the piston reaches the bottom of its stroke and starts to move back up, the intake valve closes and the air-fuel mixture is compressed by the piston (compression stroke). As the piston reaches the top of its travel, the spark plug in the top of the cylinder produces an arc of high-voltage electricity (generated by the coil) that ignites the fuel, and this explosion forces the piston downward (power stroke). The piston is connected to the crankshaft, and the force of the piston's moving downward turns the crankshaft, which turns the driveshaft through the transmission, applying power to the wheels. As the piston reaches the bottom of the power stroke, an exhaust valve opens, and the burned gases are pushed out through the exhaust manifold and exhaust pipe by the upward movement of the piston (exhaust stroke). So the piston makes two complete up and down movements for each power stroke, or four strokes total, which is why this type of gasoline engine is called a four-stroke engine.

The electricity for the coil and spark plugs is produced by the battery, which is kept charged by the alternator, a type of generator that runs off the engine itself by a belt. The battery also supplies power to the starter, a small electric motor that turns over the engine to begin the sequence of compression and power strokes.

If the engine won't turn over, or does so slowly and laboriously, the problem is likely to be the battery. Sometimes in this case you will hear a rapid clicking coming from the engine compartment. This is the starter solenoid engaging; it means there is enough voltage to work the solenoid, but not the starter itself. The quickest way to confirm a battery problem is to turn on the headlights. If they won't come on or they shine feebly, the battery is not producing enough electricity (if you find the headlights *already* on, of course, you've uncovered the problem—you left the lights on and ran down the battery!). If the headlights work, but the motor won't turn over, check the fuse for the starting circuit.

If the battery appears to be the culprit, it might be discharged, or the cable terminals might simply be dirty, preventing voltage from leaving the battery. With a small wrench you can loosen the nut that holds on each terminal, pull it off, and use your terminal brush to scrub both the terminal and the inside of the cable connection until everything is shiny. Caution: Don't put the cables back on the wrong terminals! If the vehicle starts, congratulations! If it still won't, the battery is discharged and you need a jump.

If you suspect that an external cause—such as leaving those headlights on—caused your dead battery, you can probably drive the vehicle for several miles to let the alternator recharge the battery, and everything will be fine. If there was no such obvious fault, however, or if the

PROPER JUMP-STARTING

Position the vehicle that will do the jumping as close as possible to the disabled vehicle. Turn off its engine. Locate with certainty the positive (+) and negative (−) posts on both batteries. Connect one red clamp on the jumper cables to the positive terminal of the healthy battery, and the other red end to the positive terminal of the dead battery. Then connect the black clamp to the negative terminal on the healthy battery.

You can clamp the other black clamp directly to the negative terminal of the dead battery. However, this final connection sometimes creates a spark which, on very rare occasions, can be dangerous—batteries produce hydrogen gas, which the spark can ignite. It's better to make the final connection to another ground point on the disabled vehicle. This can be the other end of the negative cable leading from the dead battery, if it is accessible, or nearly any piece of bare metal connected directly to the body or engine of the vehicle—a bolt head, bracket, or something similar.

Once the connections are in place, start the engine of the healthy vehicle and let it run for a couple of minutes, then try the starter of the dead vehicle. If it still won't turn over, let the other engine run for several more minutes to build up a charge. You can turn on the headlights of the disabled vehicle to make sure a charge is getting through. If the lights still won't work either, try moving the ground clamp to a different spot.

problem recurs the next time you turn off the engine, you should go directly to your mechanic to have the charging system checked.

If the engine turns over normally but won't fire, the odds are it is not getting one of two things: fuel or a spark. First check your fuel gauge to ensure there is fuel in the tank. Don't laugh—it happens all the time. If you've just driven through water, the problem could be a wet distributor or other contacts. If the engine is warm, just letting it sit for a few minutes will usually dry things out enough. Otherwise, you can open the hood and use a rag to dry off the distributor cap, or even pull off the cap and carefully dry the inside. Some newer engines don't have a distributor; the spark distribution is handled entirely by computer. Fortunately, this type of system is extremely hard to short out.

Another possibility is a loose coil wire. The coil wire carries the high-voltage charge from the coil to the center of the distributor cap, from where it is "distributed" to the spark plugs. Check to ensure both ends of the coil wire are firmly in place.

Engine Misses

If your engine is well-tuned and has been running properly but suddenly starts to miss— that is, one or more cylinders fails to fire, creating a ragged sound and feel—a couple of things are worth checking. First is if you've been through some water, which might be shorting out the ignition system. In this case just waiting a few minutes will normally set things right.

The second thing to do is check the spark plug wires by pushing on each one where it

If your engine turns over normally but won't "catch" or fire, it's probably a fuel or spark problem. If you're driven through water, it might be a wet distributor or contacts; dry them off. Also check the coil contacts.

joins the spark plug at the engine and where it connects to the distributor. This might be difficult or impossible while the engine is hot.

A slightly more advanced approach to finding the cause of the miss involves letting the engine idle while pulling the spark plug wires off each spark plug in sequence. At idle a steadily missing engine will stutter once with each revolution of the engine, as the affected cylinder fails to fire. When you pull off a spark plug wire from a cylinder that isn't missing, the engine will immediately sound even rougher. Push the wire back in place and go to the next one. When you reach the cylinder that is missing, there will be no change in the engine noise when you pull off the wire. Inspect the wire itself to make sure it isn't visibly damaged (although the wire inside can break with no external sign). Then, if you have a spark plug

TIMING BELTS

Many modern overhead-cam engines use a belt to turn the camshafts inside the engine. A belt is quieter than the metal chains that used to be standard, but it is susceptible to breakage. Consult your owner's manual or ask your dealer to find out if your engine has a timing belt. If so, pay close attention to the recommended replacement interval—usually about 60,000 miles. If you're planning a long trip and you've got more than 50,000 miles on the vehicle, consider having the belt replaced early.

If a timing belt breaks, the engine will stop running instantly. On some engines no further harm is done, but on others a broken belt will cause the valves to hit the tops of the pistons, resulting in a very expensive repair. So don't try to push it and get "another couple thousand miles" if the book says do it now.

wrench and a spare spark plug, try replacing the spark plug. If neither of these tricks works, your only option is probably to limp home with the miss.

Fan and Alternator Belts

On the front of your engine are one or more belts that are driven by the big crankshaft pulley at the bottom of the engine and that in turn drive vital accessories such as the alternator, water pump, and fan, as well as optional components such as the power steering pump and air conditioner compressor.

Belts are subject to a lot of heat and stress and should be considered a regular maintenance item. Check them before each long trip. Look on the inside of the belt for any signs of cracking or fraying; replace the belt if in doubt—it's cheap insurance. Belts should last two to three years.

If a fan or alternator belt breaks while you are underway, you will most likely hear a clatter as the fan chews up the belt and then spits it out on the road. If the alternator belt has broken, a dashboard warning light will probably come on to alert you. You must stop immediately and replace it, since the engine is now running off the battery and will discharge it quickly.

Each belt has some device to facilitate adjusting tension and removal. This can be a slotted bracket for the alternator, for example, or a separate "idler pulley," so called because it serves no function other than tension adjustment. In any case, if a belt has broken you'll need to locate the tension adjuster for it and back it all the way off to get the new belt on. Then tighten the tensioner until the belt is snug—you can determine proper tension by pressing on the belt between two pulleys. A firm push should depress the belt only a half-inch or so. Sometimes you will have to remove another belt or even two to replace the one that broke all the way in back—one of those laws of nature.

Coolant Leaks

Coolant leaks generally take the form of split hoses, since these are the soft parts of the cooling system. You can temporarily repair a split hose with radiator tape, which is designed to be waterproof. When you notice steam coming from under the hood, stop, turn off the engine, and locate the source of the leak. Wait for things to cool down, wrap the hose with the tape, and top up the coolant reservoir. Drive the vehicle for a few miles, then check again to make sure the tape is holding, and to see if any more coolant needs to be added.

Occasionally the radiator can spring a leak. Usually this will be a pinhole caused by a rock or internal corrosion. A can of radiator repair compound dumped directly into the radiator will often stop it effectively. If you don't have any, a handful of oatmeal will sometimes do the trick—the grain migrates naturally to the hole and swells to fill it. Make sure you have the leak repaired and the system flushed as soon as possible.

Fuses

A blown fuse can be the cause of numerous failures, from a dead engine to a dead radio. If the vehicle suffers any sort of electrical failure, the first thing to rule out is the fuse dedicated to the circuit that has failed. Your owner's manual will tell you the location of the fuse box or boxes and will also have a diagram listing what each fuse controls, or a diagram will be printed right on the fuse box. Make sure you carry spare fuses in each amp range needed for your vehicle and always replace a blown fuse with one of the same rating.

Jonathan Hanson

To check your fan belts for proper tension, press on each belt between its pulleys (with the engine off!); a firm push should depress the belt only a half-inch or so.

Flats

Like most other parts of our vehicles, tires have become more reliable over the years. In fact, some car makers are doing away with spare tires altogether in some of their models, relying instead on tires designed to be driven on safely even after a puncture has let all the air out. Four-wheel-drive vehicles, however, are more susceptible to flats than are road cars, given the rough and debris-prone nature of most backroads.

Many people give no forethought to the possibility of a flat, assuming they'll be able to figure out the procedure when and if it's needed or that they'll just pick up the cell phone and call for assistance. If you're headed out of AAA reach, however, you'd do well to make sure in advance that you can successfully jack up the vehicle and install the spare without outside help.

The first thing to do is locate the jack that came with your vehicle and try it out in the driveway. This accomplishes two things: It confirms that all the parts to the jack are present and working, and it tells you whether the jack is worth a darn—many standard jacks aren't. If you can't easily raise the vehicle on a level, paved surface, it will be next to impossible to do so in mud, sand, or rocks. Even if the jack works well, you should strongly consider buying a Hi-Lift jack (see Chapter 5, page 131). The Hi-Lift is stronger and more versatile than any standard unit, and makes it easier for someone of marginal strength to raise a heavy vehicle. Whatever jack you use, you should have a big base plate for backroad use (see Chapter 2, page 32).

Once you've got a good working jack, you'll need a working wheel nut wrench (also called a lug wrench). Try the wrench that came with the vehicle (usually a single bar bent at an angle) and see how easy it is to loosen a nut on one wheel. If it's difficult or impossible, buy a heavy-duty T-shaped wrench or, even better, an 18- or 20-inch-long socket handle (called a breaker bar), with a short extension and a socket that fits your lug nuts (buy a spare socket, too). One common problem with lug nuts occurs when a tire mechanic tightens them so tight using an air wrench that even with a good hand wrench they can be nearly impossible to remove. If you can't loosen the nuts with a T-wrench or a breaker bar, take the vehicle to your tire store and ask that the lug nuts be loosened and then hand-tightened to the proper torque setting.

Spare tire mounts vary tremendously in convenience. Spares that mount in the cargo area inside the vehicle are the cheapest for the manufacturer. A salesman for a $40,000-plus sport utility I once drove told me, "It keeps the spare clean." I laughed, and asked him what happens when you have to take off the filthy, mud-caked flat and heave it into your nice clean cargo area after removing the nice clean spare. He clearly hadn't thought of that.

I like swing-away racks that mount the spare above the rear bumper so it doesn't take up luggage space. The problem with these, as well as the inside mount, is that you have to lift the flat tire several feet off the ground to switch places with the spare. This can be difficult or impossible for some people.

Mounts that position the tire under the vehicle, behind the rear bumper, might not seem very convenient, but they eliminate the need to lift the tire more than the few inches necessary to get it in place on the axle. You use a crank or lever to lower the tire to the ground; then you can slide it out and roll it to the right corner.

All under-the-vehicle mounts are not equal. I once helped someone in a Ford truck who couldn't make heads or tails of the owner's manual instructions. I got the tire off, but the procedure involved using the jack handle first as a wrench and then as a big lever to slowly pry the tire to the ground. In contrast, on our Toyota you just insert the crank in a slot under the bumper and turn; the tire lowers effortlessly (the same Ford, by the way, had the factory-supplied jack mounted *inside the engine compartment*, where it was too hot to touch for 20 minutes after stopping).

So—you're driving along innocently, enjoying the scenery on a remote trail, and you hear that unmistakable sound of a tire losing air, followed by the floppy feel at one corner of the vehicle. Here's how to handle the situation with minimum fuss.

HELP YOURSELF

Roseann recalls:

When I was 16 my mother and I drove from Arizona to Texas to visit her parents, just the two of us. On the way back, in the middle of a freezing rain-about-to-turn-to-snow storm in the middle of absolutely nowhere west Texas, we got a flat tire on the freeway. We switched on the flashers and opened the hood. We waited ten minutes. No one stopped to help. Twenty minutes. Heck (that's not actually what we said, but you get the picture). So we put on all our warm clothes, emptied the hatchback (the spare was under the rear deck), dug out the jack, fumbled with the instructions, got frustrated because not only did everything seem so hard to figure out, but our fingers were numb and nearly useless. Then I saw a highway patrol car approaching. Good—now we won't have to figure this out, I thought. But he shot past, not even slowing down. Heck (that's not actually what we said). Well, my mom said, her old Texas drawl coming back, let's just git this thang dun! We did finally get the car jacked up, between the two of us got the lugs off, heaved the tire in the back and got the new one on. Meantime dozens of cars passed us. We headed for the nearest town so we could get the lugs properly tightened, and there was the cop, sitting warm and cozy in a fast-food joint sipping coffee. I vowed right then and there never, ever to rely on anyone to help me. I would always be prepared.

In the years since, I have been lucky—I've had to deal with flats only twice on my own in the backcountry. Given the amount of time I spend traveling backroads alone, this is remarkable. I always keep a breaker bar handy, and I make sure I can easily manage my vehicle's spare by myself (my current truck has an easy-to-use under-vehicle mount). In a pinch, if you forget a breaker bar, try standing on the end of the too-short lug wrench to get it to move (be careful not to strip the lugs—don't jump forcefully, just gently apply weight).

My latest flat happened fairly recently, miles from nowhere on the top of a southern Arizona mountain. I had things under control when a nice elderly man appeared off a trail and offered to help. I let him (can't be rude), but I started getting worried when he appeared to know more about chivalry than flat changing. When he started tightening the lugs in the wrong order (around the clock rather than opposites), I had to sweetly step in and take over. I thanked him profusely and assured him I'd be fine as he walked away, shaking his head slightly, probably muttering, "Girls these days!" Yes—thank goodness, I can take care of myself!

A T-shaped wheel nut wrench is an excellent tool for your tire-changing kit.

Jonathan Hanson

First, find the nearest level spot on which to park. It won't hurt the tire to drive a few yards at a walking pace. Apply the parking brake and put the transmission in park (automatic) or reverse (manual). Find something to block the tires at the opposite end of the vehicle from the flat. Rocks are great, so are logs, but use something. Block the tires on both sides of the vehicle, and block both the front and back of the tires.

Remove the spare tire from its mount—it's safer to do this before you jack up the vehicle. With your wheel nut wrench, break loose the wheel nuts on the flat tire until they *just* turn readily. It's much easier to do this with the weight of the vehicle keeping the wheel from turning. Loosen the nuts in a star pattern, moving from one nut to the opposite one rather than going around in a circle. Then position your jack and its base plate. If you're using the stock jack, follow the instructions as to where to place it; if you've got a Hi-Lift jack, you'll be using the bumper. Raise the vehicle and remove the lug nuts and wheel. If you find you can't lift the spare into place, try lowering the jack until the wheel will just slide over the studs while still on the ground, then raise it again to ensure the wheel gets seated properly. Tighten the lug nuts, again using a star pattern, until the whole wheel turns with the wrench. Then lower the jack a bit to put more weight on the tire, and repeat the procedure. Finally, lower the vehicle fully to the ground and finish tightening the nuts. It's difficult to tighten them too much by hand, so crank as hard as you can.

TIPS FOR TIRE CHANGING

- Use a good jack with a base plate, and buy a good lug wrench.
- Park the vehicle as level as possible.
- Block the tires, set the parking brake, and leave the transmission in park (automatic) or reverse (manual).
- Remove the spare before jacking up the vehicle.
- Loosen the lug nuts slightly before raising the vehicle.
- Loosen and tighten the nuts in a star pattern.

Glossary

approach angle—The angle between the front tire and the bottom of the front bumper or valance, indicating the steepest angle the vehicle can climb without dragging the bodywork.

axle, live—An axle that connects both wheels by a rigid tube, with the differential at or near the center.

brakes, antilock—A brake system that prevents the wheels from locking if the brake pedal is pushed too hard.

deep-cycle battery—A battery designed to be repeatedly discharged and recharged; applications include winches, refrigerators, lights for campers.

differential—A gear cluster that splits power from the driveshaft to each wheel, while allowing each wheel to turn at different speeds through turns.

driveshaft—A tubular shaft that transfers power from the transmission or transfer case to the differential.

gas shock—A shock absorber that uses nitrogen gas to keep the damping oil at the proper working viscosity.

hubs; locking hubs—Devices that connect each front wheel to its axle. Locking hubs permit the driver to disconnect the front wheels from the axles so they roll freely, saving gas and wear on the drivetrain.

isolator—A device that allows the vehicle's alternator to charge two batteries at once, but it will not allow either battery to discharge the other.

low range—A set of gears in the transfer case that lowers the overall gearing of the transmission.

shift-on-the-fly—A four-wheel-drive system that allows the driver to shift into four wheel drive while the vehicle is moving.

torque—The twisting force applied by the engine; low-speed power useful in backroad or towing situations.

traction control—A computer-controlled system that senses tire slippage and reduces power to the affected tire.

transfer case—An auxiliary transmission to reduce the gearing of the main transmission, allowing the vehicle to operate at very low speeds on trails.

transmission—A manually or automatically controlled set of gears that allows the vehicle to operate at different speeds.

APPENDIX II

Resources

Equipment Suppliers

Vehicle Accessories

ARB (USA: Air Locker, Inc.)
564 Valley Street
Seattle, WA 98109
(206) 284-5906

B.F. Goodrich Tires
PO Box 19026
Greenville, SC 29602
(800) 521-9796

Bilstein
Western Sales
8845 Rehco Road
San Diego, CA 92121
(800) 537-1085

Eastern Sales
P.O. Box 320
Wallingford , CT 06492
(800) 745-4636
www.bilstein.com

Bloomfield Manufacturing
Company
(Hi-Lift jacks)
P.O. Box 228
46 W. Spring Street
Bloomfield, IN 47424
(800) 233-2051
(812) 384-4441
www.hi-lift.com

Borla Performance Industries
5901 Edison Drive
Oxnard, CA 93033
(805) 986-8600
www.borla.com

Cabela's
One Cabela Drive
Sidney, NE 69160
(800) 237-4444
www.cabelas.com

Camping World
Three Springs Road
Bowling Green, KY 42102
(800) 626-5944
www.campingworld.com

Con-Ferr Mfg.
123 S. Front Street
Burbank, CA 91502
(818) 848-2230
www.con-ferr.com

Hella
P.O. Box 2665
Peachtree City, GA 30269
(800) 247-5924

Hi-Lift (see Bloomfield
Manufacturing Company)

JAOS 4WD and S.U.V. Equipment
Manufacturing
525 S. San Gabriel Blvd.
San Gabriel, CA 91776
(626) 309-1009

Jacobs Electronics
500 N. Baird Street
Midland, TX 79701
(915) 685-3345
www.jacobselectronics.com

K&N Engineering
P.O. Box 1329
Riverside, CA 92502
(800) 858-3333
www.knfilters.com

KC HiLites
Avenida de Luces
Williams, AZ 85046
(800) 528-0950
www.kchilites.com

Overlander Outfitters
5592 Buckingham Way
Huntington Beach, CA 92649
(800) 288-4068
www.overlander.com

Mickey Thompson Performance
Tires
P.O. Box 227
Cuyahoga Falls, OH 44222
(216) 928-9092

Optima
17500 E. 22nd Avenue
Aurora, CO 80111
(303) 340-7440

Performance Products
(catalogs for Toyota,
Chevy/GMC, Ford)
7658 Haskell Avenue
Van Nuys, CA 91406
(800) 553-2840
www.performanceproducts.com

PIAA Corporation
15370 SW Millikan Way
Beaverton, OR 97006
(800) 525-7422

Pirelli Armstrong Tire Corp.
500 Sargent Drive.
P.O. Box 2001
New Haven, CT 06536
(800) 243-5105
www.pirelli.com

Ramsey Winch Company
1600 N. Garnett
Tulsa, OK 74116
(918) 438-2760
www.ramsey.com

Rancho Suspension USA
6925 Atlantic Avenue
Long Beach, CA 90805
(213) 630-0700

The RoadStore
3000 Northfield Place,
   Suite 1000
Roswell, GA 30076
(800) 771-7999
www.roadstore.com

TJM Bull Bars/Hella
P.O. Box 2665
Peachtree City, GA 30269
(800) 247-5924

Truckvault (Armadillo)
211 Township Street
Sedro-Woolley, , WA 98284
(800) 967-8107,
(360) 855-0464
www.truckvault.com

Warn Industries
12900 S.E. Capps Road
Clackamas, OR 97015
(503) 786-4462
www.warn.com

WeatherTech Cargo Liners/
   MacNeil Automotive
2435 Wisconsin Street
Downers Grove, IL 60515
(800) 441-6287
www.macneilauto.com

Roof Racks

Overlander Outfitters
5592 Buckingham Way
Huntington Beach, CA 92649
(800) 288-4068

Packasport
2121 Franklin Blvd.
Eugene, OR 97403
(800) 359-9870
www.packasport.com

Rail-N-Rack
400 Oakwood Road
Lake Zurich, IL 60047
(800) 243-9592
www.seaportmachine.com/
   made.htm

Sports Rack Vehicle Outfitters
   (many brands sold)
2401 Arden Way
Sacramento, CA 95825
(800) 722-5872
www.sportsrack.com

Thule (pronounced "TWO-lee")
42 Silvermine Road
Seymour, CT 06483
(800) 238-2388
www.thuleracks.com

Yakima Products
P.O. Box 4899
Arcata, CA 95521
(800) 348-9231
www.yakima.com

Trailers

Trailer Lite Corporation/
   TL Engineering
919 Tupelo Wood Court
Thousand Lakes, CA 91320
(800) 854-8366

USA VenturCraft
P.O. Box 1039
Abilene, TX 79604
(800) 472-2901
www.VenturCraft.com

Camping

Byer of Maine
P.O. Box 100
Orono, ME 04473
(800) 338-0580
www.byerofmaine.com

Cabela's
One Cabela Drive
Sidney, NE 69160
(800) 237-4444
www.cabelas.com

Camping World
Three Springs Road
Bowling Green, KY 42102
(800) 626-5944
www.campingworld.com

Campmor
P.O. Box 700-C
Saddle River, NJ 07458
(800) 226-7667
www.campmor.com

Camp Trails/Johnson
   Worldwide Associates
1326 Willow Road
Sturtevant, WI 53177
(800) 572-8822
www.jwa.com

Coleman
3600 N. Hydraulic
Wichita, KS 67219
(800) 835-3278

Duluth Pack/Duluth Tent and
   Awning
P.O. Box 16024
Duluth, MN 55816
(800) 777-4439

Eureka/Johnson Worldwide
   Associates
1326 Willow Road
Sturtevant, WI 53177
(800) 572-8822
www.jwa.com

High Gear/Top Bunk
1250 E. Nashville Church Road
Ashland, MO 65010
(800) 575-2865
members.aol.com/HGsTopBunk

Kelty/American Recreation
6235 Lookout Road
Boulder, CO 80301
(800) 535-3589
www.kelty.com

L.L. Bean
Freeport, ME 04033
(800) 221-4221
www.llbean.com

Lafuma America
16745 Saticoy, #112
Van Nuys, CA 91406
(800) 514-4807
www.lafuma.fr

Marmot
2321 Circadian Way
Santa Rosa, CA 95407
(707) 544-544-4590
www.marmot.com

Moss Tents
P.O. Box 577
Camden, ME 04843
(800) 859-5322
www.mosstents.com

Nalgene/Nalge International
75 Panorama Creek Drive
Rochester, NY 14602
(800) 446-2543
www.nalgene.com

No Rinse Shampoo
  (N/R Laboratories)
900 E. Franklin Street
Centerville, OH 45459
(800) 223-9348

R & M Specialty Products
P.O. Box 1683
Windsor, CA 95492
(707) 838-3869

REI
1700 45th Street East
Sumner, WA 98390
(800) 426-4840
www.rei.com

Sierra Designs
1255 Powell Street
Emeryville, CA 94609
(800) 635-0461

Thermarest/Cascade Designs
4000 1st Ave. S.
Seattle, WA 98134
(800) 527-1527
www.cascadedesigns.com

Gauges and Electronics

Garmin International
9875 Widmer Road
Lenexa, KS 66215
(800) 800-1020
www.garmin.com

Magellan Systems
960 Overland Court
San Dimas, CA 91773
(909) 394-5000
(800) 707-7841
www.magellangps.com

Standard Communication
P.O. Box 92151
Los Angeles, CA 90009
(310) 532-5300

Trimble Navigation
645 N. Mary Avenue
P.O. Box 3642
Sunnyvale, CA 94088
(800) 767-4822
www.trimble.com

Maps & Atlases

U.S. Forest Service
See Land Agencies, below.

U.S. Geological Survey
12201 Sunrise Valley Drive
Reston, VA 20192
(800) USA-MAPS
www.usgs.gov

DeLorme Mapping
P.O. Box 298
Yarmouth, Me 04096
(800) 452-5931
www.delorme.com

Magazines

Automobile Magazine's
*Field Guide to Sport-Utility
  Vehicles, Pickups, & Vans*
120 E. Liberty Street
Ann Arbor, MI 48104
(313) 994-3500
www.automobilemag.com

Four Wheeler
3330 Ocean Park Blvd.
Santa Monica, CA 90405
(800) 311-4458
www.fourwheeler.com

Petersen's 4-Wheel & Off Road
6420 Wilshire Blvd.
Los Angeles, CA 90048
(800) 800-4294

Open Road
The 4WD Adventure Magazine
  from Road & Track
1499 Monrovia Ave.
Newport Beach, CA 92663

Chevy Outdoors
Circulation Department
30400 Van Kyke Ave.
Warren, MI 48093-2316

Land Rover Owner International
c/o Mercury Airfreight
  International Ltd.
2323 Randolph Avenue
Avenal, NJ 07001
web.idirect.com/~lroshop/
  lromag.htm

General Interest Books on the Outdoors

*See Chapter 3 for more listings of
  camping and backroad-related
  books.*

*Backwoods Ethics: Environmental
Issues for Hikers and Campers* and
*Wilderness Ethics: Preserving the
Spirit of Wildness,* by Laura and
Guy Waterman (Woodstock, VT:
Countryman Press, 1993).

*EcoLinking: Everyone's Guide to
Online Environmental Informa-
tion,* by Don Rittner (Berkeley,
CA: 1992).

*The Essential Outdoor Gear Man-
ual,* by Annie Getchell (Camden,
ME: Ragged Mountain Press,
1995).

Essential Sea Kayak Touring, by
Jonathan Hanson (Camden, ME:
Ragged Mountain Press, 1998).

*How to Shit in the Woods: An Envi-
ronmentally Sound Approach to a
Lost Art* by Kathleen Meyer
(Berkeley, CA: Ten Speed Press,
1989).

*Medicine for the Outdoors:
A Guide to Emergency Medical
Procedures and First Aid,* by Paul
S. Auerbach, M.D. (Boston:
Little, Brown, 1991).

*Ragged Mountain Guide to
Outdoor Sports*, by Jonathan and
Roseann Hanson (Camden, ME:
Ragged Mountain Press, 1997).

Simple Tent Camping, by Zora and
David Aiken (Camden, ME:
Ragged Mountain Press, 1996).

*Soft Paths: How to Enjoy the
Wilderness Without Harming It,*
by Bruce Hampton and David
Cole (Mechanicsburg, PA: Stack-
pole Books, 1995*).*

*This Land is Your Land: A Guide
to North America's Endangered
Ecosystems,* by Jon Naar and Alex
J. Naar (New York: Harper
Perennial, 1993).

*The Ultimate Adventure Source-
book: The Complete Resource for
Adventure Sports and Travel,* by
Paul McMenamin, et al. (Atlanta:
Turner Publishing, 1992).

Adventurous Traveler Bookstore
(800) 282-3963
books@atbook.com
www.AdventurousTraveler.com

Land Agencies
Bureau of Land Management (BLM)

For a listing of state offices of the Backcountry Byways program, see Chapter 3, page 43.

Alaska State Office

222 W. 7th Avenue, #13
Anchorage, Alaska 99513-7599
(907) 271-5960

Arizona State Office

222 North Central Avenue
Phoenix, AZ 85004-2203
(602) 417-9200

California State Office

2135 Butano Drive
Sacramento, CA 95825
(916) 978-4400

Colorado State Office

2850 Youngfield Street
Lakewood, Co. 80215-7093
(303) 239-3600

Idaho State Office

1387 South Vinnell Way
Boise, Idaho, 83709
(208) 373-4020

Montana and the Dakotas

Montana State Office
222 North 32nd Street
P.O. Box 36800
Billings, Montana 59107-6800
(406) 255-2885
mtinfo@mt.blm.gov

Nevada State Office

850 Harvard Way
P.O. Box 12000
Reno, NV 89520

Eastern States

7450 Boston Boulevard
Springfield, VA 22153
(703) 440-1600

Southern States (Alabama, Arkansas, Florida, Georgia, Kentucky, Louisiana, Mississippi, North Carolina, South Carolina, Tennessee, Virginia)

Jackson Field Office
411 Briarwood Drive, Suite 404
Jackson, MS 39206
(601) 977-5400

Midwest and Northeast (Connecticut, Delaware, Illinois, Indiana, Iowa, Maine, Maryland, Massachusetts, Michigan, Minnesota, Missouri, New Hampshire, New Jersey, New York, Ohio, Pennsylvania, Rhode Island, Vermont, West Virginia, Wisconsin)

Milwaukee Field Office
310 West Wisconsin Avenue,
Suite 450
Milwaukee, WI 53203
(414) 297-4400

U.S. Forest Service

National Headquarters

U. S. Department of Agriculture
Auditors Building
201 14th Street, S.W.
Washington, DC 20250
(202) 205-1760

Region 1, Northern Region

(Montana, northern Idaho, North Dakota, northwestern South Dakota)

Federal Building
P.O. Box 7669
Missoula, MT 59807
(406) 329-3511

Region 2, Rocky Mountain Region

(Colorado, Kansas, Nebraska, South Dakota, eastern Wyoming)

P.O. Box 25127
Lakewood, CO 80225
740 Simms Street
Golden, CO 80401
(303) 275-5450

Region 3, Southwestern Region

(Arizona, New Mexico)

Federal Building
517 Gold Avenue, SW
Albuquerque, NM 87102
(505) 842-3300

Region 4, Intermountain Region

(southern Idaho, Nevada, Utah, western Wyoming)

Federal Building
324 25th Street
Ogden, UT 84401
(801) 625-5605

Region 5, Pacific Southwest Region

(California, Hawaii, Guam, Trust Territories of the Pacific Islands)

630 Sansome Street
San Francisco, CA 94111
(415) 705-2870

Region 6, Pacific Northwest Region

(Washington, Oregon)

333 SW 1st Avenue
P.O. Box 3623
Portland, OR 97208
(503) 803-2200

Region 8, Southern Region (Alabama, Arkansas, Florida, Georgia, Kentucky, Louisiana, Mississippi, North Carolina, Oklahoma, Puerto Rico, South Carolina, Tennessee, Texas, Virgin Islands, Virginia)

1720 Peachtree Road NW
Atlanta, GA 30367
(404) 347-4178

Region 9, Eastern Region (Illinois, Indiana, Iowa, Maine, Maryland, Massachusetts, Michigan, Minnesota, Missouri, New Hampshire, New Jersey, New York, Ohio, Pennsylvania, Rhode Island, Vermont, West Virginia, Wisconsin)

310 W. Wisconsin Avenue, Rm 500
Milwaukee, WI 53203
(414) 297-3600

Region 10, Alaska Region

Federal Office Building
709 W. 9th Street
P.O. Box 21628
Juneau, AK 99802-1628
(907) 586-8863

Forest Service Website

www.fs.fed.us

U.S. Fish and Wildlife Service

Region 1, Pacific (Oregon, Washington, Idaho, Nevada, California, Hawaii and the Pacific Islands)

911 N.E. 11th Avenue
Portland, OR 97232
(503) 231-6828

Region 2, Southwest (Arizona, New Mexico, Oklahoma and Texas)

P.O. Box 1306
Albuquerque, NM 87103
(505) 248-6282

Region 3, Great Lakes-Big Rivers

(Illinois, Indiana, Iowa, Michigan, Minnesota, Missouri, Ohio, and Wisconsin)

1 Federal Drive
Fort Snelling, MN 55111
(612) 713-5400

Region 4, Southeast (Alabama, Georgia, Kentucky, Mississippi, North Carolina, South Carolina and Tennessee)

1875 Century Blvd.
Atlanta, GA 30345
(404) 679-7289

Region 5, Northeast (Connecticut, Delaware, Maine, Maryland, Massachusetts, New Hampshire, New Jersey, New York, Pennsylvania, Rhode Island, Vermont, Virginia, and West Virginia)

300 Westgate Center Drive
Hadley, MA 01035-9589
(413) 253-8200

Region 6, Mountain-Prairie

(Colorado, Kansas, Montana, North Dakota, Nebraska, South Dakota, Utah, and Wyoming)

134 Union Blvd.
Lakewood, CO 80228
(303) 236-5322

Region 7, Alaska

1011 E. Tudor Rd., Rm. 229
Anchorage, AK 99503
(907) 271-2737 (Alaska Public Lands Center)

USFWS Website

www.fws.gov

Driving Schools

Following are some geographically diverse off-pavement driving schools. Also contact the United FourWheel Drive Association for its club-sponsored series of schools around the country (see page 167 for the contact information).

The Adventure Company
8855 Appian Way
Los Angeles, CA 90046
(213) 848-8685
www.concentric.net/~Adventur/
This company offers on-the-road training with its fleet of four-wheel-drives, including Mercedes, Land Cruisers, Jeeps, and an old Willys. Trip destinations include Death Valley, the Rubicon, and a 21-day Baja expedition.

Bill Burke's Four Wheeling America
2134 S. Humboldt Street
Denver, CO 80210-4619
(303) 778-9144
www.bb4wa.com
Bill Burke, a 1991 Camel Trophy driver, is a veteran off-pavement driver. His school offers a variety of custom and regular classes, as well as guided trips.

Bridgestone Winter Driving School
P.O. Box 774167
Steamboat Springs, CO 80477
(970) 879-6104
www.winterdrive.com
From December to early March, the Bridgestone school teaches all the skills you will need for winter driving (its track includes a huge artificially created ice lake). Training vehicles are included in the courses.

California Association of 4WD Clubs
3104 O Street, #313
Sacramento, CA 95816
(800) 4x4-FUNN
www.cal4wheel.com
Cal-4's Four-Wheel Drive Safety Course teaches beginners the basic skills they need to become good off-pavement drivers, with an emphasis on sound judgment. Courses are held near Sacramento, Hollister, and Gorman.

Camp Jeep
(800) 789-5337
www.jeepunpaved.com

Jeep Jamboree
Jeep Jamboree USA
P.O. Box 1601
Georgetown, CA 95634
(530) 333-4777
www.4x4now.com/jjgen.htm
This annual August mega-camp (more than 1,000 Jeep enthusiasts bring their own vehicles to Camp Hale, Colorado) includes Jeep 101 for beginners, as well as trail drives, lifestyle events, and entertainment.

Ecological 4-Wheeling Adventures
2234 Catherine Place
Costa Mesa, CA 92627
(949) 645-7733
www.4x4now.com/sfdc.htm
Harry Lewellyn, aka "Silver Coyote," runs introductory through advanced courses in the desert Southwest, and longer trips into Baja. Ecological 4-Wheeling also publishes a newsletter, and offers evening talks throughout southern California.

Independent Trail
241 Oak Hill Drive
Concord, NH 03301-8601
(800) 750-7460
Independent Trail offers beginner through advanced courses near Chicago and Lake Geneva, Wisconsin, and in the future, Atlanta. Courses are run from May to October.

Land Rover Adventure
Outfitters
Land Rover N.A.
4390 Parliament Place
Lanham, MD 20706
(800) 726-5655, ext. 13
This is the official Land Rover North America driving school and expedition service. Past North American expeditions have included the Great Divide Expedition and the Moab Desert Expedition, and overseas destinations are also included in their offerings. Range Rovers, Discoveries, and Defender 90s are the training vehicles.

The Off-Road Adventure
P.O. Box 369
Andes, NY 13731
(800) 935-0761
Courses are offered at the historic 2,000-acre Broadlands Estate southwest of Albany, New York. Several levels are offered, including Level One (introductory), Level Two (intermediate, including winching and recovery), and Level Three (advanced, expedition skills and survival).

Rovers North Off-Road
Route 128, Box 61
Westford, VT 05494-9601(802) 879-0032
www.roversnorth.com
Instructors at this Land Rover-oriented school are certified off-pavement drivers, through Land Rover in England. One- and two-day courses teach all aspects of off-pavement driving; custom packages are available. Students drive Rovers North's Range Rovers, Discoveries or Defender 90 training vehicles.

Western Adventures & 4x4 Driving School
2324 Kelly Avenue
Ramona, CA 92065
(619) 789-1563
www.4x4now.com/4wstrwa.htm
Frenchie La Chance offers 21-day guided trips all over the West and Mexico, as well as full-day off-pavement driving courses. Private lessons are available.

West Coast British Off-Road Experience
190 Airway Boulevard
Livermore, CA 94550
(510) 606-8301
WCB Off-Road specializes in "no-frills" and cost-effective off-pavement driving courses.

Organizations

American Automobile Association
www.aaa.com
Search the association's website for the office nearest you or look in your Yellow Pages.

United Four-Wheel Drive Associations
Four-Wheel Drive Awareness Program
6351 Upham Street
Arvada, CO 80003
(303) 423-5938
(800) 44-UFWDA
www.ufwda.org

Clubs

There are hundreds of four-wheel-drive clubs across North America—obviously we can't list them all here. The best way to find one near you is to contact the United Four-Wheel Drive Associations (see above) or check out UFWDA's web site, which lists dozens of regional groups.

Conservation Organizations

National Audubon Society
700 Broadway
New York, NY 10003
(212) 979-3000
www.audubon.org

National Wildlife Federation
1412 16th Street, NW
Washington, DC 20036
(202) 797-6800
www.nwf.org

The Nature Conservancy
1815 North Lynn Street
Arlington, VA 22209
(703) 841-5300
www.tnc.org

Sierra Club
730 Polk Street
San Francisco, CA 94109
(415) 776-2211
www.sierraclub.org

The Wilderness Society
900 17th Street, NW
Washington, DC 20006
(202) 833-2300
www.wilderness.org

Index